Contemporary Fly [...
of BRITISH COLUI ...

by Art Lingren

Frank Amato
PORTLAND

All inquiries should be addressed to:
Frank Amato Publications, Inc.
P.O. Box 82112 • Portland, Oregon 97282 • 503-653-8108
www.amatobooks.com

Book Design: A.D. Huntsinger
Photography: Art Lingren, unless otherwise noted

Printed in Singapore
1 3 5 7 9 10 8 6 4 2

Softbound ISBN: 1-57188-375-4
Hardbound ISBN: 1-57188-376-2
Limited Edition Hardbound ISBN: 1-57188-377-0

Table of Contents

Greg Gordon with a lively Skeena summer-run.

A box of the author's favourites.

Dedication

To Frank Amato; a man with a passion for fish,
fly-fishing, fly-tying and fly-fishing related history.
No one person in North America has done more to
chronicle the art and craft of North American fly-tying in
the late 20th and early 21st centuries than has Frank
and his staff at Amato Publications.
All of us who have a passion for the art and craft
of fly-tying owe Frank our heartfelt thanks.

Acknowledgements

To all of those who took the time to
dress flies and do the write-ups for this book,
and to Rob Way, who read my draft manuscript
and provided helpful comments.

Introduction

*W*hen I wrote *Fly Patterns of British Columbia,* which was published by Frank Amato Publications in 1996, my goal for that book was to chronicle British Columbia's rich fly-fishing heritage. Inseparable from British Columbia's fly-fishing history is the art and craft of fly-tying. For both fly-fishing and fly-tying we need to know our roots to really appreciate where we are today.

In *Fly Patterns of British Columbia* I feature those patterns that show British Columbia's rich fly-tying history, with flies that trace the development of fly-tying with B.C.-originated fly patterns from the first, dressed by John Keast Lord in 1863 after being inspired on the banks of the Moyie River in eastern British Columbia by the trout in that river, to some of the more recent ones developed in the 1970s and '80s. Patterns chosen for inclusion in that work, the pattern had to meet some or all the following criteria:

- Be documented in writing
- Display some original thought process
- Be of some historical importance in British Columbia fly development
- Be available commercially
- For contemporary patterns, have been in use for about 10 years.

In documenting that part of our fly-tying heritage, I relied on the words penned in articles and books by the fly-fishing writers of the day or their diaries if they existed. The book's two-page Bibliography documents those many written sources. However, in the many communities near waters where trout, salmon and steelhead swim, and in the larger centers such as Vancouver and Victoria, there are fly tiers developing flies for their local or favourite waters and fish. British Columbia fly-fishing and fly-tying heritage is rich, however it has become richer over the past 20 years because of the many good contemporary fly tiers, some of whom have contributed flies to this book. This is not a comprehensive listing of the province's best and most well-known fly tiers, however many are included in this book. The samples obtained, and the ingenious thinking that has gone into the creations shown on these pages, are evidence of the inventive fly-tying talent that exists in this province. That talent consists of all age groups, from Ken Ruddick, founder of Ruddicks' Fly Shop, at 84 years old and still dressing flies to Doug Wright, age 15, the youngest, but yet with a number of years of fly-tying under his belt. With 60 years at the vise, Bill Jollymore enjoys the longest reign at the fly-tying bench. Indeed the talent displayed in this book spans many generations and years.

We have many game fish to pursue with our flies and in this book you will find innovative patterns for a host of British Columbia game fish such as:

- Sea-run cutthroat
- Freshwater salmon flies for coho, chum, chinook, sockeye and pink

A selection of Spey flies featured in the book.

Top-quality hackles add quality to dry flies.

- Must have a following with a reasonable period of use (plus or minus two years minimum),
- Recognize those who came before, if the pattern is borrowed from another. (Very little is new or original; we borrow and adapt ideas from others and incorporate them into our creations.)
- No flavours of the month: a book takes a minimum of two years before it will be on shelf and a flavour of the month will have fallen into disuse,
- Commercially available,
- Innovative pattern favoured by fly-fishing guide, knowledgeable fly tackle store representative, or experienced fly-fisher,
- Thought process in development must display some originality,
- Prefer B.C.-originated flies, dressed by competent fly tiers who are ardent fly-fishers, or well-known fly-tying authors
- Be a tribute to the art and craft of fly-tying.

The earliest record listing materials and dressing an artificial fly dates back to Aelian, who lived during the last part of the second and into the early third century in Macedonia. The English translation of Aelian's Greek words says that, "They fasten red (crimson wool) round a hook, and fix on to the wool two feathers which grow under a cock's wattles, and which in colour are like wax." (p. 188, *Fishing From the Earliest of Times*, 1921, by Willaim Radcliffe).

Since that time fly tiers have been adapting dressings by using different colours and materials to dress flies to catch game fish. Fly tying is a craft in continual evolution. The evolution in the last quarter century has been truly amazing with the on-going

Camping is part of the fly-fishing experience.

- River rainbow trout, cutthroat, and char with flies in the dry, wet and nymph groups
- Interior stillwater rainbows, cutthroat and brook trout with patterns to cover Chironomid, dry-fly, traditional cast-and-retrieve and trolled sunk-fly techniques
- Steelhead to cover five presentation techniques
- Saltwater salmon: coho, pink and chum with shallow-water saltwater flies and bucktails

British Columbia is a large land mass, which if superimposed on the Northwest states would include all of Washington, Oregon, California as far as San Francisco plus parts of Idaho and Nevada. The province is divided into eight freshwater fisheries management regions and I thought it appropriate to list flies from fly tiers from the region in which they live, rather than the game fish the fly was originally designed to catch. However, many fly-fishers develop flies for their favourite waters in other regions. For example I live in Region 2 but I use my patterns in all regions of the province that I visit. Many of the flies found grouped in a region will work in other waters. In the Index I have sorted flies designed for salmon, steelhead and trout. There is also a fly tier Index. Fly patterns are grouped by region by tier's name or club. Individual tiers in each region are listed alphabetically, followed by participating clubs.

However, unlike for *Fly Patterns of British Columbia* I asked potential contributors in this book to consider the following criteria when recommending flies:

introduction of synthetic fly-tying materials that tiers can't resist incorporating in their creations. At times nostalgia takes hold in some sectors of the fly-tying community, which reverts back or re-discovers old patterns that work as well or perhaps even better when fished with the improved fly-fishing equipment we enjoy today. A good example of rediscovering the past is the rebirth of 150-year-old Spey flies within the steelhead fly-fishing community. However, in a craft that has evolved over hundreds of years, very little is new or original. We borrow and adapt ideas from others and incorporate new materials into our creations and give them different names, yet all flies owe their origins to the one described by Aelian about 1800 years ago. I have used the terms "adapted" and "originated" in the sub-heading below each fly's name. I am not sure they are the right words, as there are a host of other words that could be substituted, such as conceived, designed, developed, altered; and maybe one of these descriptors might suit some flies better. There are a number of patterns that are quite similar in appearance—the Chironomid and bloodworm patterns used in British Columbia are legion and there are a number of samples in this book and as well a number of other patterns such as caddis emergers, damselfly emergers, and Woolly Buggers that owe their origins to other flies. So I use the term "originated" lightly; for example, if I list a Blood-red Woolly Bugger contributed by Joe Flytier and all he has done is change the colour of the original Woolly Bugger, Joe Flytier is credited with the term "originated by."

I have used the term "intended use" and by that I mean, for which fish was the fly originally intended and for what fishing technique, i.e., wet fly, dry fly, nymph, etcetera.

I assumed many roles in preparing this book: compiler, writer, editor, and main photographer. I was mainly concerned about highlighting fly tiers, not wanting to eliminate a good tier because he may be uncomfortable with putting words on paper. For those who are not writers or had difficulty with the written word I put together their section either by consulting with them and making notes, or expanding their brief written submission. Other fly tiers supplied their information in written form, some of which went into the book verbatim, but many submissions I edited to make the content more concise and ensure the format was consistent. Many tiers provided fairly detailed tying instructions. This is a fly pattern book, not a fly-tying book, and to maintain conciseness, tying instructions have been severely edited or not included in the recipe section. I am the main photographer, but many of the pictures that appear with a fly tier's biography were supplied by the tier or a friend.

From the flies listed in this book, one can chose patterns that suit virtually every fish that swims in British Columbia waters. Some flies are for very specific waters while others have a more universal use. By exploring the text under the comment section following the recipe of a pattern, you will find that some fly-fishers have shared their hush-hush secrets and logic behind their fly's success. Everything you will need to satisfy your heart's fly-fishing desire can be found somewhere in the pages of this book. Enjoy!

Art Lingren
March, 2004

NOTE: *There are some materials specified in this book's fly recipes that are difficult to obtain or illegal to possess in the United States and other countries. Examples include polar bear, seal fur, and heron feathers. If you wish to dress a particular fly that calls for one of these banned materials, check with your local fly fishing shop and they can recommend a suitable substitute.*

Bill and Lori Jollymore: Bill is a master fly tyer with 60 years at the tying bench.

Shawn Bennett

Vancouver Island born and raised, Shawn was introduced to fishing at an early age by his father. Introduced to the fly tier's craft in 1985 through a course offered by the Haig-Brown Fly Fishing Association in Victoria, he became a fly tier before he took up the sport of fly-fishing. In 1995 Shawn and his wife, Lise Peters, started a company called Moonlight Flies, specializing in saltwater flies for Pacific fin fish species such as coho, chinook, black rockfish, lingcod and other saltwater sport fish. Incorporating epoxy in many of their patterns, they have become known for their innovative, durable, and quality flies, not available elsewhere. At one time they were distributing flies to over 15 stores in the Pacific Northwest. However, commercial tying has now become less of a priority for Shawn. He has been pioneering saltwater flies and fly-fishing techniques on Vancouver Island's West Coast and has been instrumental in developing the fly-fishing program for Weigh West Marine Resort, where he is currently the Marine Operations Manager, as well as a fly-fishing guide. Shawn has also held seminars/presentations on saltwater fly-fishing and fly-tying at sportsmen shows and fly-fishing clubs throughout B.C, Washington and Oregon.

CATFACE STREAMER
Designed and contributed by Shawn Bennett

Hook: Size 1/0 to 2, Mustad 34011
Thread: Fine UNI-Thread mono (monofilament)
Body: Pearl Diamond Braid
Hackle: Dyed green grizzly, tied in along lateral line
Wing: Chartreuse over white polar bear or bucktail, with a topping of peacock herl from the eye
Beard: Red calf tail
Head: Mylar stick-on eyes, covered with a light single coat of epoxy
Intended use: Wet fly for Pacific salmon

Comments: This general-purpose attractor/baitfish imitation is best fished on an intermediate to fast-sinking line. This streamer has a moderately broad silhouette and when fished in the small bays and neighboring waters around the base of Catface Mountain Range in Clayoquot Sound, salmon may take this fly as a perch or shiner. It is productive in similar waters along B.C.'s coast. Chartreuse together with a small bit of red is a common theme among many saltwater streamers, but this pattern can also be tied in similar style with a purple, olive, or blue wing. Grizzly saddle hackle can be tied in at the lateral line, matching the same colour as wing, to give a variegated dorsal pattern.

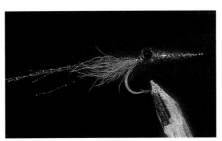

M.L. SHRIMP
Designed and contributed by Shawn Bennett

Hook: Size 4 to 8, Mustad 34007
Thread: UNI-Thread mono (monofilament)
Antennae: Calf tail & Krystal Flash
Eyes: Mono nymph eyes
Body: Diamond Braid & single coat of epoxy over entire fly
Intended use: Wet fly for coho and sea-run cutthroat

Comments: I fish this shrimp imitation/attractor pattern early in the season for juvenile coho and sea-run cutthroat. For best results, fish the fly on the bottom or in close proximity to the bottom. It is tied in attractor colours rather than natural and it also is effective late in the season fished with a slow retrieve. It can also be tied in pink, orange, and green.

CLAYOQUOT CLOUSER
Adapted and contributed by Shawn Bennett

Hook: Size 1, Mustad 34007
Thread: UNI-Thread mono & chartreuse 6/0
Eyes: Nickel-plated lead dumbbell eyes
Body: Pearl saltwater Flashabou, wrapped around hook shank from
gap to eyes over white FisHair with a red gill slash tied in just behind eyes
Wing: Chartreuse FisHair and green glow-in-dark Flashabou
Intended use: Wet fly used on sinking lines for all Pacific Ocean fish species.

Comments: This fly, originated by Bob Clouser, can be fished for a wide range of fish species. It has a dipping action when retrieved and can be irresistible to certain game fish. I tie this fly with what I consider to be the three most effective colours for coho salmon: chartreuse, pink, and orange. When retrieving line, a distinct pause between quick strips helps take advantage of the action created by the weighted eye.

MOONLIGHT SPECIAL
Designed and contributed by Shawn Bennett

Hook: Size 1, Mustad 34011
Thread: UNI-Thread mono
Body: Pearl, silver, or gold Diamond Braid
Wing: Chartreuse over white polar bear or bucktail, with couple strands of Krystal Flash
Beard: Red calf tail
Head: Pearl Mylar tubing, sleeved over head, stick-on eyes with a light coat of epoxy
Intended use: Wet fly for Pacific salmon

Comments: This general-purpose attractor/baitfish saltwater fly is an effective imitation when fished with an intermediate to fast-sinking line. This streamer can be tied in various sizes and colour blends. I favour the chartreuse when fishing deeper, but do fish the combinations of olive over purple (Art's Special), red over yellow (Mickey Finn), blue over red (Coronation), green over red (Parrot), fluorescent red over lime (Father Charles). The later the season, the sparser the fly should be tied.

FLASHY GLOW
Designed and contributed by Shawn Bennett

Hook: Size 1, Mustad 34011
Thread: UNI-Thread mono
Body: Green Sparkle Braid
Wing: Bottom is yellow glow Flashabou, top is green glow Flashabou and along the lateral line use metallic green Flashabou, followed by pearl Mylar tubing sleeved over whole fly. After head is finished, the tubing is unraveled/frayed from tail to just behind eyes
Head: Stick-on eyes with a light coat of epoxy
Intended use: Wet fly for Pacific salmon

Comments: Used on an intermediate to fast-sink line, this fly is a consistent producer for varied species of saltwater game fish. A highly visible fly, it cuts through murky water created by algae blooms in summer and tea-coloured run-off in the fall. I like to fish this pattern, like many flies, with a steep angle (to vertical) retrieve, mimicking the escape strategy of Pacific sand lance. The fly is also tied in pink glow Flashabou with white belly.

S.B. DART
Designed and contributed by Shawn Bennett

Hook: Size 2/0 to 2, Mustad 34007
Thread: UNI-Thread mono (monofilament)
Tail: White Ultra Hair, olive Antron, and Krystal Flash
Body: Silver or pearl Diamond Braid
over tail material, olive Antron & Krystal Flash laid from head to tail as dorsal. Finish the fly with a coat of epoxy mixed with glitter
Intended use: Wet fly for Pacific salmon.

Comments: A sleek narrow profile with olive back makes this a good Pacific sand lance imitation. This bait makes up a major part of Pacific salmons' diet. Using an intermediate to fast-sink line, fish the fly with a vertical retrieve from very bottom up (again to

imitate the natural as if fleeing). This fly is also effective for Dolly Varden on some Mainland rivers. The epoxy coating makes this a lasting durable fly.

Frank Dalziel

A native of Vancouver Island, Frank Dalziel presently works as a Fisheries Technologist in the Fisheries and Aquaculture Department at Malaspina University-College in Nanaimo, B.C. He was fortunate

to have a father passionate about fishing, including fly-fishing and tying flies. That knowledge was passed along at such an early age that Frank has been fly-fishing and fly-tying for over 40 years. He is a former guide and commercial fly tier who believes that fly patterns should be simple to tie, be durable, and catch fish. Frank is a member of the Mid-Island Castaways Fly Fishing Club in Qualicum Beach and has been a long-time supporter and member of the BCFFF. In addition, he is active in Trout Unlimited Canada, formerly a member of their National Board of Directors, and he is currently one of the British Columbia representatives on their National Resource Board. When not spending time at the fly-tying bench at home, Frank haunts the beaches of the East Coast of Vancouver Island in the never-ending search for beach coho and cutthroat trout.

COHO BUGGER (also known as "California Neil")
Adapted and contributed by Frank Dalziel

Hook: Size 2 to 6, Daiichi 2546 preferred (standard length) or Tiemco 9394 or Mustad 34011 may be used if long shank is desired
Thread: Fluorescent chartreuse 6/0
Tail: Fluorescent chartreuse polar bear hair, (sparse) length of hook shank with 4 strands of chartreuse Flashabou over top
Body: Fluorescent chartreuse Diamond Braid
Rib: Small green wire or clear monofilament used to bind hackle to hook (Note: Small red wire also used)
Hackle: Grizzly saddle, palmered
Intended use: Floating or intermediate line, wet fly for beach and estuary coho and chum salmon

Comments: This is an offshoot of the famous Woolly Bugger commonly known as the California Neil. Naming the fly Coho Bugger is just my attempt to give credit to the original pattern from which this fly was derived. I wish I could take credit for the idea, but Bob Weir handed me this "tweaked up" version of the Coho Woolly Worm many seasons ago. To the best of my knowledge, he was the first to introduce this version of a very effective dressing to coho fishers on the East Coast of Vancouver Island. I had given several Coho Woolly Worms to Bob sometime in the mid-1990's and weeks later, he handed me samples of this dressing, noting that he could not catch fish with the Coho Woolly Worm but wanted to know what I thought about this pattern. Consequently, I rarely use anything else when fishing coho in the Central Vancouver Island Region. The only alteration I make to the pattern that Bob gave to me is to use green or red wire to bind the hackle to the body in order to increase the useable life of the fly.

This pattern will take coho and chum salmon using any retrieve, from a dead drift to a very fast retrieve. In my opinion, this is why the fly is so effective. Long, slow strip retrieves are very effective, but successful retrieves can vary greatly from day to day. The secret to catching fish using this pattern is to vary the speed of the retrieve. At times, simply casting up-tide and maintaining a tight line with no retrieve is all that is needed to hook fussy coho.

Other variations of this dressing found around Vancouver Island beaches include patterns using silver bead or cone heads, and also fine angel hair instead of polar bear for the tail. From time to time, this fly tied using other colours can be effective.

COHO WOOLLY WORM
Adapted and contributed by Frank Dalziel

Hook: Size 4 to 8, Mustad 34011 or equivalent
Thread: Olive 6/0
Tail: Short to medium paired grizzly hen neck hackles
Body: Olive Diamond Braid
Rib: Small green wire
Hackle: Five to six turns of palmered grizzly saddle
Intended use: Floating line, wet fly for beach coho and sea-run

Comments: A copy of the original fly (unnamed, with slightly different dressing) was passed along to me by John Pewovich of Qualicum Beach. Apparently, the original dressing was used by a fellow from California named Neil (hence the name California Neil) to great advantage while fishing for coho in Clayoquot Sound. To the best of my knowledge, the original had a body of "Laser Wrap" (or equivalent). This dressing is my simplified version and it has worked very well for me over the years for coho. I also discovered a few years ago (by accident) that cutthroat trout really relish this fly, especially in the late fall along the beach.

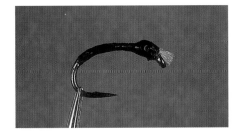

THREAD-HEAD CHIRONOMID PUPA
Adapted and contributed by Frank Dalziel

Hook: Size 14 to 18, Tiemco 2457 (or equivalent)
Thread: Dark brown 8/0
Body: Dark brown 8/0 thread
Rib: Bronze Flashabou
Thorax: Dark brown 8/0 thread built up into a ball
Gills: White Antron
Note: When finished, add several coats of lacquer or a thin coat of epoxy to thorax and body for durability
Intended use: Wet fly for Interior or coastal stillwater trout using a floating line or appropriate sinking lines (usually Type I – Type III)

Comments: Stu Slymon and I spent many years fishing White Lake near Salmon Arm. This fly is one of many that we "developed" to match the various hatches at White Lake that has proven to be valuable elsewhere. It is a very simple fly that requires few materials and catches fish very well wherever I have used it in British Columbia. Other Chironomids can be imitated by changing hook size, thread and ribbing to suit.

CARROT CHIRONOMID
Adapted and contributed by Frank Dalziel

Hook: Size 8 to 16, Tiemco 2457 (or equivalent)
Thread: Red 6/0
Body: Red 6/0 thread
Rib: Pearl tinsel sized to suit, 3 to 4 turns; counter-wrapped with fine copper wire
Thorax: Red 6/0 thread
Head: White bead (plastic or metal) or white ostrich herl (Note: Lacquer body for durability)
Intended use: Wet fly for Interior or coastal stillwater trout

Comments: I am not sure who is the originator of this pattern, but Gord Honey gave me a fly at White Lake many years ago that resembles this dressing (The original was tied using ostrich herl however, like many other tiers, I have grown fond of bead heads). I am never quite certain if fish take this as a pupae or bloodworm, but this fly seems to work well wherever I fish so I never leave home without a few of these in my box.

PINK CARDINNALE
Adapted and contributed by Frank Dalziel

Hook: Size 3/0 to 6, Partridge Single Salmon hooks, Code M (or equivalent regular shank salmon hook, TUE)
Thread: Pink 6/0
Body: Fluorescent pink chenille (add lead wire if desired)
Hackle: Fluorescent chartreuse collar
Wing: Fluorescent pink marabou, full
Intended use: Wet fly for steelhead

Comments: A fly similar to this was advertised in an Orvis catalog in 1980. I tied several and took a trip to the Vedder River to try fly-fishing for winter steelhead. At that time, we were splicing our own fast-sinking heads to running line and to be honest, the equipment was quite primitive compared to that available today. After several unsuccessful trips, I went fishing one afternoon and was working my way down a run close to the canal when my rod was nearly pulled from my hands and the reel was in overdrive! I don't have any idea how long the fight was, but I still have a picture of a beautiful silver-bright steelhead; my first taken on the fly, a Pink Cardinnale.

Years later, after hearing about Art Lingren's success with a Black G.P., I tied a Cardinnale in black but retained the chartreuse hackle. That turned out to be a very successful combination, perhaps better than the pink, which has caught many fish in various Vancouver Island rivers. Like other tiers, I get bored and try other patterns, but perhaps because I caught my first steelhead on the fly using a Cardinnale, I still have faith in this simple dressing and find that it takes fish as well today as it did almost 25 years ago.

BLUE AND GREEN BUCKTAIL
Adapted and contributed by Frank Dalziel

Hook: Size 4–8, Daiichi 2546 or Tiemco 9394 (same sizes) if a longer fly is desired
Thread: Clear monofilament, fine or ultra-fine and fluorescent red 6/0 for gills
Belly: Sparse white polar bear
Wing: Sparse chartreuse polar bear, 4 strands of chartreuse Krystal Flash, sparse silver-doctor-blue polar bear, topped with 6–8 strands of blue Krystal Flash.
Head: 1.5 mm silver or pearl prismatic tape eyes (Note: Attach fluorescent red 6/0 thread to back of head and wind to produce a thin red strip to depict gills)
Intended use: Wet fly, use with a floating or intermediate line for beach and estuary pink and coho salmon

Comments: Variations of this pattern are used by many fly-fishers for pinks and coho when they stage along the East Coast of Vancouver Island beaches. Bob Weir gave this fly to me a few years ago, and it is one of my favorite flies for pink salmon holding or feeding along beaches.

Bob Giles

A Victoria resident most of his life, Bob Giles started fly-fishing over three decades ago, when he was 11 years old. He dressed his first fly when he was 14. He was a member of the Haig-Brown Fly Fishing Association for 10 years, starting in 1985, and then

BOB GILES PHOTO

joined the Cowichan Fly Fishers in the mid 1990s. He is one of British Columbia's premier fly tiers and in 2002 he was awarded the BCFFF's Jack Shaw Fly Tying Award in recognition of his exemplary skills in the art and craft of fly-tying. When not dressing flies, he can be found wandering the banks of his favourite river, the Cowichan, casting flies to its brown, cutthroat and rainbow trout and steelhead.

ALLARD (YELLOW)
Originated by Al Allard and contributed by Bob Giles

Hook: Size 6, Mustad 34007 or 340011
Thread: Danville, black 6/0
Tail: Grizzly hackle fibres
Body: Medium, yellow chenille
Rib: Medium, flat, silver Mylar
Hackle: Grizzly hackle throat
Wing: White polar bear hair, sparse, to extend just past hook bend with 6 to 8 strands of orange Krystal Flash a little shorter than polar bear
Intended use: Wet fly for estuary coho and cutthroat

ALLARD (ORANGE)
Originated by Al Allard and contributed by Bob Giles

Hook: Size 6, Mustad 34007 or 340011
Thread: Danville, black 6/0
Tail: Grizzly hackle fibres
Body: Medium, burnt orange chenille
Rib: Medium flat, silver Mylar
Hackle: Grizzly hackle throat
Wing: White polar bear hair, sparse, to extend just past hook bend with 6 to 8 strands of orange Krystal Flash a little shorter than polar bear
Intended use: Wet fly for estuary coho and cutthroat

Comments: I first tied this fly in 1993 when coho were in good numbers around southern Vancouver Island. About a year earlier, Bruce Ferguson of Gig Harbor, WA, gave a sample to Barry Stokes but he didn't try it. I remember the day well when I tried the Allard. The fish were hard to hook that 1993 day and with the Allard I caught a fish within a few casts. That was the start of the popularity of the Allard on the Canadian side of the border. Since then this fly has taken on many variations up and down Vancouver Island, particularly on the east coast. It is a very effective fly off the mouths of creeks for newly arrived coho, when they are still quite aggressive. But it has proven to be an outstanding sea-run cutthroat trout fly up and down Vancouver Island's coast.

MARABOU SPRATLEY
Adapted and contributed by Bob Giles

Hook: Size 6 to 12, Mustad 9672
Thread: Danville, burgundy 6/0
Tail: Grizzly hackle fibres
Body: Maroon and black mohair
Rib: Medium oval gold or silver tinsel
Hackle: Grizzly throat
Wing: Burgundy or wine marabou
Intended use: Wet fly for stillwater trout

Comments: I first dressed this pattern in 1989 and it is a variation of the famous Doc Spratley Interior trout fly. It has worked well for me as a leech imitation and it works well in most lakes.

S-17 (DAMSEL EMERGER)
Originated and contributed by Bob Giles

Hook: Size 10, Tiemco 101
Thread: Danville, olive 6/0
Tail: Braided nylon leader burned on one end and coloured with Pantone pen # 4655
Body: Ginger, rabbit dubbing
Hackle: Grizzly

Wing: Very fine light deer hair, but flare butt ends over the eyes Elk Hair Caddis-style
Eyes: Burned monofilament fishing line
Intended use: Dry fly for stillwater trout

Comments: Originated in 1994 to simulate an emerging damsel, I use this fly when the damsels are hatching on Vancouver Island and Interior lakes.

RIVER DRAGON
Originated and contributed by Bob Giles

Hook: Size 4 to 10, Mustad 9672
Thread: Danville, olive 6/0
Tail: Red phase of a ring-necked pheasant rump fibres, tied short
Body: Hareline rabbit dubbing #39, dark olive brown (Note: optional underbody of lead wire)
Rib: (Optional) Oval gold tinsel
Thorax: Peacock herl
Wingcase: Mottled pheasant rump

fibres pulled over peacock
Hackle: Red phase of a ring-necked pheasant rump feather one side stripped to maintain sparseness
Head: Dark moose body hair, 90 degree to hook shank and trimmed leaving a 1/8-inch stub on each side
Intended use: Wet fly for Cowichan River jack springs

Comments: This fly came from my tying bench in 1987 and is somewhat of a contradiction due to its name. It is not a dragonfly nymph imitation but rather a fall caddis imitation. I dressed it to entice Cowichan River jack springs, which will react quite aggressively to the right fly. The River Dragon proved effective for jack springs but rainbows, cutthroat, browns, coho, springs, chums and steelhead in the Cowichan have found this pattern appealing to their tastes. As well, it has been a very effective fly on Vancouver Island and Interior lakes. However, a real surprise to me was this fly's consistent effectiveness on Cowichan River winter-run steelhead.

YELLOW, ORANGE AND RED BUCKTAIL
Originated by Charlie Stroulger and contributed by Bob Giles

Hook: Size 3/0, Mustad 34007 for front hook, trailer: size 1, Mustad 92553S
Thread: Danville's, black 6/0 or mono
Body: Double wrap of #10 flat, silver Mylar
Wing: Two strands of #10 flat, silver Mylar, two clumps of white polar bear hair on sides of hook and another on top, five or six strands of pearl Flashabou on each side, another

clump of white polar bear hair on top, followed by dyed yellow, orange, scarlet polar bear hair. (Note: after fly is complete, dry rub with Brylcream to add luster to the polar bear hair)
Head: Three or four coats of clear nail polish or lacquer
Eyes: Optional
Intended use: Trolled wet fly for saltwater coho

Comments: In the early days of the sport, fly-fishing for coho was uniquely British Columbian. It was practiced by early British visitors and evolved over a number of years from the cast to trolled fly. Moreover, with the introduction of the hairwings or bucktail as they became known, the flies became larger and eventually difficult to cast. The fly-fishers of the day found that the larger flies, when trolled, were more productive, and the term bucktailing was born to describe a trolled fly made from deer tail hair. About fly-fishing for sea-run cutthroat and coho salmon fly-fishing, Vancouver fly-fisher Frank Darling in a 1930s letter says:

We use a long streamer fly made of bucktail. Trout and salmon both take it. I use polar bear, black and brown bear hair. . . . It's a bit hard to cast, have to heave it like a spoon.

Charlie Stroulger's family lived on the Bay for most of the 20th century. As a teenager in the late 1920s and early '30s, he remembers the Bay teeming with coho and the fly-fishing he and his brother enjoyed. After Charlie took up fly-tying, he became one of Vancouver Island's premier bucktail fly dressers. Stroulger-dressed bucktails were a must if you wanted to increase your chances of success on the Bay. Charlie's legacy to the sport is his Grey Ghost Bucktail. A few years ago, when Charlie became over 80 years old, he took Bob Giles under his wing to pass on the secrets in dressing Cowichan Bay-style bucktails.

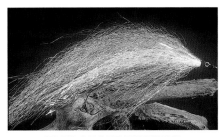

GREY GHOST BUCKTAIL
Originated by Charlie Stroulger, tied and contributed by Bob Giles

Hook: Size 4/0, Mustad 34007 for front hook; trailer: size 2/0, Mustad 92553S
Thread: Danville's, black 6/0 or mono
Body: Medium, silver, Mylar tubing
Wing: White polar bear hair built up thick at shoulder, pale pink over followed by light elephant gray, then

dark elephant grey, five or six stands of pearl Flashabou on each side
Head: Three or four coats of clear nail polish or lacquer
Eyes: Painted-on or stock eyes, apply between coats of head cement
Intended use: Trolled wet fly for saltwater coho

CORONATION BUCKTAIL
Tied and contributed by Bob Giles

Hook: Size 3/0, Mustad 34007 for front hook, trailer: size 1, Mustad 92553S
Thread: Danville's, black 6/0 or mono
Body: Double wrap of #10 flat, silver Mylar
Wing: Two strands of #10 flat, silver Mylar, two clumps of white polar bear hair on sides of hook and another on top, five or six strands of pearl Flashabou on each side, another clump of white polar bear hair on top, followed by scarlet and then royal blue polar bear hair
Head: Three or four coats of clear nail polish or lacquer
Eyes: Optional, painted on or stock, apply between coats of head cement
Intended use: Trolled wet fly for saltwater coho

BLACK & WHITE BUCKTAIL
Tied and contributed by Bob Giles

Hook: Size 3/0, Mustad 34007 for front hook; trailer: size 1, Mustad 92553S
Thread: Danville's, black 6/0 or mono
Body: Double wrap of #10 flat, silver Mylar
Wing: Two clumps of white polar bear hair on sides of hook and another on top, five or six strands of pearl Flashabou on each side, another clump of white polar bear hair on top, followed by black polar bear hair with a few strands of scarlet polar bear mixed with red Krystal Flash down each side
Head: Three or four coats of clear nail polish or lacquer
Eyes: Optional, stock red #2 stick-on, apply between coats of head cement with three coats over eyes
Intended use: Trolled wet fly for saltwater coho

PURPLE & WHITE BUCKTAIL
Tied and contributed by Bob Giles

Hook: Size 3/0, Mustad 34007 for front hook; trailer: size 1, Mustad 92553S
Thread: Danville's, black 6/0 or mono
Body: Medium, silver, Mylar tubing
Wing: Two strands of #10 flat, silver Mylar, two clumps of white polar bear hair on sides of hook and another on top, five or six strands of pearl Flashabou on each side, another clump of white polar bear hair on top, followed by clumps of light and dark elephant grey polar bear hair then royal blue and burgundy purple or just purple polar bear hair
Head: Three or four coats of clear nail polish or lacquer
Eyes: Optional
Intended use: Trolled wet fly for saltwater coho

Comments: This was one of Charlie Stroulger's favourite colour combinations for Cowichan Bay coho.

ORANGE & WHITE BUCKTAIL
Tied and contributed by Bob Giles

Hook: Size 3/0, Mustad 34007 for front hook; trailer: size 1, Mustad 92553S
Thread: Danville's, black 6/0 or mono
Body: Double wrap of #10 flat, silver Mylar
Wing: Two strands of #10 flat, silver Mylar, two clumps of white polar bear hair on sides of hook and another on top, five or six strands of pearl Flashabou on each side, another clump of white polar bear hair on top, followed by a clump of elephant grey polar bear hair and then orange polar bear hair
Head: Three or four coats of clear nail polish or lacquer
Eyes: Optional
Intended use: Trolled wet fly for saltwater coho

Comments: This colour is as good today as it was in the 1930s and 1940s when Charlie and Jack Stroulger started bucktailing on Cowichan Bay. It has a following along Vancouver Island's east and west coasts, wherever fishermen pursue coho with a bucktail fly.

BLUE & GREEN BUCKTAIL
Tied and contributed by Bob Giles

Hook: Size 3/0, Mustad 34007 for front hook; trailer: size 1, Mustad 92553S
Thread: Danville's, black 6/0 or mono
Body: Double wrap of #10 flat, silver Mylar
Wing: Two strands of #10 flat, silver Mylar, two clumps of white polar bear hair on sides of hook and another on top, five or six strands of pearl Flashabou on each side, another clump of white polar bear hair on top, followed by a clump of elephant grey polar bear hair and then topped with light blue, green and black polar bear hair
Head: Three or four coats of clear nail polish or lacquer
Eyes: Optional
Intended use: Trolled wet fly for saltwater coho

GREEN & WHITE BUCKTAIL
Tied and contributed by Bob Giles

Hook: Size 4/0, Mustad 34007 for front hook; trailer: size 2/0, Mustad 92553S
Body: Silver, Mylar tubing

Thread: Danville's, black 6/0 or mono
Wing: Two clumps of white polar bear hair on sides of hook and another on top, five or six strands of pearl Flashabou on each side, another clump of white polar bear hair on top, followed by a small amount of pink followed by elephant grey polar bear hair and then topped with dark green polar bear hair
Head: Three or four coats of clear nail polish or lacquer
Eyes: Optional
Intended use: Trolled wet fly for saltwater coho

Comments: The classic Cowichan Bay bucktail fly has a distinct hump in the wing. This hump, together with a keel-shaped head, indicates that the fly has been built up correctly and, when trolled, will come alive with that swimming action that coho cannot resist.

Jim Kilburn

Long recognized as a British Columbia fly-fishing pioneer, Jim Kilburn's "B.C. Flyfisher" articles written in the late 1960s into the 1970s show a man with an inquiring mind and a passion for the sport of fly-fishing. About Kilburn, Roderick Haig-Brown in the Foreword to *British Columbia Game Fish* published in 1970, says that he "may well be the first really solid expert of fly-fishing for trout of the interior lakes." Kilburn was one of the founding members of the Totem Fly Fishers, B.C.'s oldest fly-fishing club. He lives in Qualicum Beach where he can be found on the beaches casting after cutthroat trout, coho and pink salmon and he makes the occasional journey off the Island in pursuit of Interior stillwater trout.

HANDLEBAR FLY

Variation by Bob Hurst, Parksville B.C. and contributed by Jim Kilburn

Hook: Size 8, Mustad 34007
Thread: Monofilament
Tag: Silver tinsel
Body: Double layer of silver tinsel covered with the pinkish-red translucent plastic material that was used as tassels on the tips of a bicycle's handlebars (Note: Available in sheet form from most sporting goods stores)
Underwing: Several strands of blue Krystal Flash
Wing: White polar bear hair
Eyes: Silver
Head: Fluorescent red tying thread, epoxy head and eyes
Intended use: Wet fly for beachfront coho and pink salmon

Comments: This saltwater coho pattern, the Handlebar Fly, came to my attention in the late 1960s. The specimen enclosed is Hurst's very effective version of that pattern. It is generally fished with a floating or slow-sinking line using a steady, medium strip retrieve. An effective variation, tied by Frank English of Qualicum Beach, substitutes the white wing with yellow polar bear hair and clear Krystal Flash.

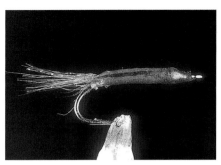

JIM'S FLY

Originated and contributed by Jim Kilburn, Qualicum Beach, B.C.

Hook: Size 6 or 8, 3 extra long
Thread: Monofilament
Body: Same as the Handlebar Fly above, but with a narrow strip of red reflective Mylar tape on either side.
Tail and Back: Pink polar bear hair or equal, pink Krystal Flash over, tied down at hook bend to form tail
Eyes: Red
Head: Fluorescent red tying thread
Cover: Clear epoxy coating over the head and body, not the tail
Intended use: Wet fly for beachfront coho salmon

Comments: Jim's Fly is another version of the ubiquitous Epoxy Minnow. I first tied Jim's Fly several seasons ago for use off saltwater beaches, where it quickly proved effective for coho salmon. The unique features of this pattern are that it incorporates the body of the Handlebar Fly, and includes a narrow strip of reflective red tape on either side of the body. I alternate this pattern with Art Limber's Candy minnow version, which has proven so successful over the years. Jim's Fly is generally fished with a floating or slow-sink mono-core line. The fly sinks quite rapidly, thus a fairly fast strip retrieve is required when fishing shallow waters.

AL'S PAL

Originated and dressed by Al Limber, Courtenay B.C., contributed by Jim Kilburn

Hook: Size 6, Mustad 34007
Thread: Fluorescent pink
Tail: Tied short, using several strands of pink polar bear hair, several strands of Krystal Flash over
Body: Underlay of pink thread, covered with holographic clear plastic
Rib: About ten wraps of fine red, oval tinsel
Cover: Thin epoxy coating over the body, not the tail
Wing: Several strands of Krystal Flash, several strands of pink polar bear hair over extending only to the beginning of the hook bend to avoid wrap-around and turning
Eyes: Prismatic silver, epoxy over
Intended use: Wet fly for schooling coho salmon

Comments: AL's Pal is another extremely effective saltwater pattern for schooling coho. It was originated by Al Limber, who also tied this sample. Limber uses this fly exclusively when fishing for coho salmon off the saltwater beaches. For best results, fish this fly with a slow-sink mono-core line. Cast beyond the school of fish, allow it to sink for about five seconds, then retrieve it rapidly through the school.

DRAGGIN' DRAGON OR THE CLIPPED DEER HAIR DRAGONFLY NYMPH

Contributed by Jim Kilburn, Qualicum Beach B.C.

Hook: Size 4 or 6, 4x1 streamer type, weighted with lead or copper wire to invert the hook when the finished fly is in the water
Thread: Grey or white monocord
Body: In a ratio of two light to one dark bands of spun deer body hair clipped to represent a dragonfly nymph; or alternatively, use one colour of deer hair and mark segments with a felt pen

Legs: Six fronds from a primary grey goose feather or substitute, tied in along the thorax (Note: Legs can be spread, then stiffened with glue so they act as stabilizers)
Eyes: A bead-chain barbell attached with criss-cross bindings and blackened with a felt pen
Intended use: Wet fly for rainbow trout

REED RUNNER

Contributed by Jim Kilburn, Qualicum Beach, B.C.

Hook: Size 6 or 8, 3 extra long
Thread: Grey or white monocord
Tail: Deer hair
Body: Spun deer hair, clipped to represent an insect's abdomen, and marked accordingly with an appropriately coloured felt pen

Hackle: Cock (brown, badger or grizzly hackle) or deer body hair tied full and heavy, with fibres long enough to deflect the weeds past the hook (Note: Stiffen with clear sprayed varnish or equivalent, if necessary)
Intended use: Wet fly for rainbow trout

Comments: These last two flies are snag-resistant freshwater trout patterns that have been lurking in my fly box since the late 1950s. I tied them out of necessity in order to discourage snags, weeds, and reeds from stealing my flies. Although I tied them without being influenced by any particular pattern, the concept has doubtless been used by preceding generations of anglers faced with the same fouling problem. At any rate, both patterns are of clipped deer hair. The inverted one is tied to represent a dragonfly nymph dragging itself over the bottom marl or through chara weed. The heavily hackled one represents nothing in particular, and is designed to deflect its way through standing reeds. Although I've never previously named them, I suppose they could be respectively called the Draggin' Dragon and the Reed Runner, for lack of something more descriptive. At least, those are the names I've given them in the text.

In a follow-up letter in January 2004, Jim, concerned about fouling up the mud more with the term "originator" and with pattern names writes:

Regarding the Reed Runner, I have no proof that I originated this pattern, although I tied it in the late '50s and have used it ever since; similarly, the Draggin' Dragon. However, this fly has about 35 years of recorded history to back it up (see *The Compleat Kilburn*, "The Lake From Top to Bottom," page 57) and is probably 10 or more years older than that. It is therefore probably safe to say that I originated it. However, I'm reluctant to make such a claim for either pattern since I have no positive proof. Therefore, I have used Contributor rather than Originator in the attached dressings for these flies. Further to the Draggin' Dragon, it is possible that this fly might be capable of stirring up more than the mud. For instance, in Doug Wright's article *(BCFFF Fly Lines* Volume 4, 2003) Doug mentions a Phil Rowley dragonfly imitation called the Draggin'. To me, this implies that the name Draggin' Dragon should be changed—perhaps to the Dragon Dredge or simply the Dredge, or it could even be named The Clipped Deer Hair Dragonfly Nymph as it was named in the above-mentioned article. Take your pick.

I fish this fly with a sink-tip line and a very slow retrieve.

Comments: This is a snag-resistant pattern designed for dragging through the bottom vegetation and marl common to so many B.C. lakes. The fly is designed to represent a dragonfly nymph, and I fish this pattern through the weeds with a slow hand-twist retrieve. When fishing over bottom marl, I find it is worthwhile to punctuate the slow retrieve with an occasional sharp, six-inch tug to represent the jet-propelled capability of the dragonfly nymph and to hopefully stir up a small cloud of fish-attracting marl in the process.

Art Limber

Born in Penticton, British Columbia in 1939, Art has since spent the majority of his life developing his love and natural talent for fishing. He could be seen fishing the Fraser River in British Columbia before and after school as early as age 9. This devotion to fish continues today and he can be seen

regularly fishing the water within and around Vancouver Island. Art now resides in Qualicum Bay on Vancouver Island. Art's love of angling led him to design some of his own lures and flies. He capitalized on over 35 years of producing, proving, and refining his own designs and now makes some of the finest polar bear bucktails in North America. The flies are primarily used to catch coho and spring salmon. They are trolled at approximately 5 knots on the surface of the ocean, in the wake of the motor approximately 60 feet behind the boat. Some of the patterns and colours used in Art's early designs became the forerunners for those used in the present day bucktails. His bucktails have long been prized by fresh- and saltwater fly-fishermen in the Pacific Northwest.

OLIVE WIZARD
Originated and contributed by Art Limber

Hook: Size 6 and 8, Mustad 34011 or equivalent
Thread: White Danville's Plus
Tail: Fluorescent pink Fluorofibre
Body: Diamond Braid, colour to suit
Belly: White polar bear with 4 strands of pearl Krystal Flash blended in
Beard: Fluorescent pink Fluorofibre
Wing: Rolled teal breast fibres dyed lime, medium olive polar bear mixed with 4 strands of peacock Krystal Flash
Head: Clear monofilament, 1.5 mm red or silver tape eyes (Note: Epoxy head to finish)
Intended use: Wet fly; floating or intermediate line for beach and estuary coho and cutthroat trout

Comments: This is probably the best beach fly that I have ever used in over 30 years of beach fishing. Coho take it through the entire season. Cutthroat trout take it well from mid-July until the end of the season. Fish using a fast strip retrieve.

BEACH CLOUSER
Adapted and contributed by Art Limber

Hook: Size 8 or 10, Tiemco 9394
Thread: Shell pink 6/0
Eyes: Self-centering Hour Glass Brass Eyes, micro. 1.5 mm red tape eyes, lacquer head and eyes when fly is finished.
Under-Wing: Yellow polar bear and 3 to 4 strands of pearl Flashabou
Over-Wing: Bubblegum pink polar bear mixed with 3 or 4 strands of pink Flashabou
Intended use: Wet fly; floating or intermediate line for beach or estuary salmon and cutthroat trout.

Comments: A very good fly for pink and coho salmon. It fishes well in 4 to 6 feet of water and is also good for beach cutthroat early in the season.

CANDY FRY
Originated and contributed by Art Limber

Hook: Size 8 or 10, Tiemco 9394   *Thread:* Clear monofilament

Body: Ten strands of rainbow Krystal Flash
Back and Tail: Dark green dyed, teal flank, rolled and tied down at rear.
Head: Clear monofilament
Eyes: 1.5 mm silver prismatic eyes
Finish: Epoxy entire body and back to finish
Intended use: Wet fly; intermediate or floating line for beach and estuary coho and cutthroat trout

Comments: A very good early season fly used for beach cutthroat trout during pink and chum fry migrations. This fly is also good for coho in the fall. Fish using a fast strip retrieve.

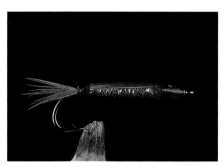

PINK CANDY
Originated and contributed by Art Limber

Hook: Size 8–10, Tiemco 9394
Thread: Fluorescent red 6/0
Tail: Fluorescent pink hackle fibres
Body: 12 strands of rainbow Krystal Flash
Back: Fluorescent pink hackle fibres tied down at rear
Head: Fluorescent red thread
Eyes: 1.5 mm. red prismatic tape eyes
Finish: Cover entire body with 5-minute epoxy
Intended use: Wet fly; intermediate or floating line for beach or estuary salmon and cutthroat trout

Comments: An excellent early season fly for pink salmon and cutthroat trout. It is the only fly that I have used to catch all five species of Pacific salmon in salt water. Coho take this fly all season long. Fish it using a fast strip retrieve.

ART'S SPECIAL BUCKTAIL
Originated and contributed by Art Limber

Hook: Size 2/0 to 4/0, Mustad 34007 for front hook; trailer: size 1 to 2/0 Mustad 92553S
Thread: Black 3/0, use fluorescent red 3/0 to tie down Mylar tubing at rear
Body: Medium silver Mylar tubing
Wing: White polar bear with four strands of pearl Krystal Flash mixed in, pale pink polar bear, light purple polar bear with four strands of purple Krystal Flash mixed in, medium olive polar bear with four strands of peacock Krystal Flash
Eyes: Hand-painted yellow with red pupil (Note: Apply several coats of lacquer over all)
Intended use: Trolled wet fly for saltwater coho

Comments: The best baitfish bucktail I have ever used. This pattern can be tied 3", 4.5" or 7" long, depending on bait size.

MARK McANEELEY PHOTO

Mark McAneeley

His reading of Roderick Haig-brown books in high school provided Mark with the inspiration to take up fly-fishing and fly-tying for steelhead. Mark developed a passion for the sport, which helped him acquire a summer job as a saltwater fishing guide in Campbell River in the summer of 1978 at the age of 17. In 1982, he became a member of the Haig-Brown Fly-Fishing Association in Victoria, and it was during his years of association with that group of fly-fishers and on the Thompson River that he met his mentors who introduced him to the double-handed rod and Spey casting. When he moved back to Campbell River he became friends with Bruce Gerhart, Bill Harrison and Dan Willard, also Spey rod enthusiasts. This is when he decided to make fishing and guiding his life-long occupation. He remains, to this day, passionately involved as a full-time, professional, freshwater guide on Vancouver Island and the Babine River, the latter for the Silver Hilton Steelhead Lodge.

BLACK WAKER
Adapted and contributed by Mark McAneeley

Hook: Size 2, Tiemco 7999
Thread: Black
Tail: Moose mane
Body: Deer hair dyed black, spun and clipped
Wing: White calf tail split and angled forward
Intended use: Waked dry fly for summer-run steelhead

Comments: Influenced by Lani Waller at the Silver Hilton Steelhead Lodge, the majority of our guests use the Waller Waker as their searching pattern when fishing a dry fly. This is my stripped-down version of the original developed by Waller. It is my favourite as a searching pattern, because with a riffle hitch, it will wake all day and is very visible to the angler and the fish. The white wings are more visible under good light conditions, when the sun is high and behind you. The large black body makes the fly more visible under tough light conditions, especially in the morning and late afternoon when there is often a silvery glare on the water.

THE CLOSER
Adapted and contributed by Mark McAneeley

Hook: Size 6, Tiemco 2302
Thread: Black
Tail: Blue Krystal Flash
Body: Silver Mylar
Hackle & Head: Deer hair dyed black, spun and clipped
Wing: Two grizzly hackle tips
Intended use: Waked dry fly for summer-run steelhead

Comments: This is a version of the Muddler that I developed for stubborn fish that will boil at the Waker but refuse to take it. I have used it with great success on the Babine River. First I try it with a riffle hitch and, if the fish refuses, I try it without the hitch.

JUICY LUCY SPEY – PURPLE
Adapted and contributed by Mark McAneeley

Hook: Size 3/0 to 2, Daiichi 2025
Thread: Red
Tag: Five turns of fine silver, oval tinsel
Body: Fluorescent, pink floss back half, purple seal fur front half
Rib: Number 14, silver Mylar with fine silver oval tinsel wrapped beside Mylar
Hackle: Purple, palmered over seal fur body section
Collar: One purple marabou feather wound sparsely followed by two turns of guinea fowl
Wing: Fluorescent orange-dyed, golden pheasant breast feathers tied in to lay flat over body
Intended use: Wet fly-fished with a floating line for summer-run steelhead

JUICY LUCY SPEY – BLACK
Adapted and contributed by Mark McAneeley

Hook: Size 2/0 to 2, Daiichi 2025
Thread: Black
Tag: Five turns of fine silver, oval tinsel
Body: Blue floss back half, black seal front half
Rib: Number 14, silver Mylar with fine silver oval tinsel wrapped beside Mylar
Hackle: Black, palmered, over seal fur body

Collar: One black marabou feather wound sparsely followed by two turns of guinea fowl
Wing: Purple-dyed golden pheasant breast feathers tied to lay flat over body

Intended use: Wet fly-fished with a floating line for summer-run steelhead

Comments: I developed both of these fancier, sparser Spey-style flies for fishing summer steelhead with floating lines in 1992. I have had great success on the Bulkley and Babine rivers with both of these patterns. When the rivers are very low and clear, I have had some success on the Gold, Nimpkish and Salmon rivers for winter steelhead when fished with a floating line.

JUICY LUCY
Adapted and contributed by Mark McAneeley

Hook: Size 2/0 to 2, Tiemco 7999
Thread: Fluorescent orange
Body: Fluorescent, orange floss
Rib: Gold Mylar
Hackle: Fluorescent orange marabou followed by fluorescent pink hackle

Wing: Six strands of pearl Krystal Flash, topped by two fluorescent orange-dyed golden pheasant breast feathers tied in to lay flat over body
Intended use: Wet fly for winter-run steelhead

Comments: I first started tying and fishing this fly in the winter of 1986. Before this I fished the orange G.P. almost exclusively for winter steelhead. I loved how the G.P. fished and was having very good success, but I was not fond of how long it took to tie. Since most of my winter fishing is with sink-tips, I was looking for a pattern that had a similar profile, but took a lot less time to tie. Bill Harrison first introduced me to marabou patterns, and the Juicy Lucy is an offshoot of a pattern that Bill was tying. I loved the fact that when the fly is wet it has a similar "shrimpy" profile as the G.P. and only takes a fraction of the time to tie. I came up with the name Juicy Lucy when I commented on how "juicy" the fly looked in the water. I also tie this pattern in both purple and black & blue.

JUICY LUCY – PURPLE
Adapted and contributed by Mark McAneeley

Hook: Size 2/0 to 2, Tiemco 7999
Thread: Red
Body: Purple floss
Rib: Silver Mylar
Hackle: Purple marabou followed by purple hackle

Wing: Six strands of pearl Krystal Flash, topped by two fluorescent orange-dyed golden pheasant breast feathers tied to lay in flat over body
Intended use: Wet fly for summer-run steelhead

Comments: Developed in 1987 for summer-run steelhead, I have had good success with it on winter-runs as well.

JUICY LUCY – BLACK & BLUE
Adapted and contributed by Mark McAneeley

Hook: Size 2/0 to 2, Tiemco 7999
Thread: Black
Body: Blue floss
Rib: Silver Mylar
Hackle: Black marabou followed by teal blue marabou

Wing: Six strands of pearl Krystal Flash, topped by two purple-dyed golden pheasant breast feathers tied in to lay flat over body
Intended use: Wet fly for summer-run steelhead

Comments: Developed in 1987 for summer-run steelhead, I have had very good success with it for winter-run steelhead. With the tube-fly craze that has been happening on the Skeena system in the last couple of years I have been tying all three of these patterns on tubes with great success. To this day these are still my "go to" patterns when fishing with sink-tips for steelhead. Steelhead from the Campbell, Salmon, Nimpkish, Cowichan, Gold, Squamish, Wakeman, Bulkley, Kispiox and Babine rivers have all been taken on all three of these patterns.

Barry Stokes

Born in Victoria, Barry Stokes has lived his entire life on Vancouver Island. He has been fly-fishing for 25 years and a member of the Haig-Brown Fly Fishing Association for 23 years. He has taught fly-fishing, fly-tying, casting and rod building over a number of years, and has built rods and tied flies commercially. Currently he is the manager for Islander Reels in Saanichton. Barry was the first fly tier to be honoured by the BCFFF for his tying skills and in 2001 received the Jack Shaw Fly Tying Award. He enjoys all types of fly-fishing, but has a special attraction to fly-fishing for sea-run cutthroat.

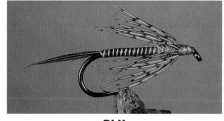

PLK
Adapted and contributed by Barry Stokes

Hook: Size 10 to 14, Tiemco 5262
Thread: White 6/0
Tail: A few pheasant tail barbules
Body: One brown and one white moose mane wound up hook

Thorax: Grey Ice Dub
Hackle: A few turns of Hungarian partridge
Intended use: Wet fly for stillwater trout

Comments: This is a possible variant of a Sylvester Nemes pattern. I dressed this fly to target trout feeding on large "bomber" chironomids. It is an effective fly fished at all depths and best fished slowly. As well, this fly has proved effective when trolled very slowly.

OLIVE CRIPPLED DAMSEL EMERGER
Adapted and contributed by Barry Stokes

Hook: Size 8, Tiemco dry fly
Thread: Light olive 6/0
Tail: Pale olive braided mono (use olive Pantone pen)
Body: Pale olive dubbing
Hackle: Grizzly, palmered
Wing: Pale olive dyed deer hair
Intended use: Dry fly for stillwater trout

Comments: When damselfly nymphs are mature they swim to lakeside or shoal vegetation and climb up the stalks of reeds to hatch into adults. This fly was developed to target trout feeding on emerging damselflies that were either wind blown from reeds or knocked off by hungry trout.

PLWB (PROSPECT LAKE WOOLLY BUGGER)
Adapted and contributed by Barry Stokes

Hook: Size 8, Tiemco 5263
Thread: Black 6/0
Tail: Medium olive Woolly Bugger marabou
Body: Glo-Brite chenille, #9 (chartreuse and green)
Rib: (Opt.) green wire to secure hackle
Hackle: Grizzly, palmered with a couple of extra turns at the head
Side: Medium green Flashabou, extending to the tail's end
Intended use: Wet fly for stillwater trout

Comments: This fly is the result of testing a number of colour combinations of the traditional Woolly Bugger. The body colour is critical to the success of this Bugger variation. It has proved to be a good searching fly on many lakes.

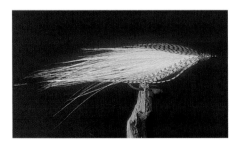

GARTSIDE SOFT HACKLE – CHARTREUSE
Originated by Jack Gartside, adapted and contributed by Barry Stokes

Hook: Size 8, Partridge Roman Moser Barbless Streamer, CS29
Thread: Monofilament
Tail: Silver Flashabou and chartreuse Krystal Flash
Body: Collar of fluorescent
chartreuse marabou
Hackle: A turn or two of mallard flank
Wing: Dark olive dyed mallard flank
Intended use: Wet fly for sea-run cutthroat

Comments: This fly was developed for sea-run cutthroat in murky water that has been stirred up with wind and wave action. It also performs quite well as a "go-to" pattern for selective or fussy cutts, especially when baitfish are present.

MONTE'S ZUMA
Originated by Ian Montgomery, tied and contributed by Barry Stokes

Hook: Size 2/0 to 1, Mustad 34011
Thread: Fluorescent pink 6/0 Danville's
Tail: Frayed-out pearl tinsel tubing
Body: Small pearl tinsel piping
Belly: White polar bear hair
Sides: Blue Fluorofibre along lateral line
Wing: Bubble gum pink over white polar bear hair
Intended use: Wet fly for ocean coho

Comments: This fly was developed for casting to coho in the ocean. When this fly was first put together, a number of colour combinations was tried but this one proved to be the winner and has become a standard at Weigh West Marine Resort. It also works well "bucktailed" for selective and fussy fish.

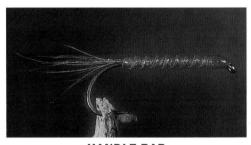

HANDLE BAR
Tied and contributed by Barry Stokes

Hook: Size 4 to 8, Partridge Sea Streamer CS11
Thread: Fluorescent pink
Tail: A few strands of hot pink polar bear hair and pink Krystal Flash
Body: Fluorescent red (pink) Edge Bright over silver tinsel
Intended use: Wet fly for pink salmon

Comments: Bruce Ferguson of Gig Harbor, Washington, introduced me to this fly, which is without doubt my most effective pink-salmon beach fly. This fly is most effective when fished slow or dead drift. [Note: See Jim Kilburn's section for the origin of this fly, which although very simple has many variations.]

Cowichan Fly Fishers
Formed in 1991, the Cowichan Fly Fisher club is based in Duncan and its home river is the famous Cowichan. Few rivers on Vancouver Island are as rich in aquatic life and as a result the river is home to all species of salmon as well as rainbow, cutthroat, winter steelhead and the introduced brown trout. Fly tying is an important part of the club activites. The club has a number of excellent tiers as is shown by the flies contributed by Sylvia Dean, Barry Alldred, Kenzie Cuthbert and Ken Thorne.

Barry Alldred

has lived his entire life in the Cowichan Valley and threw his first Alldred-dressed flies onto that river when he was 14 years old. His brother introduced him to steelhead the year before he started fly-fishing, and fishing for that game fish soon became his passion. In the mid-1970s he moved to Duncan where on the lower Cowichan he met and was befriended by Haig-Brown Fly Fishers Association's Mike Dunn, Guy Lawrence and Gary Stuart who introduced him to steelhead fly-fishing. In 1978 he became a member of that club. In the mid to late 1980s when the summer-runs were running well on the Campbell, Barry spent time on that river learning the secrets of double-handed rod fly-fishing from Mark McAneely. In 1990 he was one of the charter members of the Cowichan Fly Fishers and started his Squaretail Guide Service. When not pursuing steelhead, he can be found on Interior lakes searching for rainbows or on Vancouver Island beaches for pinks and coho salmon.

Kenzie Cuthbert

began fishing at the age of 11, has had 25 years fishing experience and guides on both fresh and salt water. He owns Cowichan River Wilderness Lodge, located on the banks of the Cowichan River. He joined the Cowichan Fly Fishers in 1997.

Sylvia Dean

was born and raised on Cowichan Lake on Vancouver Island and has spent her entire life in that southern part of the Island where she spends her pastime fishing its many lakes and rivers. She, along with her three brothers, learned to fish on their father's knee, but Sylvia turned to fly-fishing around 1980 and began tying flies around 1985. She was hooked on tying when she caught a 15-inch trout on one of the flies she tied. She has been a member of the Cowichan Fly Fishers since 1991.

Ken Thorne

is a lifelong fisherman who grew up on the banks of the Cowichan River and Cowichan Bay. For the past 14 years he has lived on Fuller Lake and that is the water where he tests his flies. He spends considerable time each year on the lakes of B.C.'s interior and Cariboo. He likes to fish for bass on Vancouver Island, as well as stillwater trout. Coho in salt water are a favourite, but his passion is for summer-run steelhead in wild settings. He is a keen fly tier, specializing in durable, fish-producing patterns that represent life forms that fish feed on, rather than patterns that attract. He joined the club in 1994 and has taught fly-tying within the club for the past number of years.

STEELHEAD DOC SPRATLEY
Adapted and contributed by Barry Alldred

Hook: Size 1/0 to 6, Partridge Bartleet
Thread: Danville's, black 6/0
Tip: Red tying thread
Tail: Polar bear hair
Butt: Red floss
Body: Black dubbing over seven wraps of 0.035 lead
Rib: Oval silver tinsel
Hackle: Guinea fowl beard
Wing: Black bear hair with a few strands from a golden pheasant red breast feather
Intended use: Wet fly for winter steelhead

Comments: The steelhead Doc Spratley has seen many versions over the past 40 seasons, most for use on Interior waters. This fly is another variation of the famous Doc Spratley coming from Barry's tying vise in 1998. He uses it for steelhead and brown trout on the Cowichan.

COWICHAN SUNRISE
Adapted and contributed by Barry Alldred

Hook: Size 1/0 to 6, Partridge Bartleet
Thread: Danville's, red 6/0
Tag: Holographic tinsel
Tail: Hot orange Fluorofibre
Butt: Peacock herl
Body: Fluorescent hot orange Ultra Chenille
Rib: Holographic tinsel
Hackle: Orange throat
Wing: Orange polar bear hair
Intended use: Wet fly for winter steelhead

Comments: First dressed by Barry in 1998 as a variation of the popular Washington State Skykomish Sunrise, developed by George McLeod.

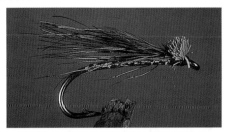

BLUE & GOLD ROLLED MUDDLER
Adapted and contributed by Kenzie Cuthbert

Hook: Size 6, Eagle Claw L1197N F
Thread: Black
Body: Flat gold prismatic tinsel
Wing: Sparse mix of deer hair and blue tinsel
Head: Flared deer hair
Intended use: Wet fly for coastal trout and salmon

Comments: This is another variation of Tom Murray's well known Rolled Muddler fly. This adaptation came from Kenzie's tying vise in 1999 and he has found it effective on Vancouver Island waters for trout and salmon.

MUDDLED MICKEY
Adapted and contributed by Kenzie Cuthbert

Hook: Size 6, Eagle Claw L1197N F
Thread: Black
Body: Flat gold prismatic tinsel
Wing: Sparse mix of red and yellow craft hair with a few deer hairs
Head: Flared deer hair
Intended use: Wet fly for coastal trout and salmon

Comments: A variation of the famous eastern Mickey Finn, which was popularized as a sea-run cutthroat and coho fly by the Totem Fly Fishers in the late 1960s. This is a recent adaptation coming from Kenzie's vise in 1999 and has proven effective for trout and salmon on Vancouver Island waters.

DEER HAIR DUD
Adapted and contributed by Sylvia Dean

Hook: Size 12
Thread: Black 6/0 or 8/0
Wing: Deer hair
Intended use: Dry fly for rainbow, cutthroat and sea-run cutthroat trout

Comments: This fly was originated by a nameless old man on Northern Vancouver Island. It is my favourite dry fly for trout and I have used it with great success on lakes all over Vancouver Island. Like the Mickey Finn, it seems to work when nothing else will. I have used it with a dry line, but also quite successfully with a 10-foot sink-tip. It has been a consistent producer from the first cast.

MUSKRAT EMERGER
Originated and contributed by Ken Thorne

Hook: Size 14 to 18, Mustad 80200BR
Thread: Black
Tail: Eight to 10 lemon woodduck fibres over one strand of pearl Krystal Flash
Body: Dubbed silver muskrat underfur
Rib: Fine copper wire
Wing: One fine grizzly hackle tip with a small tuft of pumpkin-coloured cul de canard over tie-in point
Hackle: Two turns of grizzly, wrapped and then swept slightly back and tied down
Head: Black thread coated with black lacquer
Intended use: Dry or wet fly Chironomid for stillwater trout

Comments: Developed on Fuller Lake in 1996, I have used the Muskrat Emerger successfully on many Vancouver Island lakes, as well as lakes in the Cariboo and Kamloops area. I developed this fly for a number of reasons. Vancouver Island stillwater trout often key on emerging Chironomids, providing the fly-fisher with either a very frustrating or rewarding surface or surface film fishing. My search for a consistently productive pattern to match the hatching insect led me to much observation, both on Fuller Lake and in my aquarium. By observing pupae just under the surface film in pre-emergent states, I witnessed the following key characteristics:

- Prominent hollow shuck with diffracting qualities and ribbing or segmentation marks
- Prominent black shiny head
- An amber colour present in the wing case and newly emerging wing (Note: This colour fades quickly as the wing dries and is usually not apparent in adult Chironomids)
- Very straggly legs
- Pronounced movement during actual shucking phase
- Gas sheath on body, often very noticeable, especially when Chironomids have ascended from deep water.

This pattern, which owes some of its inspiration to Randall Kaufmann's Timberline Emerger, was designed to reflect these characteristics, and has proven very successful. It can be fished dry on top, or pulled under and fished wet just below the surface. The muskrat dubbing holds a bit of air and has a good silvery appearance. Do not apply floatant or sinkant to this fly.

MOOSE MANE EMERGER
Originated and contributed by Ken Thorne

Hook: Size 14 to 18, Mustad 80200BR
Thread: Black
Tail: Eight to 10 lemon woodduck fibres over one strand of pearl Krystal Flash
Body: One light and one dark moose mane hair, tied in at thin end and wrapped side by side up hook shank and coated with Flexament or nail hardener
Wing: One fine grizzly hackle tip with a small tuft of pumpkin-coloured cul de canard over tie-in point
Hackle: Two turns of grizzly wrapped and then swept slightly back and tied down
Head: Black thread coated with black lacquer
Intended use: Dry or wet fly Chironomid for stillwater trout

Comments: This fly came from my vise in 1998. Under some water or light conditions Chironomid emergers do not have the body-covering gas film, and more realistic-looking segmented body works best. Moose mane fibres provide good segmentation, are naturally tapered and come in a range of dark and light colour tones. I have used moose mane-bodied Chironomid pupa patterns with good success prior to adapting the fly body to that of an emerger. This pattern has been very effective on Vancouver Island lakes and has also been a consistent fish catcher for me on lakes in the Cariboo and Kamloops areas.

My favourite way to fish this Moose Mane Emerger and the Muskrat Emerger is on a slow-sinking line (type II or slime line) and sight cast to surface-feeding fish. The small size and natural buoyancy of these patterns allows me to fish the fly dry or in the surface film for the first half of the retrieve, and then just under the surface for the rest of the retrieve.

RED TERMITE
Originated and contributed by Ken Thorne

Hook: Size 8 and 10 Mustad 9671
Thread: Black
Body: White closed-cell foam, coloured with rustic brown permanent marker
Wing: Six to eight strands of black and one or two strands of pearl Krystal Flash sweeping back along sides
Hackle: Ginger
Intended use: Dry fly for stillwaters or river trout and steelhead

Comments: On Vancouver Island, termites hatch in good numbers, usually around the beginning of September. Trout and summer-run steelhead love them and the lack of a good pattern prompted me to experiment with termite imitations. The foam-bodied Red Termite came from my vise in 1998 and has proved to be a very effective and durable fly. Stillwater dry flies don't require as much buoyancy, but the foam body really helps on a river, permitting the use of a heavier wet-fly hook which is a boon for holding steelhead.

FOAM-BODIED SEDGE
Originated and contributed by Ken Thorne

Hook: Size 6 to 12, Mustad 9671
Thread: Pale yellow
Body: Tied on the hook's underside, a thin strip of light or bright green closed cell foam for stillwaters and green or bright yellow closed-cell foam for summer-run steelhead
Wing: Four clumps of stacked, well-marked deer hair
Hackle: Ginger
Intended use: Dry fly for stillwater trout and summer-run steelhead

Comments: First tied in 2000, I designed this fly as an imitation of the stillwater traveling sedge. As a stillwater fly it performed well, but it has become a very successful fly for Vancouver Island summer-run steelhead as well. This is an improved adaptation of the numerous standard B.C. sedge patterns. I wanted a fly as effective as the Mikulak or Traveling Sedge pattern, but one that would float all day long and not succumb to water logging from fish slime or damage by fish teeth. This fly's shape provides a

good silhouette to the fish, the mottled wing diffracts light well, and together with the segmented, foam body makes for a realistic, buggy-looking, sedge imitation.

Island Waters Fly Fishing Club

The Island Waters Fly Fishing Club was founded in 1985 and is based in Nanaimo on lovely Vancouver Island. It is the home club of the self-proclaimed world's greatest fly-fisherman, Bill Brown, now deceased. The purpose of the club is as follows:

- To practice, further and promote the art of fly-fishing
- To practice and promote fish conservation and enhancement
- To encourage fellowship and sportsmanship amongst anglers

The flies dressed by club members Dave Connolly, John O'Brien and Peter Huyghebaert, show inquisitive minds that result in flies that are good examples of the art and craft of fly-tying.

Dave Connolly

has been a member of the Island Waters Fly Fishers since 1994 and served as the club president in 2002 and 2003. He has been fly-fishing for approximately 40 years. He started fly-fishing for grayling and rainbow trout in the Peace River Country in the 1960s on rivers such as the Pine, Murray, Parsnip and Upper

Peace. He moved to Kelowna in 1971 where he fished many of the lakes in the South and Central Okanagan. He was a member of the Lonely Loons Fly Fishing club in Kelowna. During those years he learned to tie flies and has enjoyed the hobby ever since. In 1983, Dave moved to Nanaimo where he has enjoyed fly-fishing for pink and coho salmon on the Central Island beaches, drifting the Cowichan and taking regular trips to the Interior lakes and rivers for trout.

Peter Huyghebaert

started fly-fishing in 1966. From Brook trout in Algonquin Park, he went on to fish the East extensively during his Air Force career: from New York's Ausable and Salmon; New Brunswick's Miramichi, Cains, Nashwaak, Renous, Dungarvon and St. John; Newfoundland's Salmonier, Indian, Little Salmonier and Renews; Quebec's Matane, Puyjalong, Romaine, Godbout and George (Ungava Bay) to

rivers on Baffin Island and in Scotland. During that "Eastern" time, he mastered the art of fly-tying with guidance from superb New Brunswick tiers such as Frank Wilson and Wally Doak. He instructed basics to classics level fly-tying courses while earning his BSc in biology (fish) from UNB. He is a re-founding member (1983) (along with Dr. Eden Bromfield and Paul Marriner), as well as Past President and Life Member of the Ottawa Fly-Fishers. Since his retirement to Nanaimo in 1994, he fishes the Kamloops and Chilcotin areas for trout in the spring and fall and fills his summers saltwater fly-fishing on Vancouver Island. He joined the IWFF in 2001 and was elected Vice President in 2003.

John O'Brien's

JOHN O'BRIEN PHOTO

dad started him fishing before potty training and at age 12, John would bike 100 miles to Banff to fish in the Park. He lived in Prince Rupert from 1969-1974 and fished the usual Skeena system rivers. On returning to Calgary he started fly-fishing in earnest. During the late 1970s, besides the Bow River, his love of the sport took him to the waters in the Rockies and B.C. Interior, including Tunkwa Lake with its great Chironomid hatches. Because of the wide range of fishing opportunities such as salmon, steelhead and smallmouth bass, as well as the natural beauty of Vancouver Island, he moved to Nanaimo in 1980. He has owned and worked in fly and tackle shops since moving to the Island and has guided on fresh and salt water and tied flies commercially. He has been teaching fly-fishing, casting, tying and rod building for over 20 years. With the help of the World's Greatest Fly Fisherman (the late Sir Bill Brown) and Roy Sorensen he was instrumental in the 1985 formation of the Island Waters Fly Fishers Club and served as president the first two years. His favorite fisheries these days are the pink and coho salmon off the Island's beaches.

DAVE'S BEAD HEAD WOOLLY BUGGER
Originated and contributed by Dave Connolly

Hook: Size 6 to 12, Mustad 9671 and size 4, Mustad 3906
Thread: Olive or clear mono 6/0
Tail: Olive marabou with 2 or 3 strands of body material added
Body: Arizona Diamond Braid, #4, peacock or #17, olive peacock
Hackle: Olive green saddle, palmered
Head: 3/16" brass bead for larger hooks and 5/32" brass bead for small hooks
Intended use: Wet fly for lakes and rivers

Comments: I started tying this variation of the Woolly Bugger in 1996. In my opinion, it is much more versatile than the standard version. It is easy to use in shallow water with a dry line as it sinks well with the bead head. As well, it works well fished deep on a sinking line. Its materials, especially the Arizona Diamond Braid body, are very "buggy" and attractive. If I were to choose one wet fly to cover most situations, this would be it. I have tied several variations, the most effective using black marabou and black hackle with either #5 Black Peacock or #7 Ruby Black Arizona Diamond Braid. The fly can also be tied with barbell eyes so that it lies upside down and fishes weedless. These black variations work well, but the long-term, steady producer is the olive.

I have been using this fly extensively for seven-plus years and have found it to be a consistently excellent producer for cutthroat, rainbow, brook and brown trout, as well as grayling. More often than not it equals or out-produces other patterns that are used at the same time.

This fly has caught fish in virtually every lake I have used it. On Vancouver Island it has worked well in Fuller, Chemainus, First and Second Nanaimo, Quennel, and Horne lakes. In the Interior of the province, I have used it in the Merritt, West and East Kootenays, Kamloops, Chilcotin, Cariboo and Peace River areas with great success. On one trip with this fly I had a great evening of fishing on Atlin Lake at the mouth of the Atlin River, catching 14" to 18" grayling.

In addition to the lakes I have used this fly with good success on the Cowichan and Big Qualicum rivers on Vancouver Island, the St. Marys and Elk rivers in the East Kootenays and the Thompson River near Kamloops.

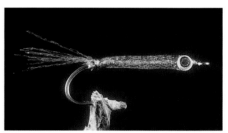

NILE STREAK
Originated and contributed by Peter Huyghebaert

Hook: Size 10 to 6, Mustad S74S SS or 34011
Thread: Fire-orange 8/0
Body: Pearl Mylar tube
Throat: 4-5 strands pearl Krystal Flash
Wing: 4-5 strands chartreuse Krystal Flash under 3 to 4 strands of blue
Eyes: Prismatic stick-ons (fly is then coated from head to tail tie-in with epoxy)
Intended use: Saltwater salmon beach wet fly for pinks and coho

Comments: This fly is tied in a similar manner to that of Keith Fulsher's Thunder Creek series in that the throat and wing are tied in facing forward and then bent back and tied in just before the bend of the hook. The Streak was developed as an easier-casting, rugged and realistic needlefish imitation. It has proven its mettle on the beaches of East Vancouver Island for both coho and pinks. Fish it on a floating line whenever you see schools of needlefish close to the beach.

OVERKRILL
Originated and contributed by Peter Huyghebaert

Hook: Size 8 to 4, Mustad C47S D
Thread: Fire-orange 8/0 or 6/0
Tail: Hot pink polar bear
Body: Small, medium or large pearl chenille, hot pink
Rib: Small or medium silver tinsel (varnished type)
Shellback: Fluorescent Pink Lazer wrap tied in facing forward, then folded back over the body and tied down with the tinsel and trimmed
Intended use: Saltwater salmon beach wet fly for pinks and coho

Comments: This fly is a further evolution of the ubiquitous pink beach fly. It is simple to tie, uses primarily artificial material which stands up well in salt water, looks good to the angler as well as the fish and has proven deadly on pinks and coho. This is the first fly I tie on for beach fishing, switching only if fish are showing and are not in a "pink" mood.

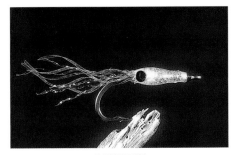

SQUIDLY
Adapted and contributed by Peter Huyghebaert

Hook: Size 8 to 4, Mustad S71S SS or 34007
Thread: Fire-orange 8/0
Tail: 4-5 strands of pink Krystal Flash
Under Body: Build up slightly with small unwaxed dental-floss (on larger versions)

Body: Pearl Mylar trimmed to leave 4 to 5 strands extending to the tail
Eyes: Red prismatic stick-on, then epoxy coat from the tail tie-in to the hook eye
Intended use: Saltwater salmon beach wet fly for pinks and coho

Comments: This fly was adapted from one used by an unknown fellow fly-fisherman from the Courtney area in 1998. His version consisted of a Mylar tube on a hook with a few strands protruding. The fly worked quite well but only for one or two fish before the body was torn off. I added the pink Krystal Flash, built up the bend area somewhat with floss, added eyes and also the epoxy finish. It is now a very rugged coho and pink beach fly that imitates a small squid, gammarid or immature baitfish which is superb for cruising coho along the beaches of East Vancouver Island.

GREEN & BLACK MEANY
Originated and contributed by Peter Huyghebaert

Hook: Size 4 or 2, Mustad S74S SS or 34011
Thread: Black 6/0
Throat: Strands of chartreuse Krystal Flash
Wing: White polar bear, under chartreuse polar bear, under green Krystal Flash
Cheeks/Eyes: These are prepared

from ring-necked Pheasant "clutch" feather, wetted with head cement, stroked into shape, with small prismatic eyes applied to suit. Coat with 5-minute clear epoxy and tie in after eyes have hardened, with a coat of epoxy applied over the head and eye area
Intended use: Wet fly for offshore coho

Comments: This fly has evolved over a number of years from more heavily dressed polar bear bucktails to a sparsely tied, much slimmer, easy-to-cast, durable coho fly which has proven itself in Barkley Sound. The primary baitfish colours in the area are green/white, black/white and blue/white, so one of these two flies will always fit the bill if you can get the size right. It fishes best on a floating ghost-tip line with a nine-weight rod being just about right for the job. For the black version, just replace the chartreuse polar bear with grey and the green Krystal Flash with black.

BLACK ANGEL/GREEN ANGEL
Originated and contributed by Peter Huyghebaert

Hook: Size 1/0 or 2/0, Mustad 34007(casting) or 34011(trolling)
Thread: Black, 3/0
Body: Pearl Diamond Braid (epoxy-coated for durability)
Wing: White polar bear hair under grey polar bear under black Angel hair

Sides: A few strands of pearl Flashabou on each side
Cheeks/eyes: Dark green pheasant rump, prismatic stick-on eyes, epoxy covered
Intended use: Saltwater salmon, chinook & coho on downrigger

Comments: These two flies were tied to imitate the baitfish on the west coast of the Island. They were originally used to cast for coho, with the larger sizes fished off a downrigger for both coho and chinook. The two-inch-long flies are reasonable to cast, however, slim, sparsely tied flies have proven much better for the casting job. These two flies in the larger sizes (4 inches +) still do a great job used on a downrigger for coho and chinook about 5-6 feet up the cable from a dummy flasher and about 5-10 feet further out. Use a fly reel with a good drag, just in case you hook into that tyee! For the green version, use chartreuse polar bear and peacock Angel Hair and a lighter shade of green rump feather.

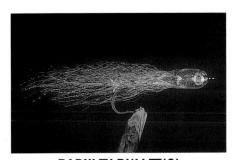

BARKLEY BULLET(S)
Originated and contributed by Peter Huyghebaert

Hook: Size 1 to 1/0, Mustad S74S SS or 34011
Thread: Fire-orange 6/0
Body: Mylar tubing over the bare hook (epoxy-coated for durability)
Throat: White polar bear

Wing: 8 to 9 strands of pearl Krystal Flash under chartreuse polar bear under 8 to 9 strands of chartreuse Krystal Flash
Eyes: Prismatic stick-ons, 3mm
Intended use: Wet fly for offshore coho

Comments: The wing and throat are tied forward, then reversed and temporarily tied down while the head is epoxied. This fly was designed to be a 2- to 2-1/2-inch-long, easy-casting imitation of the prevalent baitfish in the Barkley Sound area on the West Coast of Vancouver Island. Casting heavy Clousers to surface-feeding coho is no longer required since the Bullet has a similar, less-pronounced "jigging" action in the water and is completely non-fouling. The fish like it as well or better than a Clouser style and in comparison it is a real joy to cast. For the black version, simply change the chartreuse polar bear hair to dark grey and the chartreuse Krystal Flash to black (and apply 15 to 20 strands).

BLACK CARPENTER ANT
Originated and contributed by John O'Brien

Hook: Size 10, Mustad 94840 or Tiemco 103BL
Thread: Black 8/0
Body: Foam ant body or foam strip
Hackle: Metz brown micro saddle hackle
Wing: Brown cock hackle tips
Intended use: Dry fly for trout

Comments: Over the years I have tied many ant patterns and all worked to some degree but most either did not last long, or float well or very long. I found through working in fly shops and tackle shops and being able to order and try products like float foams or foam ant bodies that they do all of the above with the added advantage of being easy to tie. This is important because when fish are actively feeding on these large ants they lose all fear, and you will go through a dozen flies in a big hurry. The ants on Vancouver Island are usually available to the fish on the hottest days in May and June, but only for a few days. Consequently, the large numbers of these insects that fall in the water make the fish go crazy and a good ant pattern will catch many and large fish. I have caught three-pound rainbows with at least 200 ants in their belly. I fish these dry and cast to the rises trying to guess which way the fish is moving. Because I have seen good hatches in July and August I carry these flies with me at all times during the summer. Fishing the black ant hatches on the Island is for me always one of the highlights of the year. I have my fly box filled with dozens of ant patterns and am ready to go at the first sign of a hatch. Don't miss this one.

friendly and seemed to know one another. By the time the bugs started to appear in large numbers, most of the guys were casting and catching nice rainbows. As the evening progressed, the bug numbers grew and the fish became more visible. The fellow next to me must have felt sorry for me and suggested I use about a size 12 Doc Spratley but with the wing cut off. I happened to have some with me and he suggested I use a fairly slow retrieve and a floating line. That fly imitates a Chironomid pupa, which were hatching at the time, he added. Doing as instructed I caught several fish right away and was quite impressed. As the evening got darker, the bite seemed to slow. However, the fish were still surfacing, making loud splashes very close to the boat, but not many were taking the altered Spratley. I switched to a #10 Tom Thumb. A bit too large, I thought. After several refusals, I managed to hook and land one fish. By this time it was getting dark, but when I looked around there had to be at least 20 boats in this one area. This hoard of local fly-fishers came every evening to fish this bug hatch. In coming to fish the hatch, they produced a hatch of their own and this "fly-fishermen hatch" was quite a sight.

Years later, as I sat tying flies and thinking about the Chironomid hatches on one of the local lakes, I understood why the Doc Spratley worked as a pupa. But why did the fish stop biting just before dark? When I studied the insects and learned about the emerging stage, it dawned on me that from the fish's view (below the surface) the Tom Thumb may indeed look like an emerging insect. Reflecting on this revelation I wanted to tie an emerging Chironomid and asked myself what would the fish view from below. They would see a pupa struggling to break through the surface film. After looking at the Spratley and Tom Thumb, I decided to combine the two and developed what became known as John's Thumb. But this did not truly explain the fly's origins properly so I decided to rename the fly 50/50: half Tom Thumb, half Doc Spratley. This fly is very effective during Chironomid hatches just before dark or on overcast days. The one drawback is that it is fairly fragile, so you will need to have at least a dozen for an evening's fishing. As well, I tie them up to size 24 for midge hatches. Cast near or to the rises, but do not retrieve.

50/50 (JOHN'S THUMB)
Originated and contributed by John O'Brien

Hook: Size 8 to 24, Tiemco 100BL or any fine-wire, regular-shank, dry-fly hook
Thread: Black, waxed nylon 6/0 for size 8 & 10 hooks and 8/0 for size 12 and smaller hooks
Tail: Guinea fowl fibres
Rib: Fine silver Mylar
Body: Black polypropylene yarn
Back and Wing: Natural deer hair
Intended use: Dry fly for stillwater rainbow trout

DURA BOATMAN
Originated and contributed by John O'Brien

Hook: Size 8, Tiemco 2457 pupa hook or equivalent
Thread: Black 8/0
Back: Thin Skin/scud back or a strip of dark green 1/4"-wide latex
Body: Glow Bright chenille, medium white
Paddles: Dark green, black or dark brown Super Floss or rubber legs
Thorax: Metallic silver chenille
Intended use: Wet fly for stillwater rainbow trout

Comments: Back in the '70s when I fished the Interior trout lakes like Tunkwa, a strange thing occurred which I called "the fly-fishermen hatch." I fished hard all day and saw and caught only a few good-sized trout on shrimp flies. Just after supper I noticed quite a number of boats launching at the campsite and all seemed to be headed for the far Northeast corner of the lake. All the fly-fishermen anchored in or near the weed beds and looked like they were waiting for something to happen. Most were quite

Comments: The water boatman has been imitated many times with some very effective designs. Unfortunately some are very hard to tie and, because fish hit these flies very hard, they tend to break a few off. It's important for me to have a fly that is simple, durable and works well; this fly has all those features in spades. The materials used in this fly help the fly sink and add sparkle to the underside to simulate the air bubble that the boatman carries with it, allowing it to breathe under water. On Vancouver Island, boatmen are very active in the spring and are one of the early insect food sources in lakes from February through April. I use a floating line and an Airflow sinking leader, either clear intermediate or slow sink. Casting to the rise produces good results. Once you find an area where boatmen are active, fish will be close by; for example in weed beds and shoals, which are best. Let the fly sink a few seconds then use a four-inch jerky retrieve, which simulates the paddling motion of the boatman. I tie them with silver or gold tinsel chenille and both seem to work equally well. The Dura Boatman works well in the fall on lakes in the Interior and the Rockies, when you find the water boatman flights occuring.

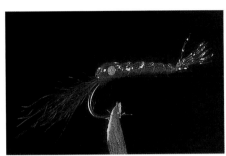

JR'S PINK EUPHAUSID
Originated and contributed by John O'Brien

Hook: Size 6 & 8, Daiichi X452 or Tiemco 411S/800S
Thread: Pink 6/0 waxed nylon to match body
Tail: Pink polar bear
Back: Pink Krystal Flash
Eyes: Small, clear monofilament eyes
Body: Pink steelhead yarn and metallic silver chenille
Intended use: Wet fly for salmon

Comments: When I first moved to Vancouver Island I was introduced to beach fishing for sea-run cutthroat at places like the Oyster River, Black Creek, Qualicum Bay, etc. My good friend Terry Petras took the time to show me the spots and when and how to fish them. It was a very special time and a unique learning experience. Fishing all that summer I eventually came across pink salmon but had limited success catching them on a variety of pink flies. Upon investigating the food sources for Pacific salmon I found that krill (euphausids) were their main food source and pink krill the predominate color.

This explained why pink flies worked so well, although most did not resemble the krill in size and shape. I set out to match the hatch, so to speak. I checked with the Pacific Biological Station in Nanaimo, obtained information from them and found pictures from books as well. Also I obtained samples from the stomachs of fresh coho, pink and chinook, caught in the Straight of Georgia's Nanaimo area. I also witnessed several so-called shrimp "hatches," for lack of a better term. Krill by the billions and it sounded like popcorn popping with the salmon gorging themselves. After learning more about krill and witnessing salmon feeding on them, I realized how important krill are to the salmon's diet. I tied many patterns prior to this one, but none came as close to imitating the euphausid shrimp like this pattern. I've had more 30-fish days with this fly beach fishing than any other fly I've tried in the last 20 years.

For salmon beach fishing I use Air Flo clear, intermediate sinking leader looped to my six-weight floating line, with 6-pound-test tippet. I try to cast 10 to 15 feet in front of the schools if possible and then use a very slow retrieve. I usually don't fish unless I see fish and only cast to them if I can reach them. If too far away I let them come to me. Low slack and incoming-to-high slack seem to be the best fishing tides. Morning tides are better than later in the day. In flowing river estuaries I fish the same tides but use a fast-sinking braided or poly leader to counter the current. I've caught all salmon species, sea-run trout, both cutthroat and rainbows, as well as summer-run steelhead on this fly. I tie it in several different shades of pink for different light conditions and I never leave home without them.

Fly-fishers searching for salmon in an estuary on a Queen Charlotte Island river.

Kelly Davison

KELLY DAVISON PHOTO

Kelly has been an active participant in the fly-fishing community for most of his adult life. He is a long-time supporter of the British Columbia Federation of Fly Fishers, the Steelhead Society of B.C., and the Atlantic Salmon Federation. He is also a founding director of the Fraser Valley Guides Associaton. He worked at Ruddicks Fly Shop for a number of years when they were located in Burnaby, after which he moved to Babcock's Fly & Tackle in Coquitlam, where he sells tackle and guides on the Lower Mainland's Fraser River system for salmon and cutthroat trout. In 2004 he became the co-owner and renamed the store to Sea-Run Fly & Tackle. He contributed "The Sea-run Cutthroat Trout" section in the *West Coast Fly Fisher*, published by Hancock House in 1998.

KELLY'S ICE CREAM CONE
Originated and contributed by Kelly Davison

Hook: Size 8 to 20, 2x long
Thread: Black 6/0 or 8/0
Body: Black thread covered with flat pearl Mylar and then with super floss
Rib: Red copper or fine silver wire
Head: White metal bead; preference is for tungsten because it is heavier
Intended use: Chironomid wet fly for trout in Fraser River backwaters and area lakes

Comments: This is a simple-to-tie and effective Chironomid pattern. The metal bead adds weight to help it sink quicker and, as well imitates the white gills of the Chironomid pupae.

KCK (KELLY'S COHO KILLER) YELLOW
Originated and contributed by Kelly Davison

Hook: Size 8 and 6, 3x long
Thread: Red 6/0
Tail: Red hackle fibres
Body: All yellow plastic chenille
Hackle: Brown saddle
Wing: Mallard flank with four strands of pearl Krystal Flash
Intended use: Wet fly for coho salmon

KCK YELLOW BUTT, RED BODIED

Hook: Size 8 and 6, 3x long
Thread: Red 6/0
Tail: Red hackle fibres
Body: Rear third yellow plastic chenille, remainder red plastic chenille
Hackle: Brown saddle
Wing: Mallard flank with four strands of pearl Krystal Flash
Intended use: Wet fly for coho salmon

KCK PURPLE BUTT, RED BODIED

Hook: Size 8 and 6, 3x long
Thread: Red 6/0
Tail: Red hackle fibres
Body: Rear third purple plastic chenille, remainder red plastic chenille
Hackle: Brown saddle
Wing: Mallard flank with four strands of pearl Krystal Flash
Intended use: Wet fly for coho salmon

KCK SALMON RED

Hook: Size 8 and 6, 3x long
Thread: Red 6/0
Tail: Red hackle fibres
Body: Salmon-red plastic chenille
Hackle: Brown saddle
Wing: Mallard flank with four strands of pearl Krystal Flash
Intended use: Wet fly for coho salmon

Comments: The all-yellow version is basically a modernized version of the Professor. The different colour combinations have worked well for me in salt and fresh water when coho are staging in estuaries, stillwaters, slow pools and backwaters.

SEA-RUN DRY
Originated and contributed by Kelly Davison

Hook: Size 6 to 10, 2x fine
Thread: Black
Tail: Deer hair
Body: Dubbed red seal fur tag and amber seal fur or seal substitute

Hackle: Ginger, palmered
Wing: Deer hair, tied down, flared and trimmed at front
Intended use: Dry fly for sea-run cutthroat

Comments: This is primarily a beach cutthroat pattern. It works especially well when there is a slight wind ripple on the water. The red tag was added by Rafe Mair who claims it improved the fly's effectiveness.

Art Lingren

For nearly 40 years Art has pursued the game fishes of British Columbia, during the last 25 years with the fly only. He has written a number of fly-fishing-related books and articles on British Columbia. His main passion is steelhead fly-fishing and he prefers to target the free-rising summer-runs. He has traveled to and caught summer-and winter-run steelhead from streams in all regions of the province where those fish can be found, as well as in all the West Coast states from Alaska to California.

LINGREN'S INDISPENSABLE
Originated and contributed by Art Lingren

Hook: Size 10 to 1/0, Partridge low-water salmon, Tiemco 7999, or Gamakatsu T-10-6H.
Thread: Black 6/0
Tail: Black squirrel, with or without a few strands of black, pearl or red Krystal Flash
Body: Black mohair

Rib: Silver oval tinsel
Hackle: Black, palmered
Wing: Two black-dyed golden pheasant breast feathers tied-in to lay flat over body
Intended use: Wet fly for winter-run steelhead

LINGREN'S MARABOU INDISPENSABLE
Originated by and contributed by Art Lingren

Hook: Size 10 to 1/0, Partridge low-water salmon, Tienco 7999, or Gamakatsu T-10-6H
Thread: Black 6/0
Tail: Black squirrel, with or without a few strands of black, pearl or red Krystal Flash
Body: Black mohair

Rib: Silver oval tinsel
Hackle: Marabou collar, about three or four turns
Wing: Two, black-dyed golden pheasant breast feathers tied-in to lay flat over body
Intended use: Wet fly for winter-run steelhead

LINGREN'S LOW-WATER INDISPENSABLE
Originated and contributed by Art Lingren

Hook: Size 4 or 6, low-water salmon hook
Thread: Black 6/0
Tail: Black squirrel, with or without a few strands of black, pearl or red Krystal Flash
Body: Black mohair
Rib: Silver oval tinsel

Hackle: Black, palmered, one side stripped
Wing: Two black-dyed golden pheasant breast feathers tied-in to lay flat over body
Intended use: Floating line, wet fly for summer-run steelhead in low, clear water and poor light conditions

Comments: In the dawn of 1984 I had the notion that winter steelhead would respond better to a large black fly over the traditional bright ones in use, so I dressed a few Black General Practitioners and put them in my fly box. I took my first winter steelhead with my new black fly on February 13, 1984. Using black flies for winter steelhead was a novel idea back in 1984 and even today you will hear fly-fishers claim that you must use bright flies for winter steelhead. How misled they are. At that time, my favourite winter steelhead pattern was Colonel Esmond Drury's orange General Practitioner. Golden pheasant feathers play a critical role in Drury's fly, so much so he considered giving his fly a name with Golden Pheasant (GP) in it, but decided against it and opted for General Practitioner (GP). A wise decision, as the choice of name can often determine how the fishing community accepts or rejects a fly. Drury's fly caught the attention of Bob Taylor back in the 1960s and he ordered some from Hardy of England for use on our western waters. The complete story of the General Practitioner introduction to the Northwest can be read in my 1996 book *Fly Patterns of British Columbia*.

Drury's GP is an excellent fish catcher and I used it as a model for my Black General Practitioner. However, rather than a polar bear tail, I used black squirrel, I changed the rib from gold to silver as silver suits black flies better, and for the wing I discovered some black feathers on a woodduck cape that would lay flat and provide the desired silhouette. I kept the red golden pheasant breast feather over the tail and the golden pheasant tippet eyes. The fly worked like a hot dam and in that first year I caught steelhead from eight winter and summer-run rivers on Vancouver Island, the Lower Mainland, Thompson, and Dean. Winter steelhead really responded well to the Black GP, and summer-runs liked it as well or better. Other game fish like it too and there is not a British Columbia game fish that swims in the waters I have fished that I have not caught on the Black GP. As of this writing, I have used this fly successfully in all regions of the province that I have fished, as well as rivers in Alaska, Washington and Oregon, 81 waters in total. My standard is dressed on a number two hook, but I have dressed it on hooks up to 5/0 for steelhead and down to size 10 for trout.

Since its inception, I have altered the original fly's dressing considerably. As the Black GP evolved over the years some of the first things to go were the golden pheasant red breast feather in the tail and the tippet eyes. I sometimes add a few strands of black, red, pearl, silver, or chartreuse Krystal Flash in the tail to add colour and, at times, I do like to dress the Black GP on red Gamakatsu hooks. The Krystal Flash and red hooks add sparkle and colour to the fly. However, just plain black without the colour works just as well. I realized early on that the golden pheasant red breast in the tail and tippet eyes were superficial components and that the critical components that attracted a response from the fish were the Black GP's long, supple squirrel tail, the flowing body hackle and its attractive dark silhouette. As the fly evolved, Bob Taylor would look at the most current version and comment on the lack of golden pheasant in the fly. He is one of the few people who knew how important a role golden pheasant played in Drury's GP and that fly's name. With the golden pheasant breast feather and golden pheasant tippet feather eyes gone from my fly and with my use of woodduck or hen hackle feathers for the wing, Bob questioned my GP name and hinted that I should either reinstitute golden pheasant into the fly or consider a different name. In more recent years, after one supplier started dying golden pheasant capes black, I used the golden pheasant black-dyed breast feathers for the wing but do not layer them in as did Colonel Drury. I dress my black version now with two black-dyed golden pheasant breat feathers tied in at the hook eye. Even then when Bob commented on my wayward GP I would respond with "but there is golden pheasant in the wing" and it is still a GP.

During a recent spring 2004 coastal cutthroat fishing trip with Taylor, the subject of a Black GP name change rose to the surface again. We were hoping to hit the main salmon-fry emergence and planned on fishing silver-bodied fly patterns. We did have some days when the cutts and Dolly Varden were slashing the surface after fry but, when the surface was quiet, surface-fished fry patterns provoked few responses. I can't say how many trips I have been on where I was told that you need to have a certain fly to be successful, but by trip's end the anglers in the party I was with have discarded their recommended pattern for the Black GP. The spring cutthroat trip turned out the same. Some of the guys left their supply of Black GPs at home or had too large a fly to fish on our trout rods. Their facial expressions revealed their despair as they witnessed the cutts and Dolly Varden attacking my Black GP. I, being a generous spirit, took pity on the poor souls and dished out an allocation of Black GPs—regular and marabou versions—dressed on size 6 and 8 hooks to Bob Taylor and Charlie Brumwell. And catch fish they did. It was after this 2004 spring cutthroat trip that the name change came up again and because the Black GP has become indispensable to me, I asked Bob if he thought the name The Indispensable was

appropriate. He replied that this fly is such a part of you that you should call it Lingren's Indispensable.

Regular, marabou, and low-water versions of my Indespendable, as well a barbell-eyed version dressed on hooks ranging from 2/0 to 10, line the foam ridges in my fly box and like the advertisement for the American Express card says, I never leave home on a fishing trip without a supply of Lingren's Indispensable. This fly has become an indispensable part of many a fishing trip.

WOOLLY BEAR BOMBER
Originated and contributed by Art Lingren

Hook: Size 12 to 4, Tiemco 7989, Partridge Wilson or low-water salmon
Thread: Black 6/0
Tail: Black squirrel
Body: Spun and clipped black deer hair
Hackle: Brown furnace, palmered
Wing: None, but deer hair set and trimmed so that it protrudes upwards at hook eye
Intended use: Waked-fly for summer-run steelhead

Comments: This is an offshoot of the famous Canadian Atlantic salmon Bomber developed by Reverend Elmer Smith back in the 1960s. This fly has been used successfully for summer steelhead on the Dean, Thompson, Bulkley, Kispiox, Copper and Deschutes (Oregon), with fairly good incidental catches of rainbows and bull trout. It is a good producer. One day last summer in the first five minutes of fishing Newfoundland's Codroy River this fly took one of the few Atlantic salmon taken on that river that morning.

BLACK AND GREEN – BUTT BLACK
Originated and contributed by Art Lingren

Hook: Size 12 to 4, Partridge Wilson salmon dry fly, Tiemco 7989 light wire salmon or low-water salmon
Thread: Black 6/0
Tip, Tag, Tail & Butt: Fine oval silver tinsel followed by black or chartreuse floss, a few guinea fowl fibres and black ostrich herl
Body: Rear third of black floss, remainder black seal fur
Rib: Oval silver tinsel
Hackle: Black from second turn of tinsel, one side stripped to maintain sparseness
Wing: Black squirrel
Intended use: Floating-line, wet fly for summer-run steelhead

Comments: This fly, originated in 1983, has been one of my staple patterns for use on a floating line for summer-run steelhead. I vary the size depending on water clarity, temperature and velocity. The clearer and warmer the water, the smaller the size I fish. It has done me well on about ten or so rivers, including the Dean, Thompson, Campbell, Morice, Methow and Thompson. As well, it has proven useful when used in the right water conditions for rainbows and cutthroat and on Harrys River in Newfoundland for Atlantic salmon.

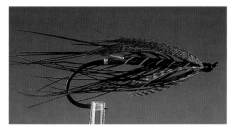

BLACK SPEY
Originated and contributed by Art Lingren

Hook: Size 6 and 4, Partridge Wilson salmon dry fly
Thread: Black 6/0
Tip, Tag, & Tail: Fine oval gold tinsel, followed by black floss and a small red/orange feather
Body: Black floss
Rib: Oval gold tinsel

Hackle: Black heron or substitute from second turn of tinsel, one side stripped to maintain sparseness
Throat: Teal flank
Wing: Bronze mallard
Intended use: Floating line, wet fly for summer-run steelhead

Comments: Coming off my fly-tying vise in 1988, this pattern owes its origins to the Black Spey pattern listed in Arthur Knox's book *Autumns on the Spey* (1872). It is one of my favourite floating-line flies for Thompson River summer-run steelhead.

CLARET & BLACK SPEY
Originated and contributed by Art Lingren

Hook: Size 4, 6 and 8, Tiemco 7989 or Partridge salmon dry fly
Thread: Black 6/0
Tip, Tag, & Tail: Fine oval gold tinsel, followed by dark claret floss and a small red/orange feather
Body: Dark claret floss
Rib: Oval gold tinsel

Hackle: Black heron or substitute from second turn of tinsel (max. three turns), one side stripped to maintain sparseness
Throat: Teal flank
Wing: Black squirrel
Intended use: Floating line, wet fly for summer-run steelhead

Comments: The Claret & Black was first dressed in 1983. I prefer to dress it now with a long, flowing hackle typical of today's Spey patterns, although with a hairwing, it is not a traditional Spey fly with crossed ribbing and bronze mallard wing. Steelhead on the Coquihalla, Campbell, Thompson and Bulkley rivers have risen from the depths to take the fly as it swam enticingly over their lies.

AS SPECIFIED # 1 & 2
Originated and contributed by Art Lingren

Hook: Size 8 to 4, low-water salmon
Thread: Black 6/0
Tip, Tag, & Tail: Fine oval gold tinsel followed by purple floss and purple hackle fibres
Body: Rear third of purple floss, reminder purple seal fur
Rib: Oval gold tinsel

Hackle: Black from second turn of tinsel, one side stripped to maintain sparseness
Throat: Teal or widgeon flank
Wing: Bronze mallard on #1 and black squirrel on #2
Intended use: Floating-line, wet fly for summer-run steelhead

Comments: My earliest steelhead fly creation first dressed in 1982, this fly remains a staple floating-line pattern for summer-run steelhead, with successes on the Morice, Thompson, Dean, and Campbell rivers.

BOMBER
Originated by Reverend Elmer Smith, adapted and contributed by Art Lingren

Hook: Size 12 to 4, Tiemco 7989, Partridge Wilson or low-water salmon
Thread: Black 6/0
Tail: Fox squirrel
Body: Spun and clipped deer hair

Hackle: Brown furnace, palmered
Wing: None, but deer hair set and trimmed so that it protrudes upwards at hook eye
Intended use: Waked fly for summer-run steelhead

Comments: In 1967, Reverend Elmer Smith developed the Bomber for Miramichi River Atlantic salmon and it was so successful that, over many years, a number of variations of that fly have been dressed. A stable waked fly on many British Columbia summer-run streams, this is my simplified version. I have used it successfully for summer steelhead on the Campbell, Dean, Thompson, Bulkley, and Copper rivers, with fairly good incidental catches of other fish.

SKEENA STEELHEAD BEE
Originated and contributed by Art Lingren

Hook: Size 12 to 4, Tiemco 7989, Partridge Wilson or low-water salmon
Thread: Black 6/0
Tail: Fox squirrel
Body: In three equal sections of brown, yellow and brown seal fur

Wing: Fox squirrel flared along the fly's sides with stubs protruding over hook eye
Intended use: Waked fly for summer-run steelhead

Comments: A variation of Roderick Haig-Brown's famous Steelhead Bee and a bee used by Rob Brown, who writes under the name of The Skeena Angler, this fly owes its name to those two sources. It is my alternative Skeena system, waked-fly pattern that I use when I have an eager steelhead that rises to my Bomber but doesn't take. Sometimes a change to a smaller fly with a different silhouette that creates less surface disturbance will do the trick.

BEAD-HEAD LITTLE BUGGER
Originated and contributed by Art Lingren

Hook: Size 12 to 16, nymph hook
Thread: Black 8/0
Tail: Webby, black hackle fibres
Body: Black seal fur
Rib: Fine gold oval tinsel followed by peacock herl
Hackle: Black, palmered
Head: Tungsten 2.7 mm bead
Intended use: Wet fly for river and stillwater trout

Comments: This fly, dressed on small hooks with a bead head and Woolly Bugger-type tail, is a variation of Roderick Haig-Brown's Black Caterpillar, developed by Haig-Brown in the 1930s. Haig-Brown thought that peacock herl, when added to a fly, held a magical allure to trout. With this small fly and Haig-Brown's original, dressed on size 8 to 16 hooks, I have taken trout from the Skagit, Vedder, Harrison and Fraser, as well some Interior lakes and even more recently on a trip south to Oregon for summer-run steelhead.

Harold Lohr

Harold Lohr has been fly-fishing since his early teens and has pursued salmon, trout and steelhead all over the province of British Columbia. He has developed specialized flies for both salt and  fresh water, some which are available through Umpqua Feather Merchants under their contract tier program. Harold has taught beginner to advance fly-tying courses, written magazine articles and participated in two instructional videos on fly-tying and fishing techniques. In the past he has been a manufacturer's rep for various product suppliers. Presently, he works for Redl distributors, where he manages their flies and fly-tying products.

HAROLD LOHR PHOTO

LOHR'S BROWN B.H. CHIRONOMID
Originated and contributed by Harold Lohr

Hook: Size 10 to 18, Tiemco 200
Thread: White and black 8/0
Body: Brown scud back
Rib: Bronze micro tinsel, UNI
Thorax: Black-dyed peacock herl
Head: Black tungsten bead
Gills: White marabou
Intended use: Wet fly, Chironomid imitation for rainbow trout

Comments: This fly can be fished using a floating line with or without a strike indicator, or fished on a full-sinking line using the

deep method. This pattern has been a steady producer for me and is my "go to" Chironomid pupa pattern whenever I fish lakes in the Interior and Cariboo regions of B.C.

LOHR'S DAMSEL NYMPH
Originated and contributed by Harold Lohr

Hook: Size 10 to 14, Tiemco 3761
Thread: Olive 8/0
Extended Underbody: Ten-pound Maxima, Ultra Green Mono
Extended Body: Light olive marabou segmented with light olive monocord
Body: Light olive marabou
Rib: Fine gold wire
Wing Case: Light olive turkey biot quill
Thorax: SLF dubbing, stillwater and stream series
Legs: Pheasant tail dyed light olive
Eyes: Light olive Ultra Chenille
Intended use: Wet fly, damsel imitation for rainbow trout

Comments: This fly can be fished with either a floating line or full-sinking line in and around the weeds, drop offs, and shoal areas. It can be tied in several colours to suit local conditions. This damsel nymph takes selective-feeding trout that are targeting migrating nymphs.

LOHR'S SCUD
Originated and contributed by Harold Lohr

Hook: Size 14 to 18, Tiemco 200
Thread: Gray 8/0
Tail: Olive dun Hare-Tron dubbing fibres
Body: Olive dun Hare-Tron dubbing
Rib: Small, light olive Spanflex
Legs: Picked-out dubbing
Shellback: Clear scud back
Antennae: Olive dun Hare-Tron dubbing fibres
Intended use: Wet fly, scud imitation for rainbow trout

Comments: This *Gammarus* imitation can be fished in several ways with a floating, sink-tip or full-sinking line or even under a strike indicator. Over the years I have fooled some very nice fish using this fairly realistic scud pattern. I tie this fly in several other colours to match scuds found in lakes that I fish. The key to this fly's fish appeal is the super-soft Hare-Tron dubbing, which helps to keep the fly from swimming upside down, a common problem when a scud imitation is dressed with stiffer dubbing fibres.

LOHR'S CONE-HEAD LEECH
Originated and contributed by Harold Lohr

Hook: Size 6 to 14, Tiemco 5263
Thread: Black 6/0
Tail: Dark olive Woolly Bugger marabou and dark olive grizzly marabou
Body: Spectrum and brown-olive mohair plus dubbing 40/60 blend
Intended use: Wet fly, leech imitation for trout

Comments: This versatile leech imitation can be fished using several lines. I use a floating line for shallow water, and then go with full-sinking lines for deeper water. I usually slip a tungsten bead into the cone head when dressing the fly. This added weight gives the fly a more undulating motion on the retrieve. This fly has been a consistent producer, working well for rainbows, brook trout, steelhead and even coho.

LOHR'S MID-STAGE ALEVIN
Originated and contributed by Harold Lohr

Hook: Size 8 to 12, Tiemco 300
Thread: Clear mono
Tail: SLF Hank, gray
Body: Silver Diamond Braid with olive, mottled, oak Thin Skin and minnow back
Egg Sack: Glue gun bead using pearl, neon fire-orange and dark roe glue sticks
Eyes: Silver prismatic 1.5 mm eyes
Finish: Epoxy the back, head and sides
Intended use: Wet fly, alevin imitation for trout and steelhead

Comments: After much experimenting, this design swims properly when swung through a drift and retrieved. The hook gap is not compromised by material, resulting in fewer lost fish. This is a useful and effective pattern when trout and steelhead feed on helpless alevin, fresh out of the gravel.

LOHR'S SALMON FRY
Originated and contributed by Harold Lohr

Hook: Size 6 to 12, Tiemco 300
Thread: Clear mono
Tail: SLF Hank, gray, light olive and dark olive
Body: Silver tone minnow body with olive mottled oak Thin Skin and minnow back
Eyes: Gold prismatic 1.5 mm eyes
Finish: Epoxy the back and body
Intended use: Wet fly, fry imitation for trout and steelhead

Comments: Use this fly with a floating line or sink tip in rivers and with a no-slip, loop knot. The fish will take the fly on the swing or during a straight retrieve. Vary the retrieve with fast and slow strips. Super durable and realistic, this minnow has caught all kinds of cutthroat, Dolly Varden, bull trout, rainbows and even the occasional steelhead.

LOHR'S PRAWN
Originated and contributed by Harold Lohr

Hook: Size 2/0 to 6, Tiemco 7999
Thread: Hot pink 6/0
Tail: Fluorescent pink polar bear and hot pink Ice Fur
Body: Fluorescent pink Cactus Chenille
Rib: Pink Super Floss
Legs: Cotton candy Angel Hair
Shellback: Pink scud back
Eyes: Prawn eyes, coat with epoxy before tying in to avoid disintegration in water
Intended use: Wet fly for winter-run steelhead

Comments: This fly needs to be fished with a sink-tip in order to get the fly down quickly. Steelhead have taken this prawn pattern during the dead drift and on the swing; as well a few steelhead have followed the fly and struck on the retrieve.

Kevin Longard

has been fly-fishing and tying flies for the past 23 years. This passion has culminated in the birth over a decade ago of Skagit River Flies and Materials, a wholesaler of fly-tying materials, books, flies, and accessories. Kevin also teaches fly-fishing, both as a certified fly casting instructor, and on-the-water instruction. He guides helicopter fly-in trips to remote alpine lakes in the Lower Mainland. Along with New Productions, Kevin has produced three instructional videos: *Flies For B.C.*, *How To Fly Fish Lakes*, and *More Flies For B.C.*, and appeared on the Safari West Video Series providing tips. As a writer, Kevin has contributed to *B.C. Outdoors*, *The Reel Angler*, *Steelheader News*, *The Outdoor Edge* and *Home Waters*. He was also one of the authors of *Fly Fishing B.C.* Kevin is an ordained minister and is currently employed as a social worker. Kevin, his wife Sandy and daughter Courtenay reside in Chilliwack, B.C.

BODILESS CADDIS
Originated and contributed by Kevin Longard

Hook: Sizes 8-16, standard shank dry (Mustad 94833 or equal)
Thread: UNI-Thread 6/0 black (olive, yellow also good)
Body: The tying thread
Wing: Medium-fine deer hair
Intended use: Dry fly midge or caddis pattern for stillwaters and rivers

Comments: Developed around 1990, this fly was originally tied as a result of Skagit River trout chewing Tom Thumbs apart so quickly. Tom Thumbs float well and dry with minimal false-casting. The other fly that is very successful on the same water is the Elk Hair Caddis, but on the Skagit's broken surface, the Elk-Hair Caddis would easily drown. In addition, both of these flies took more time to tie than I wanted to spend during the lazy days of summer. When I tied the Bodiless Caddis I was hoping for an easy tie that floated and dried well and had an under-profile of a caddis, but a high-profile wing as it entered the fish's cone of vision for mayfly representation. The Bodiless Caddis floated like a cork and took a "gummin'" that Tom Thumbs could never handle. Black has been the standard thread color for me. (It worked for Mr. Thumb all these years!) Note: Years after devising this pattern I came across a related pattern by Ted Trueblood, but other than this I am not aware of any history of this pattern.

I have successfully used this pattern as large as #6 but it gets uglier as it gets bigger and I prefer aesthetically pleasing flies. I have sold this fly at many Lower Mainland fly shops for years and taught the pattern in fly-fishing and fly-tying courses. It has been featured in many B.C. publications including Karl Bruhn's *Fly Fishing British Columbia,* as well as *Flies for B.C.* and *How to Flyfish Lakes* videos.

Many friends, acquaintances, and clients have used this pattern both in my presence and on their own with much success. This has been a staple pattern of mine since its inception. It works wonderfully on the local streams, in interior lakes, lowland stillwaters, and incredibly well on alpine lakes, which I fish a lot. I have hooked fish up to 20+ inches on the Bodiless Caddis. It has even become my main pattern for buzzers, the adult midges on many stillwaters in our region as its "bad hair" seems to simulate the rapid wing movement of adult midges as they "air boat" across the meniscus.

DOLLY DREDGER
Originated and contributed by Kevin Longard

Hook: Size 1/0 to 4, Mustad 79458 or equal 4 extra-long hook streamer hook
Thread: Fluorescent pink or red Flymaster Plus or Ultra Thread 140
Body: Silver Mylar
Rib: Medium oval tinsel, counter wrapped
Eyes: Medium or large lead or similar plated eyes
Wing: Gold, silver, olive, or UV pearl Krystal Flash
Intended use: Wet fly baitfish imitation for cutthroat and Dolly Varden

Comments: Dollies and bulls are two of my favorite fish to chase. These super-aggressive fish live in wild areas and pure water, and they chase down minnows more consistently than any other fish. As a commercial tyer, it seems I never have enough time to tie my own flies, unless they are dead quick to do. Developed in 1994, this fly suits those needs. It seems that the larger the fly the better!

A couple of reasons I don't like Mylar braid-bodied flies are the time needed to tie them and their slow sink rate. The Dolly Dredger sinks like a rock, and can be retrieved quickly without rising from the bottom, where the quarry are lurking ready to pounce. The Krystal Flash wing results in a "big look" and flashes

brilliantly. Dollies and bull trout are protected in many of our B.C. waters so we need to take special care, thus a few words about hook sizes is appropriate. It is better to increase shank length than gape width to achieve bigger patterns as too large a gape can penetrate the craniums of fish and kill them.

This commercially-sold fly is an incredible river searching pattern and I have used it with success in the Silver-Skagit Valley, with cutthroat in the Harrison area, and I even took a beautiful summer-run steelhead from the Coquihalla two summers ago when that river had one of its infrequent openings.

EYED GLO-BUG
Originated and contributed by Kevin Longard

Hook: Size 1/0 to 4, Eagle Claw 182 or equal bronze steelhead hook
Thread: Flymaster Plus or Ultra Thread to match
Body: Roe-coloured fat yarn
Eyes: Plated lead eyes, sized according to sink rate desired
Intended use: Deeply sunk wet fly for steelhead, Dolly Varden and bull trout

Comments: I dressed this Glo-Bug fly in 1990. I am sure someone dressed it before I but I haven't found anyone who will admit to it. I needed an egg pattern in which the weight is part of the fly for use on BC's fly-fishing-only waters. This fast-sinking fly is suited to fishing pocket water. I will be the first to admit that this pattern will not go into the Ed Hewitt Hall of Fame. However this beefy fly has consistently caught steelhead for me when the fish were spooked or the water was too cold for them to move higher in the water column.

GUINEA DRAGON
Originated and contributed by Kevin Longard

Hook: Size 4 to 8, Daiichi 1730 or Skagit River Flies 7474
Thread: Olive, 6/0 UNI-Thread or Ultra Thread 140
Tail: Ring-necked pheasant tail or rump fibres
Body: Large #901 dark olive chenille, olive poly yarn as an
underbody on the abdomen, tied to form a wide, flat base
Hackle: Olive-dyed guinea fowl
Head: Olive poly yarn
Eyes: Black or olive plastic bead chain
Intended use: Wet fly for stillwater rainbow trout

Comments: This fly evolved around 1990 with incorporating ideas from a long lineage of fly tyers including James Bloom, Ken Ruddick, and Fred Helmer, who requested I dress a more simplified version of Ken Ruddick's exceptional dragonfly nymph pattern. My "tweaking" resulted in this fly. Incredibly buggy looking when wet, and despite its impressionistic style, it is a dead ringer for the lower mainland darners who inhabit lowland to sub-alpine lakes.

Unknown to me at the time I dressed this fly but apparent from many years of use, this pattern fishes upside-down. This doesn't bother the fish, but the upside-down fly gives it more potential when fished down among the weeds where the naturals live. I prefer a size 6 for my personal use, but trout will take it in any size that matches the natural. I love the look of the fly when dressed on the "stonefly" bent hooks, though they may be hard to find other than through Skagit River Flies. The Guinea Dragon is sold extensively throughout the lower mainland and it has been featured in various periodicals as well as Karl Bruhn's book and the video *More Flies for B.C.*

RIPPLE MINNOW
Originated and contributed by Kevin Longard

Hook: Size 6 to 12, Mustad 9672 or similar
Thread: Fluorescent fire orange or chartreuse 6/0 UNI-Thread
Body: Silver, gold or rainbow diamond braid
Wing: Pearl or pearl-olive Flashabou, or gold or silver holographic with an overwing of peacock herl
Eye or Beadhead: Black permanent marker directly on UNI-Thread head, or no eye, but bead head to match
Intended use: A general baitfish wet fly used for all salmonids

Comments: I first developed this pattern in the mid to late 1980s as a simple cutthroat pattern for spring Fraser/Harrison River fishing. At that time I was really intrigued and wanted to be able to catch trout right through the winter and into spring on our local rivers. This simple pattern was very effective, easy to tie, and in its original dressing (silver body, pearl Flashabou, and peacock herl) was a great imitator of the emerging chum fry so prevalent in these waters. This was one of those patterns (and I realize there were many!) that spun off the saltwater bucktails etc. and was adapted to anadromous fish in fresh water. Over time, this and other similar patterns were also used in lakes, particularly where forage fish are prevalent items on a trout's menu. I have used and sold many variations over the years, however, the best combinations are reflected in the array of variations in the materials above.

KRYSTAL CAREY
Originated and contributed by Kevin Longard

Hook: Size 6 to 10, Mustad 3906 or similar
Thread: UNI-Thread to match body colour
Body: Scintilla #16 Rich Olive or #32 Vivid Red dubbing
Hackle: Grey or blue ring-necked
pheasant rump
Overwing: Red metallic or pearl olive Krystal Flash to match
Intended use: A wet-fly caddis emerger, searching pattern for stillwater trout

Comments: About 1990 I dressed this variation of the 1920s B.C. vintage pattern developed by Colonel Carey. I felt it needed some zing and thought this variation with the fuzzy body and sparkling wing would work more specifically as a caddis pupa. Also I felt one of B.C.'s most popular flies would sell very well with these renovations. Dressed in sizes from 6 to 10, this is a good searching pattern. It is one of my flies that consistently sells well and has been featured in various periodicals and in my *Flies for B.C.* and *How to Fly Fish Lakes* videos.

Peter Morrison

has been fly-fishing for over 30 years. He has traveled North America extensively and his experience includes most every species of game fish available in Canada, as well as exotic species such as tarpon and bonefish and many other saltwater species. Peter is a former professional angling guide and a pioneering saltwater fly-angler, most notably in the quest for 'open ocean' Pacific salmon. He has worked in the fishing tackle industry for over 15 years and was a contributing author and consultant for the popular book *Fly Fishing in British Columbia*, as well as a regular columnist in the electronic publication *Western Fly Fisher*. He was selected to represent Canada in the 2nd Annual New Zealand Saltfly Tournament in 1999. Peter is certified by the Federation of Fly Fishers as a Master Casting Instructor and serves as an advisor for the federation's casting programs. Peter always looks forward to entertaining audiences with casting demonstrations and seminars.

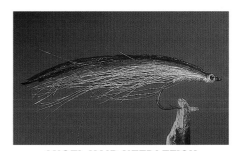

ANGEL HAIR NEEDLEFISH
Originated and contributed by Peter Morrison

Hook: Size 1 to 4, Mustad Signature C70S saltwater or substitute such as Tiemco 811S, Daiichi 2546, or Mustad 34007
Thread: Gudebrod Clear Mono 6/0 or sub Danville Fine Clear Mono
Body: Gudebrod HT metallic braid – holographic silver or substitute silver Diamond Braid
Wing: In layers of sparse white polar
bear hair or substitute, pearl/purple Angel Hair, silver holographic Angel Hair, chartreuse or electric lime Angel Hair, baitfish Angel Hair and a topping of peacock herl
Eyes: Silver/black or red/black, flat or molded holographic prism eyes
Head: Clear coat of Devcon Epoxy
Intended use: Wet fly for ocean coho

Comments: This brighter, attractor needlefish pattern is extremely effective in the sometimes occluded or tannin-colored waters off British Columbia's West Coast. It is also a good producer in areas of strong tidal current exchange. A very slow retrieve, interspersed with jerky twitches works wonders. This is a great fly to let swing through a current seam while twitching. I then continue to twitch the fly while it hangs down at the end of the swing. Hang on for big grabs!

POLAR BEAR NEEDLEFISH
Originated and contributed by Peter Morrison

Hook: Size 2 to 6, Mustad signature C70S saltwater or substitute such as Tiemco 811S, Daiichi 2546, or Mustad 34007
Thread: Gudebrod Clear Mono 6/0, or sub Danville Fine Clear Mono
Body: Gudebrod HT metallic braid – holographic silver, or substitute silver Diamond Braid
Wing: Sparse, straight fibres of white, followed by grey, topped off by purple, olive, or chartreuse polar bear hair
Sides: Two strands each side of #17 peacock Krystal Flash (tied between mid wing and over wing)
Eyes: Flat or molded holographic prism eyes silver/black or red/black substitute
Head: Coat with Devcon epoxy
Intended use: Wet fly for ocean coho

Comments: This fly is meant to imitate smaller juvenile candlefish, sandlance, or needlefish that can be found in the onshore waters of the west coast of Vancouver Island and the northwest coast of British Columbia. The irridescence of these small feed fish is captivating. When you inspect one of these shiny morsels, you can see clearly the olive-purplish hues, and sometimes chartreuse, in the little fish's makeup. Best results are obtained with a slow steady retrieve. But an occasional pause or a quick twitch will often entice a take. Always observe and attempt to imitate what you see in nature. The take of a large coho can often feel like a gentle hesitation. A strip strike is the best method for setting the hook.

Dave O'Brien

An avid fisher since anyone can remember, Dave purchased his first fly rod at 10 years of age with paper route money. By age 13, he had wrapped his own Fenwick glass rod and purchased a Hardy Viscount reel to use with that rod. Dave took his first fly-tying class when he was 14. Once he was old enough to drive, almost every summer weekend entailed a trip to the B.C. Interior, fishing Heffley, Tunkwa, and Peterhope lakes. Dave briefly ran a summer guiding operation while studying math at UB.C. Upon graduation in 1990, he bought out Bob Young to become the principal shareholder at Michael and Young Fly Shop, where he

has been ever since. Dave has been fortunate enough to fly-fish the tropics as well as Argentina, but his main passion is Spey fishing for summer/fall steelhead in British Columbia.

WALLY
Adapted and contributed by Dave O'Brien

Hook: Size 6 to 10, TMC 5263 (If tied steelhead style, TMC 7989, typically size 4 to 8)
Thread: Black 3/0 Danville's monocord
Tail: Deer hair
Body: Poly-yarn using color of choice - cut off and add each time you add another stack of deer hair (can also use any hydrophobic dubbing for the body as well, with Superfine and Antron being popular choices)
Wing: Three stacks of coarse deer hair with all tips stacked to the same length
Intended use: Dry fly for rainbow, cutthroat and steelhead

Comments: This is an excellent all-around dry-fly searching pattern to be fished primarily on large western freestone rivers. It's extremely versatile as it floats like a cork and can be adapted to represent several large river aquatics and terrestrials such as stoneflies, caddisflies and grasshoppers. The size and coloration are chosen depending upon what the angler is trying to mimic.

We were targeting resident summer rainbows on the Thompson and this fly, an offshoot of the famous Mikaluk Sedge, was tied in the early 1980s with a golden poly body and a ton of deer hair to represent the adult golden stoneflies common to the Thompson. It's precursor, the Mikulak Sedge, is typically much smaller and tied with a more complex pattern of elk hair overwings. The body on the Mikulak is dubbed olive where the originator used gink as a dubbing wax with the seal hair. Unlike the Mikulak, most adaptations of the Wally have no hackle, with the originals tied with a Muddler Minnow style bullet-shaped head. Other original variations included rust colored for stoneflies, olive for larger traveling sedges and light yellow when the hoppers were abundant. I also adapted the pattern down to a size 12, two extra-long hook in lime to represent the lime Sally stonefly adults.

This pattern has now been fished successfully all over western North America in places such as the Madison in Montana, the Yellowstone in Wyoming, the Bow in Alberta and on many British Columbia rivers such as the Elk, Skagit, Stellako, Lakelse and Harrison. The fly has proven effective for fall cutthroat as well. I have done well on the Harrison in mid-September when the large traveling sedges are hatching. One year on the Lakelse River in the spring, a good friend cleaned up on cuttys when the stones were hatching.

The fly was later adapted for steelhead dry-fly fishing and has brought up steelhead fished both dead-drift and skated. Most of the steelhead adaptations are tied with an orange or purple butt, with the rest of the body, as well as the deer-hair wing, being black. For better buoyancy and more wiggling and gurgling as it skates across the water, I often leave 1/2 inch hanging forward after the last wing is tied, and then use Dave's Flexament on this overhang to create a rudder. Steelhead from B.C. rivers such as the Dean, Thompson, Coquihalla and Bulkley have succumbed to this waked dry fly.

WAVEY'S MICRO-PUPAE

Adapted and contributed by Dave O'Brien

Hook: Size 12, TMC 3761
Thread: Olive 6/0 Danville
Body: Olive or tan Micro chenille, size extra fine
Hackle: Hen pheasant—tied very sparse
Thorax: Peacock herl
Intended use: Wet fly for stillwater rainbow trout

Comments: This is an excellent small caddis pupae imitation that has proven very effective fishing stillwater lakes in the B.C. Interior. Typically a late spring/early summer hatch, these teeny caddis are so important yet are ignored by so many anglers who are much more familiar with the more prolific traveler sedge type caddis.

I developed this fly out of necessity when I was fishing at a popular Interior lake in early July, where only one angler was having any success. Oddly enough he was trolling around whilst all the Chironomid "experts" looked on. I asked him what he was using and he said, "a small soft hackle size 14." I also noticed at the time that there were some small tan "elk hair style" caddis buzzing along the water's edge, with some funny-looking caddis husks floating on the surface that were almost as wide as they were long. I went to shore and with what fly-tying materials I had with me at the time I dressed this fly. The hugely successful original has never needed to be modified.

It's also a very effective trolling pattern, especially when fished un-weighted on a dry line with a long leader in the shallows in the late evening.

Philip Rowley

At the age of six, Phil Rowley was introduced to coarse fishing in England and has been hooked ever since. For the past 20 years Phil Rowley has been fly-fishing stillwaters almost exclusively. His love of stillwater fly-fishing has taken him all over British Columbia and Washington in the pursuit of trout and char. A former commercial fly tier, Phil has written for almost every major fly-fishing publication in North America. His contributions also include books and numerous feature articles on fly-fishing stillwaters and stillwater fly patterns. Phil's book *Fly Patterns For Stillwaters* has become a best seller. When he is not tying flies or on the water, Phil travels western North America performing at outdoor shows, teaching a variety of seminars, speaking to fly clubs and conducting weekend fly-fishing schools. Phil's website, www.flycraftangling.com is dedicated to fly-fishing and fly-tying education.

AFTERSHAFT LEECH

Adapted and contributed by Philip Rowley

Hook: Size 6-10, Mustad R74
Thread: 8/0 Gudebrod Olive
Tail: Marabou (mix colors to suit)
Body: Aftershaft feathers (mix colors to suit)
Hackle: Dyed pheasant rump to match
Intended use: Wet-fly leech imitation for rainbow, brook trout and cutthroat

Comments: During a trip early in my stillwater fly-fishing career I had the good fortune to view first-hand the stomach contents of a leech-stuffed trout. The leeches were mottled and were an average length of 2.5 inches. Upon a closer look the leeches' slender profile stuck in my mind. A glance into my box suggested my leech patterns could use a diet. Inspired by the late Gene Armstrong series of filoplume flies, I began creating my own leech patterns using aftershaft feathers as a foundation. Gene was a fixture for years at Kaufmann's Streamborn fly shop in Bellevue, Washington. Aftershaft is the smaller secondary plume found at the base of most game-bird feathers. Ring-necked pheasant is the primary source for the marabou-like aftershaft feathers. Using a dubbing loop to control this fragile material I created a leech pattern that matched the variegated look of the natural specimens I saw. Once wet, the Aftershaft Leech comes to life, pulsing and breathing on its own. Weighting the front third of the hook with .010" lead wire provided further animation. Takes on the drop are common so be prepared while the pattern is sinking. Once at depth, use a slow hand twist or 4-inch strip retrieve. Intermediate lines are a personal favorite as these lines permit a slow horizontal retrieve without the risk of the fly line over-powering the presentation. On pressured waters or in clear conditions the somber nature of this pattern provides an added benefit, as trout that have seen a number of patterns and presentations are wary of garish unnatural patterns.

BUNNY CADDIS

Adapted and contributed by Philip Rowley

Hook: Size 6-10, Mustad C 53S
Thread: 8/0 Gudebrod, olive
Body: Seal fur dubbing and gold or caddis green Crystal Chenille spun together in a dubbing loop
Wingcase: Brown Midge Back, Stretch Flex or Scud Back
Thorax: Rabbit fur spun in a dubbing loop
Legs: Brown/black Sili-Legs
Head: Peacock Sparkle Dubbing
Intended use: Wet-fly sedge pupa imitation for B.C. Interior rainbow and brook trout. Can also suggest a dragon nymph

Comments: I am a firm believer that stillwater fly patterns should feature soft, mobile materials to suggest life, as lakes are one of the most challenging arenas to present a fly. Trout are merciless critics, scrutinizing both pattern and presentation. Most anglers have never had the opportunity to see a sedge pupa, as the pupal stage is short lived. Being fortunate enough to study sedge pupae through aquarium research enabled me to realize that there are two phases within the pupal stage that lead to the creation of the Bunny Caddis. Upon chewing its way free from its larval home the sedge pupa stumbles and undulates about the bottom substrate. To suggest this phase, patterns need to be crept on or near the bottom, almost Chironomid pace. The Bunny Caddis offers an imitative profile in conjunction with mobile materials to suggest the body motions of the natural pupa. A number of days after its initial emergence the pupa enters its second phase, a brisk angled trek to the surface for the final transformation to winged adult. Powered by the sculling motion of its elongated feather-like hind legs, the pupa moves through the water column in 4- to 6-inch bursts coupled with pauses. Use a Stillwater or Wet Tip Clear line to mimic the angled path of the pupa. A moderate 4-inch strip retrieve animates the rabbit-fur thorax and Sili-Legs in the same manner as the natural. Takes are firm during the emergence trek, most of the grabs coming as the fly pauses between strips.

CDC SCUD
Adapted and contributed by Philip Rowley

Hook: Size 8-12, Mustad C 49S
Thread: 8/0 Gudebrod, olive
Body: Mixture of CDC and Sparkle Dubbing
Rib: Fine copper wire
Shell Back: Olive Midge Back, Stretch Flex or Scud Back
Intended use: Wet-fly scud pattern for rainbow or brook trout

Comments: Stillwater trout are adept at foraging in shallow water and weed-choked environments. Patterns placed in these areas are at constant risk of fouling or snagging the bottom, frustrating anglers in the process. For fly-fishers to be successful they must overcome the intimidating challenges of these areas. Finding this puzzle a challenge, I have invested time at both the vise and on the water trying to overcome this roadblock. CDC has long been recognized for its buoyant qualities and is a common component for many dry flies. The unique qualities of CDC are well suited for sub-emergent patterns as well. Using a dubbing loop and an innovative tool developed by Swiss fly tier and angler Marc Petitjean, I was able to control and blend CDC and Sparkle Dubbing. In addition to its buoyant qualities, CDC gathers lifelike air bubbles and breathes and pulses in a marabou manner. When trout are prowling the shallows or weaving amongst vegetation the CDC Scud is my pattern of choice for these circumstances. I utilize a Stillwater or Wet Tip Clear line to drag the CDC Scud beneath the surface. While not completely weedless, the CDC Scud, powered by a varied combination of hand twists and strips, darts and glides through the underwater jungle, providing trout an opportunity to track it down.

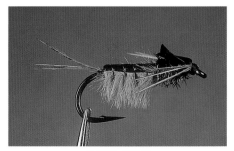

HERL MAY
Adapted and contributed by Philip Rowley

Hook: Size 12-14, Mustad R72
Thread: 8/0, Gudebrod, brown or olive
Tail: Micro Fleck Turkey Flats
Body: Light olive ostrich herl
Rib: Fine copper wire
Shellback: Mottled turkey quill or Brown Midge Back, Stretch Flex or Scud Back
Thorax: Peacock herl
Legs: Micro Fleck Turkey Flats
Wingcase: Mottled turkey quill or Brown Midge Back, Stretch Flex or Scud Back
Intended use: Wet fly; *Callibaetis* nymph imitation for rainbow trout in clear-water lakes

Comments: The mayfly reigns supreme on rivers and streams but the same cannot be said for stillwaters as the species diversity just isn't there. In the West, *Callibaetis* is the species of record and all stillwater fly-fishers should have an acute awareness of this species. Favoring the clear marl and chara lakes of the south-central plateau of British Columbia, *Callibaetis* feature prominently. Lakes such as White, Lac Le Jeune and Lac Des Roches dictate demure subtle patterns to be successful. It was with this challenge in mind that I adapted the Hurl May. *Callibaetis* nymphs are active swimmers and immediately prior to the hatch their activity level peaks, darting above the weed tops prior to emergence. During this false hatch period numerous trout cruise the shoals, searching for an easy meal. *Callibaetis* move through the water column propelled by rapid undulations of their body followed by prolonged pauses in a distinct arched position, abdominal gills fluttering. Using Micro Fleck Turkey Flat fibers for the tail and legs, I was able to duplicate the posture of both the active and resting nymphs. The ostrich herl body suggested the abdominal gills and, in a lighter coloration, blended with the shellback and wingcase to represent the light bellies and dark backs common to many aquatic invertebrates. When *Callibaetis* nymphs are on the menu the Herl May on the end of a long 15-foot leader and floating-line or Wet Tip Clear line is a proven combination. Present the pattern along the marl and chara seams. Using the chara to mask their presence, trout dart over the lighter marl, pouncing on countless *Callibaetis* nymphs.

CHROMIE
Adapted and contributed by Philip Rowley

Hook: Size 8-16, Mustad C49S
Thread: 8/0, Gudebrod, black or olive
Body: Silver Flashabou
Rib: Holographic red Mylar
Thorax: Peacock herl
Head: Black metal or tungsten bead
Gills: White Sparkle Yarn or Midge Gill
Intended use: Wet-fly Chironomid pupa imitation for rainbow, kokanee and brook trout

Comments: By the mid eighties I had been fortunate to hone my chironomid skills. Chironomids are the critical stillwater hatch all fly-fishers must be aware of. They are the number one food source during the open-water season. Diet analysis through proper use of a throat pump is a critical tactic within my arsenal, revealing key information, as the food sources collected are still alive. Live food sources display unique qualities that are the critical difference in both presentation and fly pattern. Chironomid pupae use trapped air and gases to aid both their pupal ascent and final transformation to winged adult. The trapped air and gases give the pupa a distinct silvery glow that trout focus upon. Initially these silver-bodied pupae appeared to be grey with a red rib, but it soon became apparent upon closer observation that they were silver, not grey. Dropping a silver-bodied Chironomid pupa pattern amongst feeding trout did not inspire confidence right away. I was still clinging to the traditional somber patterns then in common use. Suppressing my doubts, the Chromie fished on a floating line and long 15-foot or better leader or suspended beneath a strike indicator began to dominate my success. Reviewing my diary from the time of this fly's early development showed that the Chromie began to constantly hook fish; so much so that the Chromie is my go-to Chironomid pupa pattern, accounting for over 75% of the trout I catch and release when using Chironomids.

EARLY SEASON BOMBER
Adapted and contributed by Philip Rowley

Hook: Size 12 to16 Partridge Klinkhamer Special
Thread: 8/0 Gudebrod, black
Body: Mylar (silver, gold, green or red)
Rib: V-Rib-color to complement color scheme
Secondary Rib: Fine wire
Wing case: Pearlescent Mylar
Thorax: Peacock herl

Legs: Pheasant tail Angel Hair
Wing Pads: Orange Super Floss
Gills: White Sparkle Yarn or Midge Gill
Intended use: Wet fly: Chironomid pupa pattern aimed at representing the large bomber pupa common to the mud bottomed lakes of south-central British Columbia

Comments: Chironomids inhabit a wide range of stillwaters. Many of the popular lakes of south-central British Columbia feature dark muddy bottoms, ideal Chironomid habitat. Lakes such as Tunkwa and Leighton are renowned for their dense populations of large Chironomids, affectionately known as "bombers" by many. Pupae of these bomber species attain large sizes, close to an inch in length. Large Chironomid pupae offer many features to imitate: prominent gills, variegated bodies marked by bands and butts of residual hemoglobin from the larval stage, wing pads and pro legs. As with all Chironomid pupae, "bombers" utilize trapped air and gases to aid their pupal ascent, thus vibrant materials need to be incorporated to mimic this trait. I designed the Early Season Bomber with these features in mind after witnessing a bout of intense pupae predation during a brisk spring day on Edith Lake, just south of Kamloops. Wind drifting is a personal favorite technique for presenting the Early Season Bomber. Using a floating line coupled with a leader that is 25% longer than the water is deep, one should make a quartering cast to allow the ambient wind to drift the pattern through the water column. Wind drifting is an excellent method to cover water with a near static presentation. Sedge pupae, scuds, Chironomid larva, leeches, damselflies and mayflies are ideal candidates for wind drifting.

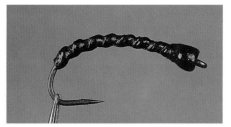

BEAD WORM
Adapted and contributed by Philip Rowley

Hook: Size 12 to 16, Klinkhamar Special
Thread: 8/0 Gudebrod, red
Body: Red or green holographic Mylar
Rib: Red V-Rib
Secondary Rib: Fine red wire
Bead: Red glass bead
Intended use: Wet-fly Chironomid larvae imitation for rainbow and brook trout.

Comments: In the absence of a hatch, experienced stillwater fly-fishers often revert to imitating a staple food source. Staples are those food items that are available all season long and are the backbone prey of foraging rainbow and brook trout. When considering staples most anglers think of dragon nymphs, scuds, damsel nymphs and leeches. Chironomid larvae are another key staple that often miss the staples list. Trout on the other hand find Chironomid larva a delicacy, seldom passing one by. On many of the mud-bottomed lakes I frequent during the open-water season, Chironomid larvae exist in epidemic proportions, many pushing an inch in length. Capable of generating hemoglobin, larvae are able to survive in oxygen-poor conditions. Red is the predominant color, which has lead to the larva's common nickname, bloodworm. In addition to red there are other colors worth considering, including maroon, olive and bright green. In the late fall, many larvae return to their natural green coloration after oxygen-depleted summer water temperatures turn them crimson red. The transformation is gradual, barber-poled combinations of red and green larvae are common. The Bead Worm is aimed to mimic the larger Chironomid larvae species. I chose reflective materials to form the slender, segmented worm-like profile of the naturals. When first venturing on the water or when fishing seems dour I often try a Bead Worm, a tactic that has proven itself for over 10 years. Keep the pattern on or near the bottom debris and ooze that the larvae inhabit. A slow-sinking intermediate line or floating line and long leader works best. Retrieves should be slow and methodical.

Ken Ruddick
has lived in the Stave Falls area for all his 84 years. For the past 40 years he has wielded a fly rod and tied flies, mostly for the rainbow trout of the Interior. He opened Ruddick's Fly Fishing Shop in 1970. Located on Dewdney Trunk Road close to his home, the business was later moved to Haney. It was British Columbia's first fly-fishing-only specialty shop. In the early 1980s, he sold the business to his son Malcolm and daughter-in-law Kathy, who since have operated it in different Lower Mainland locations. Ken continues to dress about 100 dozen flies a year, but only for special customers. When not in his fly-tying room dressing flies, he enjoys the odd trip to Bridge Lake for kokanee and can be found in the summer and fall on the Fraser system casting flies to coho and sockeye.

KEN'S DRAGON

Originated and contributed by Ken Ruddick

Hook: Size 4 or 6, Mustad 79580
Thread: Black
Tail: River otter
Body: Chenille underbody to shape nymph followed by double O dark olive chenille over a medium olive wool belly

Rib: Ten- to 15-pound nylon
Legs: Ring-necked pheasant tail
Shellback & Wingcase: Moose hair
Intended use: Wet fly for stillwater rainbow trout

Comments: Ken suggests that the body colour be changed to match the insects of the particular lake you are fishing. He assures me Ken's Dragon works in every lake where dragonfly nymphs prowl the weeds looking for prey.

BEETLE FLY

Originated and contributed by Ken Ruddick

Hook: Size 10, Mustad 9671 or equivalent 2 extra-long hook
Thread: Black
Tail: Peacock black Arizona Diamond Braid

Body: Peacock Ice Dub
Hackle: Green phase of the ring-necked pheasant
Intended use: Wet fly for stillwater trout

Comments: This turned out to be a good B.C. lake fly, but Ken originally developed it for Kathy Ruddick to use in the World Fly Fishing Competition in Australia in 2000. Ken heard that the lake where she would be fishing had a good population of water beetles.

GREY DRAKE

Originated and contributed by Ken Ruddick

Hook: Size 10 or 12, Mustad 9672 or equivalent three extra-long hook
Thread: Black
Tail: Grey squirrel
Body: Grey scud dubbing

Rib: Fine brass wire
Collar: Grizzly hackle
Intended use: Wet fly for stillwater, Interior rainbow trout

Comments: This pattern was designed for Lac Des Roche, with its good population of mayflies, and is best fished deep and retrieved quickly.

BEAR HAIR HUMPY

Originated and contributed by Ken Ruddick

Hook: Size 10 or 12, Mustad 9672 or equivalent three extra-long hook
Thread: Black
Tail: River otter
Body: Peacock herl

Rib: Black 6/0 thread
Back and Throat: Black bear hair
Intended use: Wet fly for stillwater rainbow trout

Comments: Developed in the early 1980s for Interior rainbows. When dressing the fly on a size-12 hook, add a gill of white Phentex.

BLACK OR MAROON LEECH

Originated and contributed by Ken Ruddick

Hook: Size 8, Mustad 9672 or equivalent three extra-long hook
Thread: Black
Tail: Black or maroon rabbit

Body: Black or maroon rabbit
Intended use: Wet fly for stillwater, Interior rainbow trout

Comments: Developed in the late 1980s for Interior rainbows in the lakes of Region 3. Dress the fly by building the body in segments with clumps of rabbit fur, to keep the body on the thin side for a better leech-like profile. This leech pattern's primary target fish is the rainbow trout, but it is used for cutthroat as well as coho. The black version is especially good for coho.

SHREDGE

Originated and contributed by Ken Ruddick

Hook: Size 12 or smaller, Mustad 9672 or equivalent three extra-long hook
Thread: Black
Tail: Fibres of light brown hen chicken feather
Body: Medium green seal fur mixed with about 10% yellow seal fur

Rib: Fine brass wire
Wingcase: Fibres of light brown hen chicken feather
Wing: Fibres of light brown hen chicken feather
Intended use: Wet fly for stillwater, Interior rainbow trout

Comments: This fly was made at Calling Lake in the early 1990s. It looks like a shrimp, but is dressed to imitate a sedge pupa. However, fish could take it for a shrimp, damselfly nymph or sedge. It is best fished with a fast retrieve.

NO-NAME MAYFLY
Dressed and contributed by Ken Ruddick

Hook: Size 10 or 12, Mustad 9672 or equivalent three extra long hook
Thread: Black
Tail: Black hackle fibres
Body: Black floss
Rib: Fine brass wire
Wingcase: Green Flashabou
Wing: Black hackle fibres, maximum 3/8 inch long
Intended use: Wet fly for stillwater, Interior rainbow trout

Comments: I first learned of this fly on Lac Des Roche. A fellow who worked for the government was having an excellent day on the lake. Later, when packing up, I asked him what fly he was using; he was initially non-committal, but later came and gave me a sample. This fly works best in the last week of May and first weeks of June when the trout gorge on the plentiful mayfly nymphs and newly emerged adults. [**Note:** this pattern is very similar to the Idaho Nymph.]

KENS' TOM THUMB
Originated and contributed by Ken Ruddick

Hook: Size 6 to 12, Mustad 90240
Thread: Black
Tail: Deer hair
Body: Grey deer hair
Collar: Grizzly hackle
Wing: Grizzly hackle fibres and deer hair, mixed
Intended use: Dry fly for stillwater, Interior rainbow trout

Comments: This fly is a good sedge imitation and works particularly well as a mayfly imitation.

DONATELLI SPECIAL
Originated by George Donatelli, tied and contributed by Ken Ruddick

Hook: Size 10 or 12, Mustad 9672 or equivalent three extra long hook
Thread: Black
Tail: Deer hair, sparse

Body: Light grey scud dubbing
Rib: Fine brass wire
Thorax: Orange seal fur
Wingcase: Mallard flank
Wing: Mallard flank, short about ¼ inch long
Intended use: Wet fly for kokanee

Comments: This is a particularly effective wet fly for Bridge Lake kokanee.

BEAD-HEAD MUDDLER
Originated and contributed by Ken Ruddick

Hook: Size 6 or 8, Mustad 9672 for freshwater, stainless steel for ocean
Thread: Black
Tail: Red
Tip: Red
Body: Light brass Mylar
Collar: Red band of tying thread
Wing: Mixed, of mallard flank and pearl Krystal Flash
Head: Gold coloured tungsten bead
Intended use: Wet fly for coho salmon

Comments: An effective fly for coho at Tofino on Vancouver Island and on Fraser River sloughs.

PINK FLY
Originated and contributed by Ken Ruddick

Hook: Size 8, Mustad 9672 or equivalent three extra-long hook
Thread: Pink
Tail: Pink rabbit and pearl Krystal Flash
Body: Hot pink plastic chenille
Head: Brass or copper bead
Intended use: Wet fly for salmon

Comments: A good wet fly for Fraser River coho, pinks and sockeye.

ROE FLY
Originated and contributed by Ken Ruddick

Hook: Size 6 or 8, Mustad 9672 or Mustad 79580
Thread: Black
Tail: Red hackle fibres
Body: In equal parts of red and orange plastic chenille
Wing: Six to eight fibres of pearl Krystal Flash, grey mallard, with optional overlay of white fox
Intended use: Wet fly for Fraser system coho

Comments: This is a particularly effective fly when fished deep and dead-drifted to bottom-dwelling coho.

Rick Stahl

grew up in an outdoor-orientated household. At the tender age of six, Rick received his brother's hand-me-down fly-tying vise and he became obsessed with the allure of the fly, leading him to a lifetime passion for the sport. He spent his summers chasing Kamloops trout with his family in the Merrit/Kamloops region, often spending weeks on end going from lake to lake. During the rest of the year he chased anything that swam within bicycling distance of home. At 11 years of age he caught his first steelhead, thus a whole new world opened up. At 17, Rick became a full-time employee of a local tackle shop in Abbotsford, by 21 he owned part of the shop and at 23, the entire shop. He closed the store after a few years, traveled and began a career as a fly-tackle industry representative. This lasted a short while before he was commissioned to open a fly shop in Washington. After two years,

RICK STAHL PHOTO

he returned to B.C. and found a home at Michael & Young Fly Shop where he has maintained a regular job for the last six years. Between all this, Rick managed to open his own guiding business. With guiding, working and family, he manages to spend 125 to 200 days on the water per year.

THE PORNOMID OR VIDMID
Originated and contributed by Rick Stahl

Hook: Size 10 to 18, Tiemco 2302
Thread: Black 8/0
Body: VHS tape cut into thin stips
Rib: Red saltwater Krystal Flash, tied pearl side up
Head & Thorax: Bevelled black bead
with two white dots painted on each side
Gills: White Poly Yarn
Intended use: Wet fly for Interior rainbow trout

Comments: The red saltwater Krystal Flash mimics hemoglobin (tint in the blood) that is present in the pupal stage of most natural midges.The VHS tape reflects colour well, and gives off a great shine, again very similar to the natural grays that seem to be in almost every lake. I usually coat the fly with Hard as Hull (Acrylic

Polymer/Clear nail polish), which protects the fragile body, ribbing and white paint, making the fly almost indestructible.

Developed in the spring of 1998, when I was not trying to simulate any particular chirinomid in particular, this fly quickly turned into my go-to midge on the Interior lakes. This is one of the best "searching" midge patterns that I have found. It has often out-performed other chironomids that should have been closer to the naturals that the fish were keying on.

PARR (CONED & EPOXY VERSIONS)
Originated and contributed by Rick Stahl

Hook: Size 1/0 to 6, Daiichi 2052 or equal
Body: Pearl Diamond Braid
Wing: Nat. rabbit strip (cut fairly thin) over silver and pearl Flashabou
Throat: Orange Philoplume
Head: 3/16"+ silver Hologram Dome eyes or large silver cone
Intended use: Wet fly for bull trout in the Fraser system

Comments: Developed in 1998 and introduced to Pitt River bull trout, the Parr spent most of that summer on the end of my line. During that time I discovered that chinook had a preference for this fly as well. The cone-headed version was developed to pursue bull trout and Dolly Varden in glacial rivers where the fish were primarily dependant on salmon as the base of the food chain. I wanted a weighted pattern that was slimmer than the Kiwi Muddler and quicker to tie, as we were going through scads of them while guiding. I felt that the fly offered a more realistic minnow motion by allowing free movement of the rabbit strip, as opposed to the Zonker. The white leather strip of the rabbit also showed nicely as the under belly of a minnow.

The epoxy-eyed version was developed after my successes with the weighted version and out of a need to fish shallower and/or clearer water conditions. Large prismatic eyes portray realism and "steer" fish to bite forward of the hook rather than nip the tail, promoting hook-ups. In the spring of '99 I came upon a drift fisherman gutting a hen steelhead on the Chilliwack River. I could not help but notice minnows lying in the guts on the bloody beach. Upon further examination, I determined the stomach of the fish had been packed with salmon fry up to 3 1/2 inches long, suggesting that the fish were "patterning" after minnows.

I thanked the angler and proceeded to crowd the water he was fishing, as killing the fish required him to stop fishing. I switched to the Parr and hooked up almost immediately on a large buck. This fish was hooked after at least three previous anglers had gone through the run fishing both roe and pink rubber worms. Bells began to ring. The rest of the season turned into an eye opener as I proceeded to have one of the most memorable spring steelhead seasons of my life. Time and again with the Parr pattern I have managed to hook steelies while behind other anglers using all gear types.

That summer I commissioned a commercial tier and filled a few bins with the flies at M&Y. They have all the qualities that commercial tier's love; quick, simple and effective (good money-to-time spent ratio). Sales were brisk, as it was easy for fly-fishers to see the value of having in their box a large minnow-style fly for river fishing.

BLACK DOUBLE ENDER
Originated and contributed by Rick Stahl

Hook: Size 2/0 to 6 regular salmon, Tiemco 7999 or equal
Tail: Black rabbit strip and dark blue Flashabou
Rear Body: Rear half of orange seal fur spun in a dubbing loop with a palmered, matching-colored, neck hackle
Middle Wing: Two black pheasant shoulder feathers tied Black GP style

Forward Body: Black seal fur spun in a dubbing loop with a palmered, matching-colored, neck hackle or schlappen feather
Collar: Blue guinea
Wing: Two black pheasant shoulder feathers tied GP style
Head: Turn or two of black seal fur
Intended use: Wet fly for Fraser system winter-run steelhead

Comments: Developed in 1999, because I wanted a fly that would throw a large silhouette like a Black GP, have the motion of a Bunny Leech, "push" water like a Woolly Bugger and have a little color in the butt, like a Red-butted Spade, to help the fish make up their minds to bite. I rolled all those thoughts into one and came up with the Black Double Ender. This is "the" confidence fly for your steelheading: everything that both winter and summer steelhead could ever want.

Ray Syrnyk

was born and raised in British Columbia. He caught his first fish when he was three years old fishing with his grandpa off the docks in Steveston. Growing up in Port Moody, he learned to fish the small streams in Burrard Inlet out of need to help feed the family. His first fish on the fly was caught on Machete Lake when he was nine years old. He started fly-fishing on a full-time basis in the mid seventies. He began tying in the early eighties after a two-hour lesson from Brian Mymko and a Dick Stewart fly-tying book. He has been successfully tying his own patterns and variations for the last 25 years.

RAY'S GHOST SHRIMP BUG
Adapted and contributed by Ray Syrnyk

Hook: Size 1/0, Tiemco 7999 or size 2, Tiemco 7215
Thread: Danville's Plus-light pink
Tail: Light pink polar bear hair

Eyes: Small or extra-small bead chain
Body: Light pink, four-strand floss and spun light-pink polar bear hair
Rib: Dark copper
Hackle: Chinese cock-neck dyed light

pink and light pink marabou, or light pink guinea fowl
Intended use: Wet fly for steelhead, springs, coho, Dolly Varden and bull trout

Comments: In the early ninetie's I showed my friend Rob Diston a new crayfish pattern that I had tied. He suggested that I dress a Ghost Shrimp. A few years later, returning from the Thompson River, I was discussing the pros and cons of different patterns we had been using with Aaron Goodis and his cousin Andrew Redmont. I had developed a buggy Egg Sucking Leech pattern that we found very effective. So looking for an edge I decided it was time to try tying a "buggy Ghost Shrimp", and with the spun polar bear hair and the other materials these are buggy-looking flies or BUGS! The buggier the better!!!!

I prefer to fish this fly with a floating line and long leader. By mending the cast you will give the fly a chance to sink. However, it fishes well dredged on a sinking line or tip.

RAY'S HOT PINK BUG
Adapted and contributed by Ray Syrnyk

Hook: Size 1/0, Tiemco 7999 or size 2, Tiemco 7215
Thread: Danville's Plus- hot pink
Tail: Hot pink polar bear hair
Eyes: Small or extra-small bead chain
Body: Hot pink, four-strand floss and spun hot pink polar bear hair

Rib: Dark copper
Hackle: Chinese cock neck dyed hot pink and hot pink marabou, or hot pink guinea fowl
Intended use: Wet fly for steelhead and springs

Comments: This pattern is best fished on sinking line in faster water, although I personally fish it with a floating line and long leader.

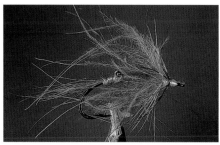

RAY'S ORANGE BUG
Adapted and contributed by Ray Syrnyk

Hook: Size 1/0, Tiemco 7999 or size 2, Tiemco 7215
Thread: Danville's Plus hot orange
Tail: Bright orange polar bear hair
Eyes: Small or extra-small bead chain
Body: Hot orange, four strand floss and spun hot orange polar bear hair

Rib: Dark copper
Hackle: Chinese cock neck dyed hot orange, and hot orange marabou or hot orange guinea fowl
Intended use: Wet fly for steelhead, coho, springs, chum, Dolly Varden, bull trout, rainbow and cutthroat trout

Comments: The original pattern mimicked a crayfish and from it came the other coloured variations. This fly works well on the Cheakamus River where I have taken winter steelhead up to 17 pounds. This fly works very well in all waters, no matter how you fish them.

RAY'S BLACK BUG
Adapted and contributed by Ray Syrnyk

Hook: Size 1/0, Tiemco 7999 or size 2, Tiemco 7215
Thread: Danville's Plus black
Tail: Black polar bear hair
Eyes: Small or extra-small bead chain
Body: Black, four-strand floss and spun black polar bear hair
Rib: Dark copper
Hackle: Black Chinese cock neck, black marabou and orange guinea fowl
Intended use: Wet fly for steelhead and springs

Comments: This pattern emulates mottled crayfish, leeches and eels. I have caught many large springs, both red and white, on this pattern.

RAY'S RED BUG OR RAY'S PURPLE BUG
Adapted and contributed by Ray Syrnyk

Hook: Size 1/0, Tiemco 7999 or size 2, Tiemco 7215
Thread: Danville's plus, red or black
Tail: Red or lilac purple polar bear hair
Eyes: Small or extra small bead chain
Body: Red or purple, four-strand floss and spun red or lilac purple polar bear hair
Rib: Dark copper
Hackle: Red or lilac purple Chinese cock neck, red or lilac purple, marabou and or red or lilac purple guinea fowl
Intended use: Wet fly for steelhead, springs, coho, Dolly Varden and bull trout

Comments: On some rivers only purple works at times, and when all else fails try a hot red!

Doug Wright

was born in Coquitlam in 1987 and, with his family spending many weeks of the year camping and fishing on the Interior lakes of B.C., has been exposed to fly-fishing his whole life. He tied his first fly at four years old under the tutelage of his father Will and has proven himself a keen student, tying commercially by the

time he was 11 years old. He spends hours doing "research" on the Internet and has also learned many finer points from family friend Phil Rowley. Doug became the youngest-ever member of the Osprey Flyfishers in 2000 at the age of 12 and also won first place in two divisions in the Logan Lake fly-tying contest in 2001. He won the BCFFF Bill Nation Award for his fly-tying accomplishments in 2003 and is a budding outdoor writer, having done step-by-step patterns in the "Osprey Flybox" (the Osprey Flyfishers newsletter), a dragonfly article for the BCFFF newsletter *Fly Lines* as well as works published in *B.C. Outdoors* and *Homewaters* magazines. Of his son's exuberance with fly-fishing, his father has said, "I've created a monster!"

AFTERSHAFT DRAGON
Originated and contributed by Doug Wright

Hook: Size 4 to 8, Mustad C53S, 3 extra-long curved nymph/dry-fly hook
Thread: 6/0 olive or brown
Tail: Pheasant tail
Under Body: Wool
Over Body: Olive or brown dubbing
Back: Olive or brown raffia/swiss straw
Rib: Medium gold or copper wire
Legs: Knotted pheasant tail
Thorax: Olive, brown or natural aftershaft/filoplume
Wing Case: Olive or brown raffia/Swiss straw
Eyes: Knotted ultra chenille
Intended use: Wet fly (nymph) for Interior rainbow trout

Comments: The Aftershaft Dragon is an effective pattern with realistic movement, imitating the Aeshindae (darner) family of dragonfly nymphs. Under careful examination, you will see that the front of a dragon nymph's abdomen noticeably pulses as it respires, and the best way I have found to suggest this motion is with the use of an aftershaft thorax. This fulfilled my needs exponentially. Because I am frequently trying to better imitate trout food sources and searching for a way to lure fish to my offerings, incorporating aftershaft feathers into the thorax seemed to be the most logical and effective way to suggest this pulsing motion. Aftershaft is the little tag feather most commonly attached to pheasant rump, and is also frequently found on partridge, grouse, and saddle hackle feathers. They pulse and undulate in the water very nicely and add life to any fly. The Aftershaft Dragon has been a successful fly when fished in waters that are generally clearer. Fish can shyly inspect the fly, rejecting any fraud that fails to score as a good imitation. Varying the dubbing used for the abdomen to a slightly brighter, flashier material regularly produces increased results in tannic or stained stillwaters.

ARIZONA DRAGON
Adapted and contributed by Doug Wright

Hook: Size 4 to 10, Mustad C53S, 3 extra-long curved nymph/dry-fly hook
Thread: Olive 6/0
Tail: Pheasant tail
Under Body: Wool
Over Body: Arizona Synthetic Peacock spun in a thread-dubbing loop, and further spun with a copper wire-dubbing loop

Legs: Knotted pheasant tail or Sili-Legs
Thorax: Peacock herl or Synthetic Peacock
Wing Case: Olive raffia/Swiss straw
Eyes: Olive or black Ultra Chenille, knotted
Intended use: Wet fly (nymph) for Interior rainbow trout

Comments: When a dragonfly nymph pattern featuring movement and shimmer is called for, the Arizona Dragon is a good solution. Utilizing Arizona Synthetic Peacock for the abdomen, the Arizona Dragon has the iridescence of natural peacock herl with the scruffy appearance of dubbing. My original Arizona Dragon called for legs of knotted peasant tail, but for such a pattern incorporating a rough, flashy body, I came to realize movement was a better counterpart than my taste for realism. Rubber hackle, Sili Legs, or straight pheasant tail or hen pheasant alone proved to be a much better choice with this pattern. The fly shimmers and moves through the water with great motion and appearance, making it a great choice for stained or murky waters.

Stalking the areas of vegetation and debris (dragonfly nymph habitat) with a full-sinking line with the Arizona Dragon on the end of your leader is a deadly tactic. With a slower-sinking line such as the clear intermediate varieties, one can use a much slower-paced retrieve, creeping the pattern alongside the edge of the structure. Try tying a few with a foam underbody and eyes, as Philip Rowley does with his Draggin. This will allow you to fish the Arizona Dragon on a full-sinking line in and around weedbeds, without the worried thought of snagging this structure. The fly line will sink to the bottom of the lake, down and dirty amongst the vegetation and debris while the fly, depending upon leader length, hovers above this structure. When retrieved, a fast strip gives the fly a diving action, heading downward towards the weight of the fly line. This is a very effective technique.

DAZZLE CADDIS EMERGER
Originated and contributed by Doug Wright

Hook: Size 10 to 14, Mustad C53S, 3 extra-long curved nymph/dry-fly hook
Thread: Gudebrod 8/0, brown or olive
Tail/Shuck: Angler's Choice Mohair Plus, Dazzle Dubbing, or Arizona Semi Seal, colour to match
Abdomen: Same as tail
Wing: Deer or elk hair
Wing Pads: Lacquered goose quill, trimmed to shape
Wingcase: 5/32" strip of brown sheet foam

Thorax: Seal, Arizona Synthetic Peacock, or other scruffy dubbing of choice
Swimmerets: Pheasant rump or hen pheasant fibers, 3 to 5 on each side
Antennae: Two fibers of pheasant rump, hen pheasant, or woodduck mallard flank
Intended use: Dry fly (emerger) for Interior rainbow trout

Comments: The Dazzle Caddis Emerger is a productive fly pattern imitating the caddis during its emergence into the winged,

moth-like adult stage. It has taken many fish for me during the exhilarating caddis hatch throughout interior stillwaters. Using a floating line with an appropriate size leader, cast to a sighted fish and apply a sharp pull as soon as it lands on the water surface. This will hopefully attract the attention of the fish towards the fly. If not, keeping a straight line, let the fly calmly lay on the surface, giving it the occasional to twitch simulate struggling, emerging movements.

When tying the Dazzle Caddis Emerger, use an appropriate amount of material for the tail. Too much will turn it opaque. Select enough material so that the tail will appear translucent when held up to a light source, allowing rays to filter through the material, yet retains a casing shape. The end result gives a realistic shuck appearance when placed in the water and held up to the sunlight, much like what a trout would most likely see.

MARABOU MAY
Adapted and contributed by Doug Wright

Hook: Size 12 to 16, Mustad C53S, 3 extra-long curved nymph hook or substitute
Thread: 8/0, colour to match
Abdomen: Marabou, colour to match
Rib #1: One strand of pearlescent Flashabou
Rib #2: Fine copper wire

Back: Pheasant tail
Tail: Pheasant tail
Wingcase: Pheasant tail
Legs: Hen saddle fibers
Thorax: Marabou
Intended use: Wet fly (nymph) for Interior rainbow trout

Comments: The Marabou May is my favorite *Callibaetis* mayfly nymph imitation. I am really happy with this pattern's effectiveness and as such it has earned a prominent place in my fly box. Two types of marabou are incorporated into this fly and both can usually be found in the same package. For the body, pick a feather with skinny, string-like marabou fibers, and for the thorax select one that has thick, fluffy strands. The marabou used for the body perfectly represents the abdomen and gills of the natural. *Callibaetis* nymphs have slender bodies with small, sparse gills along either side. The skinny, string-like marabou fibers create a perfect match, and unlike ostrich herl, suggest the abdomen and the tiny, feather-like gills with greater realism. Mayflies, as well as Chironomids, trap gases within their abdomens to aid in their ascent to the surface to emerge, and the fine copper wire and pearlescent Flashabou ribs suggest this well. The thick, webby marabou used in the thorax provides extra undulation when retrieved through the water. The back is tied "Skip Nymph style", the same way Skip Morris applies the pheasant-tail back to his popular and effective Skip Nymph. The pheasant tail is tied in at the 1/3 mark (rear of the thorax region) and is pulled down and back along the top of the abdomen. It is simply held in place with tight wraps of the fine copper wire rib.

Using either a clear wet tip or a floating fly line with long leader, try casting the Marabou May onto a weedy or marl bottom shoal; you may be surprised at the results. Use a steady, slow-paced retrieve mixed with the occasional quick, erratic twitch. This is a great fly pattern to test at your favorite clear, marl-bottommed lakes.

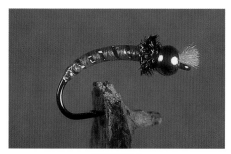

CORONA

Adapted and contributed by Doug Wright

Hook: Size 10 to 18, Mustad C49S, curved pupa/scud hook

Thread: 8/0 chartreuse or bright green tying thread

Underbody: Silver Flashabou or chartreuse tying thread (Note: An underbody is necessary for this pattern as the chartreuse Accent Flashabou is translucent)

Overbody: Chartreuse or bright green Accent Flashabou

Rib: Gold or red holographic Mylar

Thorax: Peacock herl

Head: Gold metal bead

Gills: White Sparkle Yarn

Coat: Coat the abdomen with brushable super glue for an extra layer of durability and shine

Intended use: Wet fly (pupae) for Interior rainbow trout

Comments: The Corona is best used in clear, marl-bottommed lakes where small, bright green Chironomid are commonly found. It has been a very good producer at White Lake near Salmon Arm. This pupae imitation is best fished suspended below a strike indicator about one or two feet off the bottom of the lake, or wind-drifted using a floating line and an extra-long leader. The wind-drift presentation covers a lot of water and is a very effective way to fish this pattern from an anchored boat. Utilizing a leader about 25% longer than the depth being fished and with the wind at your back, cast your floating line to the left- or right-hand side, quartering to the wind. Allow the breeze to sweep your line in an arc until the drift is finished and the line is straight downwind from you. At this point the fly has reached the "zone" and you have already covered a good portion of water. Now, if no fish have taken the fly, use a super-slow hand twist to retrieve the fly back towards the boat. Retrieve all of the line, as it is not uncommon for a trout to follow the fly right to the boat before deciding to bite!

Kingfisher Rod & Gun Club

Founded in 1959, the Kingfisher Rod & Gun Club consists of a variety of anglers, many of whom fly-fish for steelhead, trout and salmon with a fly. The club has been a long-time advocate for steelhead with some members active in conservation-related organizations such as the Steelhead Society of British Columbia. Their home river is the Thompson River with its world famous steelhead run which, unfortunately, has been in steady decline for years. Kingfisher Club members form the nucleus of a group of concerned Thompson River anglers who have led the charge to bring this magnificent fish back from its extreme conservation level.

The Kingfisher flies in this book come from the vises of Scott Baker-McGarva, Poul Bech, Tyler Kushnir and Dana Sturn.

Scott Baker-McGarva

Born in Trail, B.C., and fly casting since he was old enough to wave a fly rod in his arms, Scott grew up fishing storied Interior British Columbia lakes such as Paul, Jacko, Billy and others under the keen eyes of his father and both grandfathers. A descendant of famous angling pioneer Austin Spencer (Spent Spinner), much of his teen and early twenties were split between steelheading in Southern B.C. rivers, Alberta's Bow river, Interior lakes, and later a stint as a bluewater fly-fishing guide in Mexico. A decade, and then some, working in sportfishing retail, obtaining flycasting instructor certification by his mid twenties, teaching fly-tying, fly casting, the art of the two-handed Spey rod and various other angling disciplines, followed. Scott's flies have been featured in various printed and on-line publications, as well as at conservation auctions and banquets. Scott is now co-owner of the Anglers West Fly and Tackle shop in Vancouver.

Presently President of the rejuvenated Steelhead Society of B.C., Scott is also a member of the Kingfishers Rod and Gun Club, presently acting as Secretary. He also actively supports and donates flies and instruction to many other conservation organizations, such as the BCFFF and Trout Unlimited Canada. Scott presently lives in downtown Vancouver, never very far from the water.

Poul Bech

has been active in the fishing community for over three decades. He hooked his first steelhead in 1969 while fishing a dry fly for resident trout. The steelhead escaped after a long struggle, but Poul was firmly hooked. Poul learned to catch steelhead on the heavily-fished lower mainland streams in the 1970s when he worked at Harkley and Haywood Sporting Goods in downtown Vancouver. From 1977 to 1997, Poul worked as a technician for Provincial Fisheries. He has been a long-time fish conservation advocate and currently serves as vice president of the Steelhead Society of B.C. He can be found on British Columbia's lakes and streams fishing for all species of game fish, but his first love is the steelhead.

Tyler Kushnir

has been fishing since he was old enough to hold a rod. At age 10 he taught himself to tie and cast a fly when he inherited a fly rod along with a fly-tying vise and a box of feathers from his grandfather. His first steelhead came from the Gold River in 1970 and his first fly-caught one was in 1973 in the Line Fence Pool on the Campbell River—with Rod Haig-Brown giving him suggestions from the bank. Tyler took up the double-hander and fly-fishing for steelhead seriously in 1992 and has been a regular on the Thompson ever since. Tyler is presently involved with the Steelhead Society of B.C. as a Director and is now the Vice President of the Kingfisher Rod and Gun Club. As well, Tyler spends time guiding for salmon in the Queen Charlotte Islands and fishing Chironomids for trout on his favourite Cariboo lake.

Dana Sturn

has been fly-fishing since 1988. He caught his first steelhead on the Squamish River in March 1995 and has been a metalhead junkie ever since. His love of steelhead and Spey casting lead

Dana to develop the *Spey Pages* and *Spey Clave* websites www.speypages.com, now widely regarded as the most comprehensive resources for two-handed fly-rod enthusiasts on the Internet. A writer/photographer with credits including, *B.C. Outdoors* and *Fly Fisherman* magazines, Dana is also a FFF-certified fly-casting instructor who teaches and demonstrates Spey casting across Canada and the United States. Dana is a member of the Kingfisher's Rod and Gun Club and a Director of the Steelhead Society of British Columbia. He lives with his family in the heart of steelhead country near Vancouver, B.C.

ULI'S CADDIS EMERGER
Originated and contributed by Scott Baker-McGarva

Hook: Size 8 to 12, Tiemco 2312 or equal 3x fine dry-fly hook
Thread: Olive, 8/0
Tail: A trailing shuck of burnt orange Antron, goat or similar long-fibre material, extending 1/2 inch to 3/4 inch (depending on hook size) followed by a couple of turns of partridge flank and a strand of dark pheasant tail on each side

Body: A spun ginger or burnt orange deer hair clipped small, followed by mint Antron dubbing
Back: Grey closed-cell foam
Wing: Naturally grey deer hair or dark elk hair
Head: Deer or elk butts with foam back extending over hook eye
Intended use: Dry fly for Interior rainbow trout

Comments: This style of fly can be used in many combinations of both material and size, thus representing any number of emerging insects by substituting the colors and trailing shuck materials to suit. The elk wings help support the fly in the surface film, an all-important component of a good emerger pattern, while the foam head keeps a low profile without drowning. This fly can also be dressed using white foam, but darken the body with a Pantone marker and leave the head white for improved visibility on choppy water or low light.

During a typical June caddis hatch several years back, I watched dozens of pupae rise from the depths and hatch beside my pram. The morning gave us good, deep pupa action…but when the fish were on top, an equal number of fish were loudly slurping emergers like judges at a hot chili contest. The slurpers were educated larger fish, and a low-floating emerger with the obvious trailing shuck seemed to be the ticket, something confirmed by later stomach pump analysis. I had a few good emergers but nothing that gave the long silhouette I was looking for. As it was a typical high-country June day, a large thunderhead formed and chased most anglers off the water for a refueling, and myself for a quick fly-tying binge.

Stealing the wing idea from a favorite steelhead dry-fly design, I came up with a fly that perfectly hung in the film and cast the appropriate silhouette.

Soon the clouds cleared and round two started on the flats. This time I was armed with a new fly (but only one, as my angling buddies threatened me with bodily harm should I hoard the

prototypes). Until I snapped it off in the sharp jaw of a large, overly embarrassed fish, the new pattern went 8 for 8 on the shoal. Many takes of the confident head-tail rise type, but also some serious toilet flushers…

APRIL SPEY (AP FLY)
Originated and contributed by Scott Baker-McGarva

Hook: Size 3/0 to 3, Daiichi 2060, 2061, Talon C105 or spectra loop for inter-changeable hook or cut shank intruder style and use a sleeve
Thread: Black 6/0
Tag: Gold Mylar counter-ribbed with gold wire
Tail: Golden pheasant tippet, natural or dyed
Body: Rear third of bright green seal, highlander green or Chartreuse seal fur loosley dubbed followed by a front two-thirds of kingfisher blue blended into purple seal fur
Rib: Rear third flat pearl Mylar, front two-thirds flat blue Mylar, counter ribbed with gold wire

Hackle: Kingfisher blue saddle palmered over rear third, followed by heron, blue-eared pheasant, or substitute, palmered over front two-thirds
Collar: Purple-dyed blue-eared pheasant
Throat: Blue peacock breast feather
Wing: 20 to 30 strands of peacock herl, preferably taken off the stem as the tips are not broken, overlaid with 10 to 12 black ostrich herls
Eyes: (Optional) Jungle cock, laid in Ackroyd–style
Head: (Optional) Orange or blue rabbit or arctic fox dubbing
Intended use: Wet fly for summer and winter steelhead

Comments: Some flies are about triggering the imprint reaction from the sea, others from the juvenile period in the steelhead's life; this is neither…because experienced anglers often know that pattern specifics other than size and silhouette rarely matter, this fly came about because of different reasons.

My then-girlfriend told me her favorite colours… they became incorporated into a fly… blues, greens, purple and black were already steelhead favorites so to put them all together made sense. A fly in the classic Ackroyd-style with a little more movement in the wing made it even better. Wouldn't you know that not only did it work well on the Thompson, but all over up north as well. Given the gal, I'm not surprised. I'm sure a less-complex fly works just as well, but sometimes they just don't invoke half the interest on my part in tying.

DARK PRIEST
Adapted and contributed by Poul Bech

Hook: Size 2/0 to 8, Tiemco 7999
Thread: 8/0 purple
Tip & Tag: Flat silver, fluorescent

orange-yellow floss or thread over silver, with several coats of super glue and/or head cement

Tail: Golden pheasant crest
Body: Red, green, dark blue, & purple seal, well mixed, then mixed 50/50 with black seal to form an "optical black" dubbing
Rib: Flat silver tinsel
Hackle: Soft natural black, two turns
Wing: Very sparse grey squirrel with a few fibres of dark mallard flank on each side to give an illusion of substance without restricting movement of the squirrel hairs, two black Krystal Flash horns
Intended use: Wet fly for steelhead, year round

Comments: This pattern is adapted from a fly of the same name originated by the late Dick Vandemark of Bellingham in 1977. He first tied the fly as a Spey pattern with palmered heron substitute and dark mallard wings, then adapted the fly as a "low-water flymph" pattern as shown in his book *Steelhead Fly Fishing in Low Water*. My version, adapted as a true wet fly in 1999, has become my "go to" pattern for summer steelhead on the Thompson, Skeena tributaries, and for lower mainland winter-runs.

Nobody seems to tie a real wet fly for steelhead anymore, it's all marabou, prawns and intruders. I like a fly that I can fish on a floating line that will penetrate easily into and remain stable in strong currents, and still retain good mobility. That's the reason for the sparse wing, sparse hackle and heavy hook. Even on a sink-tip in winter, I prefer a fly that sinks faster than my line.

Vandemark was my fly-fishing mentor, and I inherited his preferences for multiple attractants in every fly, including a bit (but not too much) of fluorescent colour and flash, some natural un-dyed (and therefore buggier) materials, and mixed dubbings. Dick's theory behind the mixed dubbings was that a fish is attracted at a distance to a fly that seems to be mostly one color, and when the fish gets close enough to see all the different colors in the mix, it gets excited and seals the deal. I used golden pheasant crest for the tail because virtually every Atlantic salmon fly has it; so, applying the theory of evolution, I assumed that those fish must really like it otherwise fly-tiers would have stopped using it. I can assure you that steelhead like it, too!

WINTER CAROLINE
Adapted and contributed by Poul Bech

Hook: Size 2/0 to 6, Tiemco 7999
Thread: Flame 8/0
Tail: Reddish golden pheasant breast
Body: Mixed medium-olive and orange seal
Rib: Flat gold and silver wire,
Hackle: Sparse, stripped heron from second turn of wire
Throat: Reddish golden pheasant breast
Wing: Flame mallard flank, folded and on edge (a vertical, wet-fly-type wing as opposed to the usual low-set Spey wing). Two pink Krystal Flash horns
Intended use: Wet fly for winter or fall steelhead in low light or cold water, floating line or light sink-tip

Comments: This is a more colorful variation of the famous Lady Caroline Spey fly. I first used it in the 1980s for Squamish winter-run steelhead. Although I still use it for winter fishing, in larger sizes it really shines for low-light or cold-water situations on the Thompson. I've also used it successfully in Skeena tributaries, and in small sizes at first light in small summer-run streams like the Coquihalla. Spey patterns traditionally have low-set, horizontal wings. Although it doesn't look as pretty, I prefer a vertical, traditional wet-fly wing that allows the fly to sink more quickly and acts as a rudder in strong flows to keep the fly swimming in a more stable fashion. I use a heavy hook for the same reasons. My "regular" version of the Lady Caroline (my favorite steelhead fly) is tied exactly the same as the Winter Caroline, except the wing is natural brown barred mallard flank, folded and on edge, with pearl Krystal Flash horns.

BOOB TUBE
Originated and contributed by Tyler Kushnir

Hook: Size 4, Partridge Nordic Single Tube
Tube: Black air brake tubing approximately 1" long
Thread: Black
Boobies: 3/8-inch foam stick about 3/4-inch long tied in with cross wraps then clipped to shape
Body: None; the black air brake tube does the trick
Wing: High-quality deer hair, natural, black or purple
Waking Hole Note: Turn the fly bottom-up and poke a flame-heated bodkin needle through the tubing at a 45-degree slant towards the hole at the front of the tube. Start far enough back so as to ensure that the needle doesn't melt through the front edge of the tube. Work the needle back and forth to swage the hole, let it cool and you are done.
Intended use: Waked tube fly for summer-run steelhead

Comments: First tied in August 1997, as the Steelhead Boobie; a regular hooked fly, but in 2000 it became a tube fly and was renamed the Boob Tube. I needed a simple, unsinkable waking fly and I wasn't enthralled with any of the standards, so I set out on my own.

The concept is a spin-off from a British trout fly known as the Boobie. I had come across it while checking out a British trout magazine. Apparently it was a controversial and deadly fly on lakes in Britain. In fact, many waters banned it outright; needless to say, this caught my attention. It was fished as a wet flies on Hi-D lines and three-foot leaders. The long marabou tail wiggled irresistibly as the foam "boobies" moved the fly. I tied some for interior lakes and they *were* deadly. For a couple of years they were one of my "trout secrets". Then in preparation for an early trip to the Morice I was considering some waking flies. It struck me that in the first article on boobies that I'd read, there was mention that it was originally a waking pattern, - hmmm. The first Boobie was basically a Bomber with the foam "boobies" up front; it definitely floated and waked. On its maiden voyage, less than five minutes from the By-Mac launch on the Morice River, the Steelhead Boobie took a sleek 10 pound fish! I had my waker.

In 2000 when I switched to tube flies for steelhead I turned my attention to the Steelhead Boobie. I had never been really happy with the bomber shape, so I tried some alternatives. The new style was inspired by Collin Shadrech's Bulkley Mouse, which is like a giant Elk Hair Caddis. The simple tie of the flared deer hair up against the back of the "boobies" was perfect; even better, the black air brake tubing I use for most of my tubes made the perfect body.

The final piece of the Boob Tube came during that first 2000 season. Once again, reading a British magazine, this time an Atlantic salmon publication, I came across a method of riffling a tube fly. It involves a small hole on the underside of the tube a short distance back from the head end of the fly. The leader is threaded up from beneath and through this hole, then threaded down the tube and tied to the hook as usual. This brilliant technique cocks the fly up on an angle and planes the fly up onto the surface. As well, with the hole at the bottom of the tube, there is no need to worry about which side of the river you are on—as with a riffle hitch—it will wake from anywhere! The Boob Tube had arrived.

The Boob Tube is probably B.C.'s first waking tube pattern. It is a truly unsinkable waker that functions in all water types equally well. It is also a combination of a number of radical concepts, using foam, tube and riffle hole that can be successfully adapted to many other patterns. I have fished it in sizes that range from a sparsely dressed 1 1/2" to a fully dressed 2 1/2" long. While the original colour was natural deer hair with black foam eyes, a purple version with black eyes has proven effective, as has a Boob Tube with black deer hair and yellow eyes, which as a bonus is quite visible to the angler.

While this fly has been kept somewhat quiet until recently, it has had success on the Morice, Bulkley, Copper and Babine, as well as the Thompson.

Fly Fishing Techniques: This fly is used in the standard waking manner, fished under tension and followed or led through its arc as required. A unique feature of the Boob Tube is that while it is a radical waker, that is, a fly that planes up and onto the water due to its design and the force of the current, it will also float and wake in very smooth, even flows. Furthermore, with the exception of the foam, it rides *in* the surface providing a great silhouette.

An interesting variation of the two-fly "waker/dropper" technique is possible (and legal in B.C.) with the Boob Tube. Due to the construction of the fly, the leader can be pulled through the tube two or three feet and a low-water pattern can be trailed. The waking hole in the front of the tube will lock the waker in position on the leader. This is a deadly technique in tough conditions. The fish come to investigate the commotion of the waker, then take the low-water trailer.

THE DYNAMIC DUO – THE VOODOO CHILD AND THE RAGING PRAWN

Originated and contributed by Tyler Kushnir

THE VOODOO CHILD

Hook: Size 6 to 2/0, Partridge Bartleet Supreme for conventional dressed fly or size 6 to 2, Partridge Nordic Single Spey when dressed on a tube
Thread: Black
Tail: Black polar bear 1 1/2 times the length of the body followed by golden pheasant tippet and two peccary hairs. Cut a "V" out of a large natural Golden Pheasant tippet and tie in so the "V" lies on both sides of the tail. On top of this, tie two matched peccary hairs, cross and secure them so they flare out from the tail at approximately 45 degrees

Body: A 3/4- to 2-inch piece of 3/16-inch (inside diameter) air brake tubing with black or dark purple dubbing
Rib: Wide pearl Mylar, counter-wound with tying thread for durability
First Wing: Locate 1/3 of the way up the body and in two parts: first a clump of black woolly Bugger marabou, topped with a clump of the marabou-like feather from the flank of a purple-dyed golden pheasant skin

Hackle: In front of the wing, tie in a folded flank feather from a purple-dyed golden pheasant skin.
Body: Continue body and rib as before, leaving enough space for the second wing and hackle.
Second Wing: As the first wing, followed by a hackle, then whip finish and cement
Intended use: Wet fly for summer and winter steelhead

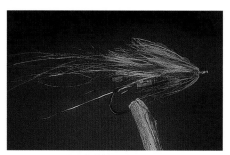

RAGING PRAWN

Hook: Size 6 to 2/0, Partridge Bartleet Supreme for conventional dressed fly or size 6 to 2, Partridge Nordic Single Spey when dressed on a tube
Thread: Red
Tail: Orange polar bear 1 1/2 times the length of the body followed by golden pheasant tippet and two peccary hairs. Cut a "V" out of a large natural golden pheasant tippet and tie in so the "V" lies on both sides of the tail. On top of this, tie two matched peccary hairs, cross and secure them so they flare out from the tail at approximately 45 degrees. polar bear 1 1/2 times the length of the body
Body: A 3/4- to 2-inch piece of 3/16-inch (inside diameter) air brake tubing with orange/red dubbing
Rib: Wide pearl Mylar, counter-wound with tying thread for durability
First Wing: Locate 1/3 of the way up the body and in two parts: first a clump of orange Woolly Bugger marabou, followed by a second of fluorescent orange
Hackle: In front of the wing, tie in a folded red-brown golden pheasant flank feather
Body: Continue with body and rib as before, leaving enough space for the second wing and hackle.
Second wing: As the first wing, followed with a hackle, then whip finish and cement
Intended use: Wet fly for summer and winter steelhead

Note: At times I will vary the colours of these flies, adding a bit more purple to the Voodoo Child and tie a pink version of the Raging Prawn, but day in, day out this Dynamic Duo will be found on the end of my line.

Comments: I developed the Voodoo Child in 1995 and took the first fish, a 12-pound buck, from the Squamish River that same year. The Raging Prawn came from my tying vise two years later and I took my first steelhead, a fifteen-pounder, from the Thompson in 1997. With these two flies my needs for a good one-two punch of a big dark fly and orange follow-up pattern were satisfied.

Like so many B.C. steelhead patterns, the origin of these flies is with the General Practitioner. However, this fly has closer ties with Art Lingren's Black GP than Esmond Drury's original. As I had a personal affinity for black flies my first focus was the Black GP. One of the problems of a single-point GP is instability on the swing, for whereas the original tied on a double-pointed hook swam very well, the single-point did not, often rolling over on the swing. Trey Combs, in his great book *Steelhead Fly Fishing,* spoke of placing more material on top of the fly to provide stability on the swing. The inspiration for the marabou wings in the pattern comes from Washington State steelheader Sean Gallagher's Black Marabou GP. The bunch of marabou on top of the hook also provides a great silhouette.

The other defining feature—the peccary feelers—come from another Washington steelheader Dec Hogan and his Winter Prawn. Where the feelers on the Winter Prawn are laid straight back, on my flies they are tied to form a distinct V-shape. The stiff hairs create a slight wiggle as the fly swims, this concept is derived from a Scandinavian tube fly that uses four peccary hairs to create a wobble. As well, the distinct black/white pattern of the peccary stands out very well in the water.

The success of the Voodoo Child inspired me to dress a counterpoint bright fly—the Raging Prawn is that fly. The orange version differs from the Voodoo Child only in colour. The Raging Prawn is not a super bright pattern. With its red body and natural golden pheasant flank hackle, it is bright but not outrageously so.

While originally tied on hooks, in 1999 the dynamic duo became tube flies. This was to take advantage of the superior hooking-to-landing ratio of short-shanked hooks. Also, the ability to simply tie on a new hook when the first becomes dulled is an advantage. Since tube length is arbitrary, the overall length of the fly (including the tail) can range from 1 1/2 to 7 inches. I have successfully fished the flies in 15 river systems in B.C. and Washington State for both summer and winter steelhead. The largest steelhead taken to date is a 43-inch buck on the Voodoo Child and a 40-inch buck on the Raging Prawn, both from the Thompson River in 2000. As a bonus, they have also been consistent producers of Dollies when searching for spring steelhead.

I have used this fly successfully fished on a sink-tip, as well as on the floating line, especially in smaller sizes. I prefer to fish black patterns for steelhead, but I believe at times there is a need for a distinct change of pace. If I get a pluck on the Voodoo Child that is not repeated, I will switch to a Raging Prawn; or if I am following a buddy who is using a dark fly I will use the Raging Prawn. I do not carry a lot of fly patterns, but I do tie these two flies in a great range of sizes and relative sparseness so I can match light and water conditions. I find that having settled on two "go to" patterns I spend very little time or brain power worrying about the right pattern—instead, I fish!

THOMPSON STONE

Designed and contributed by Dana Sturn

Tube: 1/2" – 2" air brake hose (1/8" outside diameter spaghetti line available from auto supply stores)
Hook: Size 4 or 6, Partridge Single Nordic Tube Fly Hook
Thread: Black 6/0
Tail: Black saddle
Body: Medium-diameter reddish-brown transformer wire
Hackle: Black saddle
Intended use: Wet fly or nymph for summer-run steelhead

Comments: When I started fly-fishing I read *Nymph Fishing for Larger Trout* by Charles Brooks and started using Brooks' tied-in-the-round stonefly patterns. These flies presented the same profile to a trout from any side and really worked well for me; later when I got interested in tube flies I discovered that many tubes shared

this design feature. The Thompson Stone (aka Thompson Tube) is a fly I designed in 1998 for steelhead on British Columbia's Thompson River. I first tied the tube-fly version in November 2000. It is based on the Brooks Golden Stonefly and the Steelhead Brassie, a pattern I first saw in *Flies for Steelhead* by Dick Stewart and Allen Farrow, which in turn is based on the Brassie, a wire-bodied trout fly often used to imitate midge larvae and pupae. The Thompson Stone is relatively easy to tie and requires few materials. The original has been very productive for me on the Thompson and Dean rivers, and it has been successfully used by others on the Skeena system, the Deschutes River in Oregon, and for winter steelhead in Washington State.

SPUR

Originated and contributed by Dana Sturn

Tube: 1" – 2 1/2" air-brake hose (1/8" outside diameter spaghetti line available from auto supply stores)
Hook: Size 2 or 4, Partridge Single Nordic Tube Fly Hook
Thread: Black 6/0
Tail: Black marabou
Body: Black dubbing (optional) over transformer wire
Hackle: Black saddle
Wing: Black marabou
Intended use: Steelhead wet fly

Comments: This is basically a slightly modified version of the big Marabou Spiders popularized on the Skagit River for winter steelhead by anglers like John Farrar and Dec Hogan. On a Thompson trip back in 2001 I ran out of big Black GPs and needed a quick replacement. I needed a big-silhouette pattern for first-light fishing and was too lazy to tie the GPs on tubes, so I set about finding a way to create a similar look in the water without all the bother. I had been using the Skagit flies for winter steelhead and figured that if I could make a bigger, longer Marabou Spider, that might do the trick. Marabou Spiders look big and puffy when dry, but when wet and fished in slightly streamy water they really slim down and swim beautifully, which is the GP look I was after. The Spur is simply a black Marabou Spider with the addition of a marabou tail. The fly enticed an 18-pounder the first morning I used it, and it has now become one of my most used patterns.

Totem Fly Fishers

The Totem Fly Fishers was founded in 1968 and is British Columbia's oldest fly-fishing club. Roderick Haig-Brown, the Totem's first honourary member, suggested it be a social club and that is its main focus. However, it has many talented fly-fishers whose endeavors are widely recognized in the fly-fishing fraternity. Many Totems have

served honorably in organizations such as the former Steelhead Society of B.C. and the BCFFF. The club is highly regarded and has a respected voice when it expresses its opinion on British

Columbia fisheries issues. Club members Ron Grantham, Clark Closkey, Duncan Laird, Mel Hocken, Vic Marchiel and Bob Taylor contributed to this book.

Clark Closkey

started flyfishing at about age 10, with his first rod, reel and line coming from the Surrey Co-op. That was nearly 50 years ago. Fly

tying became a passion at age 12 when his mother bought him a fly-tying kit for his birthday and he started to produce Royal Coachman and Red Ibis flies in large quantities. Soon he was supplying family and friends with flies. He has had a couple of magazine articles published over the years, as well as written an outdoors column for five years for 2 papers— *The Surrey Leader* and *Columbian*. He

also taught fly-tying and casting in night school for Surrey Parks and Rec in the 60's. He came to his first Totem meeting in 1979 and joined shortly thereafter.

Ron Grantham

has been fishing since 1964, and flyfishing since 1970. His first fly-caught steelhead was taken on the Thompson River in 1974, and, since then, he has successfully fished most of the major steelhead rivers in B.C., and several in Washington. He builds both single- and double-handed split cane fly rods as a hobby, and uses them for all his fishing. He was involved with the BCFFF in the early

years, and as a member of the Dogwood Fly Fishers in Maple Ridge prior to joining the Totem Fly Fishers in 1979. The Corbett Lake Bamboo Rod Builders' Gathering has been held every two years since 1988 and is the first of its kind in the world. Ron co-organized the event for 2004 and will be doing so again in 2006.

Mel Hocken

started out fishing as a young boy with his dad. It was on a trip to Alberta's Ram River that he was introduced to fly-fishing by an elderly fellow fly-fishing in the water in front of their camp. But it was not until he moved to Vancouver in the early '70s that some of his fly-fishing co-workers got him into fly-fishing on a regular basis. He started tying flies around 1976, after reading an article written by Jim Kilburn in the *Western Angler* magazine.

He tried to duplicate the flies in the article but was not satisfied with those attempts. He sought out some advice on how to improve his tying skills and eventually met Jack Vincent, who was working in the sporting goods section at Woodward's department store in the Oakridge Mall. It was Jack who invited Mel to Totem's meeting and sponsored his membership. Since joining the Totems, Mel has served two terms as club president. Over the years he honed his fly-tying

skills by studying magazine articles and several books on the subject. For a time he dressed flies for some of our local tackle shops. He found that tedious work, but it taught him a lot about tying a durable fly with good materials. His main interest is fly-fishing the many trout streams available in B.C., with the Elk and Skagit rivers two of his favorite destinations.

Duncan Laird

was born in the northeast of England, County Northumbria, in a small village called Ponteland. It is about 25 miles south of Alnwick, the home town of Hardy Brothers, the world-famous tackle makers. He started fishing around age 9, and was fly-fishing by 11. He came to Canada about 1965, first to Ontario, then to B.C. (Port Alice), back to Ontario and returned to British Columbia, never to move again. He was a member of

the Ospreys from 1989 to 1999, when he joined the Totems. He started fly-tying in his late teens, mostly out of necessity, and is mostly self taught, with the help of books like those by Keith Draper from New Zealand. Very basic stuff. It was not until he moved back to B.C. that he actually learned the intricacies of fly-tying. He claims B.C. is home to the finest tiers anywhere!

Vic Marchiel

has been fly-fishing and tying since 1976. Born and raised in Edmonton, he had to do a lot of driving to enjoy Alberta's better fly-fishing. He moved to the west coast in 1987 and believes that there is no place on earth that offers better accessibility to a wide spectrum of fly-fishing waters. Largely self taught at the vise, Vic credits his skills and expertise to long hours at the bench and much appreciated

information and help from fellow Totem Fly Fishers. While his favourite times are spent on a river, most of his angling time is spent on lakes. His angling in the summer is shared with his wife's dedication to her horseback riding, a hobby that marries well with his love of fly-fishing Interior lakes.

Bob Taylor

has been a fly-fisherman for 50 years and has journeyed through most of British Columbia and Washington State pursuing the mighty sea-run trouts that frequent most coast and some Interior rivers. He is the dean of the Totem's Dean River fly-fishers and has been leading groups into those wilderness waters for three decades. Taylor has long been both a supporter of the conservation movement and, before it was in vogue, a catch-

and-release fisher. He is a long-time member of the Totem Fly Fishers and supports the efforts of the Steelhead Society of B.C. and the B.C. Federation of Flyfishers, and serves as a director of the BCFFF. Taylor loves many rivers but prefers those of large size with big fish, such as the Dean and Thompson.

SIMPLE SEDGE
Originated and contributed by Clark Closkey

Hook: Size 18 to 4, 2x fine wire
Thread: Black 6/0
Tail: Deer hair (natural, brown or black)
Body: Clipped spun deer hair (same colour as tail)

Wing: Deer hair tips stroked back (same hair as tail and body)
Intended use: Adult sedge dry fly for Kamloops trout

Comments: Developed in the late 1970s, this fly was first used with great success on Sheridan Lake in the Cariboo for large rainbows. Its development came about as a result of frustration with patterns like the Tom Thumb and Humpy, with their brittle deer-hair fibres, lying length-wise along the shank, breaking when taken by the first fish, thus rendering the fly useless. But the fine floatation qualities of deer hair could not be ignored. The Simple Sedge can take twenty or more fish and still retain its shape and floating ability.

This fly has now been used with great success in New Zealand, the Yukon and throughout British Columbia in streams and lakes to take rainbow, browns, cutthroat, brook trout, Rocky mountain whitefish, Dollies, and steelhead.

GRANTHAM'S SEDGE
Originated and contributed by Ron Grantham

Hook: Size #6, Mustad 7957B, 7948A or 94840 down-eye, bronzed, forged, regular length, or equivalent
Thread: Brown
Body: Brown dubbing over .065" nylon (as used with lawn edgers)

(Note: Nylon is tied lengthwise on top of hook and extends 1/8" beyond eye)
Wing: Deer hair, tied in a clump on nylon extension in front of eye
Intended use: Waked fly for summer-run steelhead

Comments: The idea of using a front-extended body for skating flies was conceived in 1993 on the Thompson River in British Columbia while I was fly-fishing for those magnificent summer-run steelhead. Riffle-hitched flies and flies with forward-slanting wings work well enough for a while, but I wanted a fly that was attached securely and directly to the leader, and that would skate high on the water without pulling under. The pattern shown here is the final result of many trial-and-error shapes and sizes, from a mouse to a sedge, but all dressed with deer hair and a forward extension to make the fly skate better. When used with a floating fly line, this unsinkable fly will stay on the surface as long as it is moving. In principle, it acts like a kite where the line is attached to a point back of the leading edge.

The fly will skate in line with the leader, so directional changes can be made by tossing upstream or downstream mends in the fly line. Tie it on with a turle or clinch knot, but don't riffle-hitch it. Grantham's Sedge was featured in the BCFFF newsletter *Fly Lines*, September 2002, and in *B.C. Outdoors Sport Fishing and Outdoor Adventure*, Summer 2003.

HARRISON STREAMER
Originated and contributed by Mel Hocken

Hook: Size 8, Eagle Claw L52F
Thread: Black 6/0 Danville's
Tail: Fibers from a golden pheasant breast feather
Body: Pure mohair yarn, dyed pale green olive
Rib: Holographic Mylar tinsel
Throat: A few strands of white polar bear extending to the tail fibers

under a few fibers from a golden pheasant breast feather extending half way to the hook point
Wing: In three parts: yellow bucktail followed by a few strands of yellow Krystal Flash and then brown bucktail
Intended use: Wet fly for Harrison River sea-run cutthroat trout

Comments: This pattern was designed as a general-purpose streamer. The use of a variety of colours and a slimmer profile gives me a fly that cutthroat could mistake for a number of food forms.

POPKUM EMERGER
Designed and contributed by Mel Hocken

Hook: Size 12 to 18, Mustad 80250BR
Thread: Tan 8/0, Danville
Trailing Shuck: A few fibers of tan Diamond Dub
Body: Brown frostbite
Wing: A clump of deer hair tied short, natural or bleached depending on desired wing

darkness, followed by an over-wing of two small strips of pearlescent cellophane on each side of the deer hair
Collar: Two or more wraps of dark "hare's-ear" Scintilla dubbing
Intended use: Surface film dry fly for cutthroat trout

Comments: This fly is designed to represent an emerging insect in the surface film. The body design for this fly came from a technique shown to me by Phil Rowley. Phil uses unraveled frostbite for the bodies of Chironomid patterns. The use of the pearlescent cellophane in the wing is to provide some sparkle, which I believe occurs when the sun's rays hit the wings of an insect. Originally, I used Krystal Flash but found the effectiveness of the fly improved greatly when I started using the pearlescent cellophane.

DUNCAN'S FLOATING CAREY
Originated and contributed by Duncan Laird

Hook: Size 6 and 8 Mustad 9671
Thread: Olive 6/0
Body: Clipped, spun, mixed deer hair

Hackle: Ring-necked pheasant rump
Intended use: Deeply sunk stillwater wet fly for Kamloops trout.

Comments: This version of the Carey Special was developed around 1990 when I was experimenting with coloured deer hair. Deer hair was already popular for dragonflies. Its natural buoyancy is perfect for a number of presentations, however, colour variations are limited. The solid colour of the deer-hair Gomphus fly and the dubbed-over style of the Bottom Walker fly were not what I was looking for, so the obvious answer was to mix deer hair. The Carey Special style of fly seemed to me to be the right starting point and this fly has worked so well for me that I saw no reason to change the design.

Two steps are important to keep in mind when tying this fly. First, do not pack the deer hair too tightly and second, do not extend the pheasant rump hackle past the fly's body. The sparser body traps more air bubbles and the short stiff hackle barbules flex back and forth in the water instead of folding along the body. This fly is best fished with a full-sinking line and when the fly line has settled on the bottom, retrieve the fly in quick six- to eight-inch pulls as if coho fishing.

THE DOCTOR DICK
Adapted and contributed by Vic Marchiel

Hook: Size 8, Tiemco two extra long
Thread: Hot pink
Tail: White Krystal Flash
Body: Hot pink chenille over an underbody of .025 gauge lead wire wrapped on the front two thirds of the hook shank

Rib: Medium silver tinsel
Wing: White Krystal Flash to tip of tail
Eyes: Pair of large bead chain
Intended use: Wet fly for Indian River pink salmon

Comments: This pattern was inspired by the Crazy Charlie saltwater pattern. It was tied and first used on the Indian River, north of Vancouver, in 1996. The Indian is well known for its crystal clear waters. The pinks hold up in large schools and present what one would expect to be a turkey shoot. It's surprising however what reluctant takers they can be. The Doctor Dick is best fished with a mono-cord, medium-sink

saltwater line. After ensuring the pattern is well established in the lie, it should be retrieved with a quick jerky motion. The results can be remarkable! It has also accounted for rainbows in excess of 4 pounds. The pattern was named after Dr. Richard (Dick) Lupton who caught his first-ever salmon on this fly at the Indian in 2001.

TAYLOR'S DEAN RIVER SPEY
Originated and contributed by Bob Taylor

Hook: Size 6 to 2, low-water salmon
Thread: Black monocord
Tip: Fine oval silver tinsel
Tail: Golden pheasant tippet fibers
Body: Black floss
Rib: Oval silver tinsel with fine silver oval cross rib
Hackle: Grey heron or substitute wound to lay next to the oval tinsel

(Note: cross-wind the fine tinsel over the hackle)
Throat: Guinea fowl
Wing: Small woodduck breast feather, tied on flat
Head: Black
Intended use: Floating-line wet fly for summer-run steelhead

Comments: I first dressed this fly in 1997 for fishing Dean River summer-runs. I wanted a smaller fly to use with a floating line in clear water conditions. It proved to be an instant success and has been a consistent producer on waters such as the Zymoetz and Bulkley and is one of my standards for summer–run steelhead. Harrison River cutthroat trout like it as well.

TAYLOR'S BLUE SPEY
Adapted and contributed by Bob Taylor

Hook: Size 6 to 3/0, low-water salmon
Thread: Black monocord
Body: Rear third blue Diamond Braid tinsel, remainder blue seal fur, with the Diamond Braid tinsel carried over it in open turns
Rib: Oval silver tinsel, wound counter-wise over the hackle

Hackle: Grey heron or substitute, wound next to and behind the Diamond Braid tinsel
Throat: Dyed blue grizzly hackle
Wing: Two blue-dyed pheasant breast feathers, tied on flat
Head: Black
Intended use: Wet fly for summer- and winter-run steelhead

Comments: This is an offshoot of a blue fly given to me by Rob Brown of Terrace B.C. that he uses on the Skeena River tributaries. Blue is a colour favoured on some Atlantic salmon rivers, so I decided to tie up a Spey-fly version for use on our steelhead and have used it successfully on the Thompson and Dean rivers.

TAYLOR'S GOLDEN SPEY
Originated and contributed by Bob Taylor

Hook: Size 6 to 3/0, low-water salmon

Thread: Claret, used only for finishing the fly and the head; the floss is used for all of the initial steps

Tip: Fine oval silver tinsel

Body: Rear third of hot orange floss, front two thirds of hot orange seal fur dubbed onto the floss

Rib: Flat gold tinsel, followed by medium oval tinsel and fine silver oval tinsel counter-wound

Hackle: Grey heron or substitute, wound to lay next to the oval tinsel, counter-wind the fine tinsel over the hackle

Throat: Teal or lemon woodduck flank feather

Wing: Two golden pheasant red-orange breast feathers, set flat over the body

Head: Claret

Intended use: Floating- or sunk-line wet fly for summer- and winter-run steelhead

Comments: My early interest in Spey flies arose after reading the writings of British authors such as Eric Tavender's *Salmon Fishing* and the 1872 work, A.E. Knox's *Autumns on the Spey*. Later, after meeting Syd Glasso in 1967 when he lived at Forks, Washington, I was fortunate to receive a set of beautifully-tied Glasso Spey flies and, with them as models, began tying and using my own flies. In 1978 I modified the wing by replacing the hackle tip version with the golden pheasant breast feathers tied flat over the body. Later in 1979 when I showed this to Syd he said that he also had experienced problems with the winging of the Orange Heron and liked the solution.

On a 1978 trip to the Bella Coola River I christened this flat-winged version by landing two steelhead and a half dozen large cutthroat. Lee Straight promptly named it Taylor's Golden Spey, and steelhead on rivers such as the Dean, Bella Coola, Vedder, Thompson and Cowichan have taken a liking to this pattern.

The sea-run cutthroat is an attractive and sporty game fish.

Georgi and Neil Abbott

Neil and Georgi fell in love with the Logan Lake area and stole away every weekend, mostly to Leighton Lake, for many years. It was frustrating when, in need of flies, tippet material, etcetera a long trip to Kamloops or Merritt was required to find a fly shop, seriously cutting into their fishing time. It turned out to be a very convenient reason to leave their jobs and the city, to move to fishing country and open a fly shop to serve the thousands of others who frequented the lakes and had no access to any sort of fishing gear. In 1996 they opened Logan Lake Fly Shop and in 2002 a change of location found them overlooking the lake of Logan and those huge, leaping Kamloops trout.

GEORGI DAMSEL

Adapted and contributed by Neil and Georgi Abbott

Hook: Sizes 12 or 14, Tiemco 3761 or Tiemco 3761BL	**Hackle:** Hen neck or saddle, ginger/brown
Thread: Light Cahill 8/0	**Eyes:** Monofilament
Tail: Ginger or blonde marabou	**Head:** Ginger or blonde marabou
Body: Ginger or blonde marabou	**Intended use:** Wet fly for Leighton Lake rainbow trout
Rib: Fine copper wire	

Comments: The first time Georgi and I fished Leighton Lake was the early summer of 1992. In those days, Georgi was inclined to search a new lake with a damsel pattern, whereas for me it was usually a small leech. It didn't take long for me to take Georgi's lead and switch to a damsel; success was immediate but over the next year or two, Georgi developed an improved technique that consistently produced not only good numbers of trout but almost always the largest that Leighton had to offer.

Before that first summer was over, Georgi had settled exclusively on a single damsel pattern—a curious thing—tied by Mike Desaulniers who was employed by Michael & Young Fly Shop. The tail and body was tied entirely of ginger marabou, and a copper rib, burnt mono eyes and a grouse hackle at the thorax finished the fly. Tied on a size 12, TMC 3761 with a tail about three quarters of the shank length, we'd pinch the tail down to about half that or less. The bottom of the tail should be pinched off shorter yet, angled to a point at the top of the tail. This prevents the marabou from wrapping around the hook bend when casting and also slims the profile of the fly, more accurately imitating the natural as well as allowing the fly to swim.

In the spring of 1996, we opened Logan Lake Fly Shop and needed a source of ginger damsels. Fortunately, Mike was still at Michael & Young (M&Y) and we were able to purchase a fairly steady supply. It was at this time that staff at M&Y dubbed the fly the Georgi Damsel and the name stuck. The following year, Mike was working for Fly Angler Distributors, but we continued to carry Mike's original design. I'll never forget all the ginger marabou floating and accumulating around the shop as we pinched off all the tails for our customers.

In those days, most anglers fished damsels on floating lines, imitating the mature nymph. Georgi's theory was that the smaller, immature nymphs (or instars) were always present and were a preferred food source, especially following a moult. At this point, the nymphs are brighter, almost translucent and the Georgi Damsel was a perfect match. Since these instars were not emerging, it stood to reason they would be in deeper water, foraging along the bottom. Georgi's technique was to fish along the drop-offs in 6 to 12 feet of water, on the bottom, with a type III uniform sink line, any time of the year, any time of the day.

Through feedback from the shop's customers, we've heard this technique has been very successful when applied to lakes throughout western North America.

Through the late 1990s, Mike D. moved north and we lost our supply source for the pattern. We enlisted several commercial tiers to keep up with the demand and though the flies were of good quality, the pattern had become inconsistent. In 2001 we held the Logan Lake Fly Shop Fly-Tying Contest. Through the contest, we were fortunate to meet Doug Wright, a double category winner. Doug was 14 years old at the time and never had I been so impressed with anyone's fly-tying skills.

It was at this time we were redesigning the Georgi Damsel. Having spent several years studying the naturals and tying prototypes, we decided on three changes. First, get the tail right at the tying bench. Second, the eyes should be black, they should be dominant and they should be the only color contrast on the pattern. Thirdly, the contrasting grouse hackle would be replaced with a non-contrasting light ginger brown hen saddle hackle.

We approached Doug to tie for the shop, he agreed and for the past two years Doug has tied all our Georgi Damsels with the changes incorporated.

There's no doubt this "evolved" pattern is now even more successful. Over the past couple of years, it has been responsible for some of the largest trout this area has seen in a long time.

Brian Chan

has been an avid fly-fisher and fly tier for almost 40 years. He is a professional fisheries biologist who for many years managed small-lake recreational fisheries for the province of B.C. Brian is currently with the Freshwater Fisheries Society of B.C. where he is the Director of Sport Fishing Development. He has also developed a secondary career as a fly-fishing author, lecturer and video producer. Some of his more recent works include the book *Morris and Chan on Fly Fishing Trout Lakes* and

the DVD *Expert Techniques for Stillwater Fly Fishing with Brian Chan*. Brian's favourite fishing haunts are the many trout lakes surrounding his home city of Kamloops, but he can often be found wading rivers in other provinces and states as well as making forays to the North West Territories and the Yukon for a variety of fish there that also bite flies.

STILLWATER CADDIS PUPA
Adapted and contributed by Brian Chan

Hook: Size 12 to 8, Mustad Signature R72 – 2XL shank nymph
Thread: Dark brown 6/0
Body: Arizona Synthetic Peacock dubbing in natural colour
Rib: Lime green Super Floss
Thorax: Same as body
Wingcase: Cock ring-necked pheasant-tail fibres
Legs: Ring-necked pheasant rump fibres
Throat: Peacock Angel Hair
Intended use: Wet fly for Interior rainbow trout in lakes

Comments: This fly, an imitation of the Limnephilidae caddis pupa, was designed to imitate the larger species of caddis pupae that are found in many productive Interior stillwaters. These species often have a prominent bright green rib through the abdomen. Caddis pupae swim very quickly to the surface of the lake to emerge into the adult stage. Anglers should employ a fairly fast 4 to 6 inch long steady strip retrieve to imitate this action.

STILLWATER CADDIS EMERGER
Adapted and contributed by Brian Chan

Hook: Size 8 to 14, Mustad Signature C49S curved caddis/nymph hook
Thread: Dark brown 6/0 pre-waxed
Tail: Light Dun Z-lon
Body: Dark hare's ear dubbing
Rib: Pearl green Flashabou #6972
Hackle: Dark brown, dry fly
Wing: Deer hair
Intended use: Low-riding dry fly for Interior lakes and rivers

Comments: I began developing this fly in the early 1990s in an attempt to imitate a partially emerged caddis adult. During a typical caddis hatch many trout will select individuals that are in the surface film and only half emerged into the adult form. These partially hatched insects are easy prey for foraging trout. This fly is designed to sit at about a 30 degree angle on the surface film with the back two thirds of the fly submerged. The Z-lon tail represents the trailing pupal shuck of the caddis.

BLACK & RED RUBY-EYED LEECH
Adapted and contributed by Brian Chan

Hook: Size 10 to 6, Mustad Signature R74, 4XL streamer hook
Thread: Black, pre-waxed 6/0
Tail: Black/red synthetic seal fur dubbing mix
Body: Dubbed black/red synthetic seal fur dubbing mix
Beadhead : 1/8-inch copper cone head followed by medium silver-lined maroon glass bead
Intended use: Wet fly for Interior rainbow trout in lakes

Comments: The design of this fly has its roots with the Blood Leech pattern originated by pioneering stillwater fly-fisher Jack Shaw. Jack used long combed-out reddish-black mohair yarn to imitate a swimming leech. Black and red are traditionally good leech colours. The Ruby-eyed Leech uses a shorter-fibered material that is dubbed on and then picked out with a dubbing brush. The addition of the cone head and maroon glass bead provides both flash and weight to the fly. I always use a loop knot when fishing bead-headed flies so that the undulating action can be maximized.

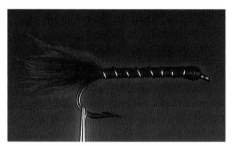

ACETATE FLOSS BLOODWORM
Adapted and contributed by Brian Chan

Hook: Size 14 to 8, Mustad Signature R74, 4XL streamer hook
Thread: Red, pre-waxed 6/0
Tail: Maroon marabou fibers
Body: Red acetate floss
Rib: Silver, gold or copper wire
Intended use: Wet fly for Interior stillwater rainbow trout

Comments: The pattern imitates the maroon-coloured Chironomid larvae found in productive stillwaters. The Acetate Floss Bloodworm has proven to be an effective and durable Chironomid larval pattern. It's effective because maroon or blood red are the most prominent colours of lake-dwelling larvae. This fly is finished by quickly dipping it into a bottle of Acetone, which melts and seals the Acetate floss, leaving a very durable and shiny finish to the fly. This fly is best fished with a floating line and long leader presentation or under a strike indicator.

BABY DAMSELFLY NYMPH
Adapted and contributed by Brian Chan

Hook: Size 10 to 14
Thread: Olive green, pre-waxed 8/0
Tail: Light to dark olive green strung marabou fiber tips
Body: Light to dark olive green strung marabou fibers
Rib: Fine silver or gold wire
Beadhead: Extra small to small gold bead
Intended use: Wet fly for Interior stillwater rainbow trout

Comments: Damselflies spend up to three years in the nymphal stage prior to emergence into the adult form. This fly imitates the juvenile stages (or instars) of damselfly nymphs. The nymphs seek cover and protection among the submerged vegetation covering the shoal or littoral zones of the lake. Trout seek out the immature damselflies, particularly during the mid- to late-fall period. I prefer to fish this fly tight to mats of vegetation or in openings within stands of long-stem bulrush. In these situations this fly is best fished under a strike indicator. Otherwise, this fly can be fished with floating and slow or intermediate sinking lines.

THE ULTIMATE CHIRONOMID
Originated and contributed by Hermann Fischer

Hook: Size 12, Eagle Claw L056M or Tiemco 2457
Thread: Black 8/0 UNI-Thread
Body: Midge or medium-sized clear Liquid Lace
Prowing: Brown or black rafia
Wingcase: Black plastic or Stretchflex
Gills: White Antron or Phentex
Head: Peacock herl
Pantone Marker: Opaque red, all around
Intended use: Wet fly for use in the lakes in the Kamloops area for rainbow trout and kokanee

LADY MCCONNELL
Adapted and contributed by Brian Chan

Hook: Size 18 to 10, Mustad Signature R30 dry-fly hook
Thread: Black pre-waxed 8/0
Tail: Undertail of white Z-lon and overlaid with tip of dry-fly grizzly hackle feather
Body: Dark green dry-fly dubbing
Shellback: Deer hair
Hackle: Dry-fly grizzly hackle
Intended use: Dry fly for Interior rainbow trout

Comments: I developed this fly in the early 1990s to imitate the partially emerged adult Chironomid. The Z-lon and grizzly hackle tip are designed to imitate the trailing pupal shuck. Over the past few years this fly has proven to be an effective imitation of fully emerged adult Chironomids, as well as mayflies in both lakes and streams.

Comments: Liquid lace filled with vegetable oil was developed by Mike Tucker from Colorado. I developed the Ultimate Chironomid in 1990 using Tucker's concept, but now use mineral oil because it is easier to fill the tubing using a small hypodermic needle. After filling, tie a knot at the end of the lace. By using white tying thread, tinsel and different Pantone markers you can achieve a variety of colours and sheens. Note: use water-based head cement, as a lacquer-based cement will eat away the Liquid Lace.

I use this fly mainly with a dry line, and a long leader up to 20 feet in length. With this fly and many others I use a small #14 swivel which helps sink the fly and results in a better turnover of the long leader. I am always on the lookout for feeding fish and then key in on that location. Most of my Chironomid fishing is done in the shallows or over a drop-off zone. In mid-summer, when it is very hot and the oxygen levels are low, I fish in 20 to 40 feet of water. Best success is obtained by fishing the fly just off the bottom. I tie my Chironomid and other flies to the leader with a loop knot so the fly hangs vertically all the time. Wind-drifting the fly gives better movement and do not strip. By using a strike indicator you can increase your success dramatically.

Hermann Fischer

is a resident of Kamloops and member of the Kamloops Fly Fishers. He has been tying flies for years and his creativity and expertise have been freely shared with an ever-widening circle of fly-fishers. His innovations in crafting new fly patterns for B.C. lakes, in conceiving and making previously unheard-of tools for tying flies, and in discovering fly-tying uses for unlikely materials, continually evoke admiration and amazement in his club members and others. Hermann's fly-tying expertise stands in the best tradition of the genre. In 2003 Hermann was the recipient of the British Columbia Federation of Fly Fishers' Jack Shaw Fly Tying Award, given to that BCFFF master fly tier who has excelled in the art and craft of fly-tying.

LIQUID LACE DAMSEL NYMPH
Originated and contributed by Hermann Fischer

Hook: Size 14, Eagle Claw L052M
Thread: Tan 8/0 UNI-Thread
Tail: Green hackle or marabou
Body: Midge, light pink, Liquid Lace
Thorax: Green ostrich herl
Wingcase: Green plastic or rafia
Legs: Ring-necked pheasant tail fibres
Eyes: Mono with sparkle over eyes
Intended use: Wet fly for trout in the lakes around Kamloops.

Comments: Developed in 1992, I dress this fly in a variety of colours and often use Ultra Chenille for the eyes. Most damselflies crawl up the stems of the toolies to hatch in the morning. So my rule of thumb is to fish this fly in the morning from about 8 to 10 a.m., when there is the most damsel activity, in about 3 to 5 feet of water and close to the bulrushes, using a floating or intermediate sinking line and with short 5 inch or sometimes longer pulls, pausing often to allow the fly to sink.

LIQUID LACE MAYFLY NYMPH
Originated and contributed by Hermann Fischer

Hook: Size 14, Eagle Claw L052M
Thread: Tan 8/0 UNI-Thread
Tail: Ring-necked pheasant-tail fibres
Body: Midge clear Liquid Lace
Thorax: Grey ostrich herl
Wingcase: Brown plastic or rafia

Legs: Hackle on each side
Eyes: Mono or chenille
Pantone: Orange at back
Intended use: Wet fly for trout and kokanee in the lakes around Kamloops

Comments: Developed in 1990, this pattern is best fished on a floating or intermediate sinking line when fished in 2 to 5 feet of water and with a slow-sinking line in deeper water. Most times you should key in on areas where mayflies are hatching, normally from the weeds to the drop-off zone. A short steady pull-retrieve works best.

BLOODWORM
Contributed by Hermann Fischer

Hook: Size 14, Eagle Claw L052M or Tiemco equivalent
Thread: Red 8/0 UNI-Thread
Tail and Front: Red Flexi Floss
Body: Midge red Liquid Lace

Thorax: Peacock herl
Pantone: Black on top
Intended use: Wet fly for trout in lakes around Kamloops

Comments: First tied in 1992, this red-bodied fly can also be dressed in green and tan. The bloodworm can be fished in any part of the water column, especially after a windy day, which stirs up the water and the naturals can be seen at various depths. I prefer to fish bloodworms on the bottom using a dry line and long leader retrieving the line with a slow, steady pull; and I mean **slow**.

HERMANN'S FOAM SEDGE
Originated and contributed by Hermann Fischer

Hook: Size 10, Mustad 9671 or 94840
Thread: Tan 8/0 UNI-Thread
Body: Light olive Diamond Dub
Legs: Three ring-necked pheasant-tail fibres on each side

Hackle: Brown, sparse
Pantone: Orange 144 with black marks
Wing: Tan foam
Intended use: Dry fly for use during the traveling sedge hatch, common on some lakes around Kamloops

Comments: Designed in 1994, the best thing about this fly is that it will float all day, unlike many other sedge patterns, and it needs no dressing. I fish it from June through July whenever the sedge hatch is on. I dress the leader with floatant to within 10 inches of the fly and, with only a few inches of leader sinking, it results in a larger wake when the fly is stripped in, especially when the water is calm. Another technique is to cast the fly out and let the wind move it. Whether stripped or wind-moved, it is a very successful fly.

HERMANN'S SEDGE PUPA
Originated and contributed by Hermann Fischer

Hook: Size 14, Eagle Claw L052M
Thread: Tan 8/0 UNI-Thread
Body: Medium clear Liquid Lace
Hackle: Grey ring-neck pheasant rump

Head: Peacock herl or dubbing
Pantone: Orange at rear
Intended use: Wet fly for rainbow trout in the lakes around Kamloops.

Comments: Developed in 1995, this pattern is similar to the Carey Special except that I use Liquid Lace for the body making it more translucent. I find it is best fished with a dry line, long leader and cast over the drop off and retrieved near vertically.

HERMANN'S BURNT SHRIMP
Originated and contributed by Hermann Fishcer

Hook: Size 12, Tiemco 2457 or Eagle Claw equivalent
Thread: Tan 8/0 UNI-Thread
Tail: Green-yellow hackle fibres

Body: Medium green Crystal chenille
Intended use: Wet fly for rainbow trout in the lakes around Kamloops.

Comments: I first dressed this fly in 1987. After I have finished the fly I cut off the chenille fibres on top and on the sides. To give the fly a smooth segmented look, hold the bottom chenille fibres between the index finger and thumb and using a cigarette lighter you singe the top and squeeze the sides together. Careful; don't burn yourself. For best results fish the fly near the bulrushes or over weeds using a dry line or an intermediate or slow sinking line.

CROCHET BOATMAN
Designed and contributed by Hermann Fischer

Hook: Size 12, Mustad 3399
Thread: Tan 8/0 UNI-Thread
Body: Tan Ultra Chenille with clear medium Liquid Lace, pearl tinsel

underneath and on back
Thorax: Grey ostrich or peacock herl
Legs: Brown hackle and light brown rubber

Eyes: Tan Ultra Chenille, colour tips black
Intended use: Wet fly designed in 1993 for rainbow trout in the lakes around Kamloops

Comments: The crochet tying technique used for this fly was developed by the Norwegian tier, Torill Kolbu. *The Fly Tier's Benchside Reference* by Ted Leeson and Jim Schollmeyer is a worthwhile book for those wanting to learn more about this fly-tying technique. For this fly I use pearl or silver tinsel underneath. The crocheting is done with one strand of Ultra Chenille and one strand of clear Liquid Lace.

Fish this fly with either a dry line or slow sink-tip. Let the fly sink to the bottom or mid-water, depending on the depth of water you are fishing and retrieve with short jerky pulls with pauses in between. This is a good fly to use just after ice-off and later in the fall in October and November after the first frosts, when the boatman insects are starting to mate.

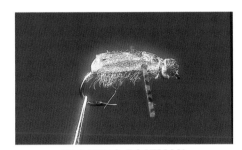

FLOATING BOATMAN
Designed and contributed by Hermann Fischer

Hook: Size 12, Mustad 3906
Thread: Tan 8/0 UNI-Thread
Tip and Under Body: Pearl or silver tinsel
Body: Light olive Diamond Dub with a 3/8-inch foam strip over
Thorax: Grey ostrich or peacock herl
Legs: Medium brown rubber
Pantone: Orange 144 over foam back, black eye tips and paint the back with Moonglow nail polish
Intended use: Surface fly, designed in 2002 for rainbow trout in the lakes around Kamloops

Comments: Tie in a strip of foam, dub body, and pull foam to front. Using fly-tying scissors, poke a small hole in the foam and pull the foam so the hook eye goes through the hole then tie off the foam underneath the hook eye, making a small head. Trim excess foam. Colour the back with the Pantone marker. Poke a hole in the foam thorax area using a small sewing needle with part of the needle eye removed, fix rubber leg material in eye and pull legs through the foam. Using a medium or fast-sinking line with a leader that is longer than the depth of water you are fishing, let the line sink near the bottom. With the long leader, the foam fly will still be on the surface. Now retrieve using a jerk-and-pause technique. The fly will dive under the water on the pull and jump to the surface on the pause, imitating the movements of the natural insect. In weeded areas, use a dry line and fish the fly on the surface.

STONEFLY NYMPH
Designed and contributed by Hermann Fischer

Hook: Size 6 or 8, Mustad 9674 or equivalent straight-eyed streamer hook
Thread: White
Tail: Yellow goose
Under Body: Shape body with white Phentex
Body: Medium clear Liquid Lace
Wing Case: Brown plastic or raffia, colour after
Thorax: Grey ostrich herl
Legs: Ring-neck pheasant tail
Eyes: Plastic—heat up and shape so they are flat
Pantone: Yellow and orange on underneath, with green tan or black on top to suit
Intended use: Wet fly designed in 1991 for trout in the rivers around Kamloops.

Comments: Add weight in the thorax area to make it sink quicker. Dress this fly with white tying thread and white underbody so that you can colour as desired. However, a stonefly imitation should have a light underneath and a darker back. Colour the underbody before wrapping the clear Liquid Lace. Fish with a dry line or sink tip and tumble the fly over the rocks.

DRAGONFLY NYMPH
Designed and contributed by Hermann Fischer

Hook: Size 6, Mustad 9672 or equivalent streamer hook
Thread: Black 6/0 UNI-Thread
Tail: Ring-neck pheasant tail fibres or peacock herl
Under Body: Shape body using a piece of old dry fly line on each side of hook
Body: Wire brush (.009 wire) grey, light brown or green polar bear or llama dubbing
Wing Case: Plastic, raffia or Stretchflex
Thorax: Peacock herl
Legs: Ring-neck pheasant tail
Eyes: Plastic—heat and shape
Pantone: Yellow and orange on underneath, with green tan or black on top to suit
Intended use: Wet fly for rainbow trout in lakes around Kamloops.

Comments: Using a dubbing machine with .009 stainless wire, spin the dubbed body. Wire brush bodies are tough and can be easily trimmed to desired shape. Fish the fly with a dry line in shallow water and with a sinking line over the drop-off. Dragon fly nymphs are bottom dwellers and the imitation needs to be fished near the bottom with a slow paused retrieve.

HERMANN'S FLAT-BODIED DRAGONFLY NYMPH (GOMPHUS)
Developed and contributed by Hermann Fischer

Hook: Size 8, Mustad 3906
Thread: Black 6/0 UNI-Thread
Body: Tan Crystal Chenille
Wing Case: Brown plastic or raffia
Thorax: Peacock or ostrich herl
Legs: Mottled turkey
Eyes: Green or tan mono—tie in under hook eye
Pantone: Light grey or green on top, green underneath
Intended use: Wet fly for rainbow trout in lakes around Kamloops.

Comments: To form this fat stubby body you need to fix two pieces of Chrystal Chenille to each side at the rear of the hook. Then with a crochet hook, twist twice and put the loop over the shank, push back and then pull tight. Repeat the procedure on the other side. Then repeat again on each side but this time twist the chenille in the crochet hook four times. Repeat for a third and fourth time but twist the chenille six times. Repeat twice more twisting the chenille four times and then do again twisting chenille twice. Trim chenille fibres from underneath. Lacquer on top center to melt the fibres together so that the body will not turn on the hook, making sure the body is centred on the hook.

I like to fish this fly over weed beds using very slow pulls. If you get hung up on the weeds, quicken your retrieve.

[**Note:** Near the end of the 1970s, the red-shouldered dragonfly nymph was assumed to be a member of the Gomphidae family and the imitation became affectionately referred to as the Gomphus. However, in the genus *Gomphus* there are only two species indigenous to British Columbia and they are restricted to the lakeshores and slow rivers in the southern interior, according to a December 1994 article called the "Gomphus that is Not" in the Haig-Brown Fly Fishing Association's newsletter, *The Steelhead Bee*.

The writer of that in-depth article, an enthusiastic angler and amateur entomologist named Loucas Raptis, attributes the misnaming of the Gomphus pattern to Alf Davy. In *'The Gilly'* (1985), Chapter IX. Dragons: The Bottom Predator, Davy writes:

> My fishing friend and companion . . . took this weed-crawling pattern, shaped it to look like Jack Shaw's seal fur Gomphus mud-dwelling nymph pattern, added some pheasant tail legs on either side . . . and it became the "Gomphus" . . . . (p. 78)

After considerable delving into the fly-fishing literature associated with the misidentification and naming the red-shouldered dragonfly nymph Gomphus, Loucas Raptis writes:

> The evidence was unequivocal: all the accounts, descriptions, illustrations, and photographs of the dragonfly adult and nymph carrying the name "Gomphus" in all contemporary fly-fishing publications in British Columbia are in fact those of the genus *Sympetrum*. This discovery was particularly striking when one considers that some authors treat the subject with apparent entomological clout and assumed air of authority, yet in fact their search has been utterly superficial. (p.3)]

HERMANN'S MINNOW FLY
Designed and contributed by Hermann Fischer

Hook: Size 6, Tiemco streamer
Thread: 6/0 black
Under Body: Pearl tinsel
Body: Medium clear Liquid Lace
Under and Over Wing: White, light green, medium green, blue and black Fish Fuzz

Gills: Red plastic
Head: Sparkle nail polish
Intended use: Wet fly for trout, salmon, steelhead and other fish in rivers, large lakes and ocean beaches.

Comments: This fly came from my vise in 1985. In the early days I dressed it with a chenille body. Now I use Liquid Lace over

a tinsel underbody, making it a much more durable fly. I alter the Fish Fuzz wings to match the colouration of the small bait fish and always develop the wings with the white underneath the body and build the wing with varying shades of Fish Fuzz around the body with the dark on top. Often I will add a strip of goose quill along the lateral line and/or jungle cock tied in at the head.

This is an effective fly for the Thompson River and a good trout fly for those superb rainbows that feed off the mouths of salmon-bearing streams on Shuswap Lake. As well it is a good fly to use on the ocean beaches for migrating salmon.

LEECH
Designed and Contributed by Hermann Fischer

Hook: Size 10, Mustad 9671
Thread: 6/0 black
Body: Rear half of red, green or blue holographic tinsel, front half of 5 to 7 turns of wire brush (0.0045 wire)

llama fibre with pearl enhancer
Collar: Red llama fibre
Head: Peacock herl
Intended use: Wet fly for trout in the lakes around Kamloops

Comments: To make a durable fly I make a dubbing brush body of llama fibres mixed with pearl enhancer on a 0.0045 stainless wire. The holographic tinsel and pearl enhancer gives the fly a translucent sheen. For best results, fish this fly on a dry or slow-sinking line over weed beds and with a fast-sinker in deeper water. Normally, a slow retrieve works best, but a fast retrieve will produce every now and then.

Bill Jollymore

Born in Nova Scotia's Cape Breton Island, Bill has been a fly-fisherman since boyhood. He started dressing flies over sixty years ago, in 1942. He tied commercially for many years, supplying flies to many well-known Atlantic-salmon fly-fishers. He moved to British Columbia in the 1950s and many of his greatest memories come from his association with the fishing and hunting industry

and those he has met during the decades on the Western side of the North American continent. He had a sporting goods shop in Kamloops back in the 1960s and he recalls days when the great fly-fishers of the day such as Heber Smith, Jack Morrill, Collie Peacock, Ray MacPherson, Bob Allen, and Ralph Shaw would be clustered in his shop swapping tales. Fly fishing has been good to Bill over the past six decades. He and his wife Lori enjoy fly-fishing and, at times can be found standing in the water, both of them casting bamboo rods to Atlantic salmon in Bill's native Nova Scotia waters or Newfoundland, or on the lakes around his British Columbia home on Lac Des Roches.

NATION'S GREEN-BODIED SEDGE

Originated by Bill Nation, tied and contributed by Bill Jollymore

Hook: Size 6, limerick
Thread: Black 6/0 or 8/0
Tail: Red swan or substitute of red goose
Body: Medium to dark olive green seal fur

Rib: Medium oval gold tinsel
Hackle: Badger
Wing: Mallard flank
Intended use: Surface fly for rainbow trout in Kamloops area and other Interior lakes

Comments: The history and glamour of this fly makes it my favorite. Bill Nation, guide, fly-fisher, pattern designer among other things, advised Rod Haig-Brown in a letter dated March 8, 1938 that this pattern was now fixed. Olive green pig's wool was used prior to seal fur. Bill varied the green by bleaching the fur with hydrogen peroxide to match light and water. The fly imitates the sedge nymph rather than the adult, holding in the surface tension waiting to hatch. As such, the green body represents the color of the nymph case. I dress the fly with floatant so it sits half submerged, half above water. I have had good results with this fly on the shoals in the dark of the moon, prior to the new moon. A great fly.

HALFBACK

Originated by John Dexheimer, tied and contributed by Bill Jollymore

Hook: Size 4 to 10, Mustad 79580
Thread: Black 6/0 or 8/0
Tail: Ring-necked pheasant-tail fibres
Body: Bronze peacock herl
Hackle: Beard of ring-necked pheasant-tail fibres

Wing-case: Ring-necked pheasant tail fibres
Intended use: Wet fly for Interior rainbow trout

Comments: John Dexheimer from Savona, B.C. gets credit for this one. Developed for Tunkwa Lake, its fame spread to other lakes in the Interior, showing great returns on Stump Lake. The original pattern called for ground hog tail for the tail and bearded hackle with pheasant-tail wing case and peacock herl body. The only commercial pattern I've seen or tied has pheasant-tail fibres tail and wing case with the tips of the wing case folded under to form a hackle beard. Another must-have pattern. I carry 60, sizes 4-10.

TOM THUMB

Unknown, tied and contributed by Bill Jollymore

Hook: Size 10, Mustad 3906B
Thread: Black 6/0 or 8/0
Tail: Coast deer-hair fibres
Body: Coast deer hair

Wing: Coast deer hair
Intended use: Dry fly for Interior rainbow trout

Comments: The inventor of this fly should get a gold medal. The originator is unknown but my good friend Collie Peacock threw the name into the air and it stuck. Two versions can be encountered. One has the body tied solid encompassing the hook and likewise, the hackle. I like the other tie, which has an open bottom on the body and hackle cocked forward. This represents the sedge after emergence, wings raised and cocked forward to dry; a vulnerable time for the insect. I have used it for brown trout in Montana, trout in New Zealand, cutthroats in tidal water in Washington State. It works. Probably more trout have met their demise to this fly than any other B.C. pattern. My favorite.

BLACK O' LINDSAY

Judge Spencer Black, tied and contributed by Bill Jollymore

Hook: Size 6, Mustad 3906B
Thread: Black 6/0 or 8/0
Tail: Blue goose
Body: Yellow wool
Rib: Medium gold oval tinsel
Hackle: Brown over blue goose beard

Wing: Mallard flank over peacock sword
Intended use: Wet fly for rainbows in Interior lakes and the Thompson River

Comments: A very versatile fly which can be used to cover a lot of angling situations. This pattern was developed by Judge Spencer Black from Lindsay, California, as a grasshopper pattern for the Thompson River rainbows. Some date the fly's development to around 1925, others between 1930-'35. The pattern has been modified by some tiers by changing the tail and hackle to blue and brown hackle fibres, to perhaps shorten the time to tie the original pattern.

I was introduced to it by John Collins of Cache Creek in 1959, and used it on the Thompson with good success. When I moved to Kamloops in 1964, I usually had six dozen in my fly shop showcase. Jack Morrill advised trying it on Heffley Lake; he knew the results would be good, how true. On Schedam or Harper Lake one evening, on three casts I caught three fish, total weight 16.5 pounds.

TUNKWANAMID

Originated by Tom Murray, tied and contributed by Bill Jollymore

Hook: Size 10 to 14, Mustad 9671
Thread: Black 8/0
Tag: Oval silver tinsel
Body: Peacock herl
Rib: Oval silver tinsel
Gills: White ostrich herl
Intended use: Wet fly for Interior lakes

Comments: An effective fly during Chironomid hatches, especially when the dark-bodied flies are hatching. This fly was originally known as the Tunkwa Lake Chironomid and was developed by Tom Murray in the early '70s, but was renamed by Dave Elliot. The Tunkwanamid name was an excellent choice and this fly is a favorite of mine. It is best fished with 12- to 16-foot leader and with a wind drift away from the boat.

Peter McVey

When not on the Dean working for Lower Dean River Lodge and since the early 1970s, Pete has operated Corbett Lake Country Inn, near Merritt. He is an accomplished steelhead and trout fly-fisher and consummate story-teller. As well he is a bamboo rod builder, a skill honed over more than 30 years of rod building. He learned that craft from one of the master English bamboo rod builders, Bob Southwell. Every two years, Corbett Lake Country Inn hosts an internationally-attended bamboo rod-builders' convention.

MCVEY UGLY

Originated and contributed by Peter McVey

Hook: Size 2 to 10, Alec Jackson-style steelhead
Thread: Black
Tail: Red wool
Body: Medium black chenille
Hackle: Soft grizzly
Wing: Black moose, teased out to lay along side of body
Intended use: Waked fly for summer-run steelhead

Comments: In his early Dean River steelheading years, McVey, with his British roots, favoured the Zulu fly, an old-time Scottish trout and salmon pattern. He soon became enamoured with taking fish on surface patterns and, in the early 1970s the black-bodied, red-tailed Zulu was transformed in what is now known as the McVey Ugly. This fly is unique in that it is the first Pacific Northwest steelhead fly with moose hair wings that angle down the shank and protrude horizontally from the body. This design adds to the fly's contact with the water surface and when fished in the traditional greased-line technique, the fly stays on the surface producing a wake. Some summer-run steelhead love to attack a waked fly. Besides McVey's experiences on the Thompson and Dean rivers, others have experienced good success with this fly on the Skeena system.

PETE'S SHRIMP

Originated and contributed by Peter McVey

Hook: Size 4, Gamakatsu red salmon
Thread: Black
Tail: Hot orange hackle tip
Body: Black chenille tip followed by red wool
Hackle: Hot orange
Wing: Lady Amherst pheasant rump feather
Intended use: Floating-line wet fly for summer-run steelhead

Comments: Peter prefers to entice free-rising, summer-run steelhead to flies fished in the surface film or just below surface. This shrimp adaptation works best when fished using the greased (floating) line technique.

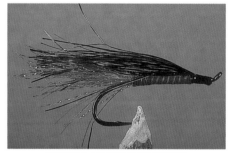

PETE'S BLUE POACHER

Originated and contributed by Peter McVey

Hook: Size 4, Gamakatsu red salmon
Thread: Black
Tail: Pink Krystal Flash
Body: Fluorescent red plastic flagging over an underbody of flat gold tinsel
Wing: Blue Flashabou
Intended use: Floating-line wet fly for summer-run steelhead

Comments: A bright fly for those light conditions which warrant a bright fly fished just under the surface. Pete says it is his "desperation fly that works well on bright sunny days." He also dresses this fly on hooks from size 6 to 10.

CORBETT LAKE SPECIAL
Originated and contributed by Peter McVey

Hook: Size 12 or 10, Mustad 9671
Thread: Red
Tail: Hot orange hackle tip
Body: Spun, dark green seal fur or chenille
Hackle: Fine gold tinsel or thread
Hackle: Hot orange throat
Wing: Teal
Intended use: Wet fly for Corbett Lake rainbow trout

Comments: This is a good all-around attractor fly. For best results, fish it fast around the lake's edges in shallow water.

CORBETT LAKE STILLBORN DAMSEL
Originated and contributed by Peter McVey

Hook: Size 12 and 10, Mustad 94831
Thread: Olive green
Tail: Olive green hackle fibres
Body: Spun olive green seal fur
Rib: Olive green thread
Hackle: Olive green
Wing: Olive green hackle tips
Intended use: Surface fly for Corbett Lake rainbow trout

Comments: Works best in Corbett Lake when the wind is blowing hard, the damsels are hatching and the trout are picking off those damsels that didn't make it.

Thunder clouds loom over a fly-fisher searching Fraser River slough for coho.

Steve Harris

is the owner/operator of Wild Rivers Fly Fishing Service and resides in Cranbrook, B.C. Through his company he teaches the art of fly-tying, fly casting, entomology and stillwater instruction. Steve is a well-known fishing guide who spends many days each year on the rivers and lakes of the East Kootenay. He is also a freelance fly-fishing writer and has contributed to several fly-fishing books and magazines.

STEVE HARRIS PHOTO

ULTRA VIOLET SCUD
Originated and contributed by Steve Harris

Hook: Size 12, Partridge YK2B
Thread: Yellow 6/0 UNI-Thread
Tail: Blended dubbing of orange Hareline and yellow UV dub
Body: Blended dubbing of orange Hareline and yellow UV dub
Rib: Yellow 6/0 UNI-Thread
Back: Clear Scud Back
Head: Tungsten bead
Intended use: Wet fly for stillwater rainbow trout

Comments: To the stillwater angler, the most important piece of equipment is a stomach pump. I try to take samples from trout on every fishing trip. One aquatic insect that comes up time after time is orange-colored scuds. Many of the lakes in the East Kootenays are gin clear and have large, sandy shoals. Sight-fishing for rainbow trout cruising the shoals is a productive form of stillwater fishing. This fly has been very rewarding to me over the last five years. The fast-sinking tungsten bead and the vigorously brushed body of the Ultra Violet dubbing, make this pattern a stillwater favourite.

EMERGING CRYSTAL MIDGE (ECM)
Originated and contributed by Steve Harris

Hook: Size 12 to 22, Tiemco 2487
Thread: Black 8/0 UNI-Thread
Tail: Two strands of pearl Krystal Flash
Body: Two strands of black Krystal Flash
Rib: Fine silver wire
Hackle: Grizzly Micro Barb
Wing: Rainy's Foam Post (parachute)
Intended use: Dry fly for rainbow trout

Comments: The ECM was developed six years ago. This is a midge pattern that works wonders on selective trout year round. The foam post and grizzly hackle keep the fly up, while the shiny body and Krystal Flash shuck resemble the struggling emerger. One afternoon in the spring of 2003, the Emerging Crystal Midge was particularly effective. I fished to a pod of large rainbow trout feeding on midges. The trout ignored my Griffith's Gnat and small Adams pattern, but they really took to the ECM. I landed three trout that afternoon on a size 22 fly. These fish were 22, 20 and 17 inches long.

PURPLE UV LEECH
Originated and contributed by Steve Harris

Hook: Size 8, Mustad 79580
Thread: Red 6/0 UNI-Thread
Body: Purple Ice UV dubbing
Wing: Purple rabbit strip tied down at hook bend
Head: Red 6/0 UNI-Thread
Intended use: Wet fly for rainbow trout

Comments: This particular pattern has been my go-to fly when the trout seem to be holding in deep water. My Black, Maroon and Olive Leech patterns have all taken the back seat when it comes to leech selection. This fly has tons of action: it pulses and undulates very naturally. Manistee Lake is a lake known for its large Gerard rainbows. These fish are hard to catch, but the Purple UV Leech has accounted for five fish over nine pounds, including a huge 13-pound trout taken in 2002.

HARE 'N' SQUIRREL WIGGLER
Originated and contributed by Steve Harris

Hook: Size 12, Fenwick NW1XL
Thread: Grey 8/0 UNI-Thread
Tail: Red squirrel tail
Body: Antron squirrel belly
Rib: Medium gold wire
Thorax: Grey rabbit fur picked out
Head: Black 1/8 inch bead
Intended use: Wet fly for trout in rivers and lakes

Comments: Doug Swisher invented the wiggle nymph idea. The Squirrel Tail Nymph is a Dave Whitlock creation. Both men are fly-fishing and fly-tying masters. During an experiment I came up with this very productive fly. It is a combination of both nymph ideas mixed with my own creative thoughts. A loop of light mono forms the hinge and allows the trailer hook to wiggle naturally. The Hare 'N Squirrel Wiggler works whereever there are trout.

This is my most productive nymph pattern, works in sizes 12, 14, 16 and 18 and it also fishes well without a bead.

GLASS CADDIS PUPA
Originated and contributed by Steve Harris

Hook: Size 12, Partridge YK2B (Sedge)
Thread: Black 6/0 UNI-Thread
Body: Orange seed beads
Hackle: Hungarian partridge beard

Head: Black super-fine dubbing
Wing Pads: Dark turkey
Antennas: Two pheasant tail fibres
Intended use: Wet-fly nymph pattern for river trout

Comments: For years I used Lafontaine's Sparkle Pupa flies to represent local caddis pupae. I wanted to find a pattern that had lots of sparkle as well as more realistic silhouette. The combination of sedge-style hook, the glass beads and the dark wing pads gave this fly a better overall profile. I fished the St. Mary's River near Kimberley as my testing ground for this pattern. The cutthroat and rainbow trout both found this pattern very appealing. This fly fishes best when it is dead-drifted or as it twitches through fast riffles.

STILLWATER CALLIBAETIS NYMPH
Originated and contributed by Steve Harris

Hook: Size 16, Tiemco 5212
Thread: Tan 8/0, UNI-Thread
Tail: Hungarian partridge
Body: Super-fine Callibaetis Dub
Rib: One strand of pearl Flashabou

Thorax: Dark green rabbit fur
Wing Case: Tan Fun Foam
Intended use: Wet fly for stillwater rainbow trout

Comments: Late May and early June is the start of the *Callibaetis* mayfly hatch on many lakes in the East Kootenay. This pattern is one I invented four years ago. It is a ringer for rainbow trout that are feeding on the migrating mayfly nymphs. Big trout move into shallow water and lurk along drop-offs to pursue the fast-moving nymphs. A clear, stillwater, fly line helps the angler get a closer approach to the fish. The fly is fished with either a quick retrieve with one-inch pulls or a floating line and suspended under a strike indicator. The slim profile and small amount of flash contribute to its effectiveness.

ROOTBEER CHIRONOMID PUPA
Originated and contributed by Steve Harris

Hook: Size 16, Tiemco 5212
Thread: Brown 8/0 UNI-Thread
Body: Rootbeer Super Floss
Rib: Copper wire
Thorax: Peacock herl

Wing Case: Pheasant tail
Gills: Miniature pearl Sparkle Braid
Intended use: Wet fly for stillwater rainbow trout

Comments: All fishing guides have their effective, proven patterns. The Rootbeer Chironomid Pupa is one that I rely on often during the spring months. As Chironomid hatches begin to intensify, the trout become more selective. This pattern in sizes 12 though 18 really works well. Some of the Chironomid fishing we do is in 30 or more feet of water. I believe the Sparkle Braid enhances the fly's appearance at that depth. A drop of Krazy Glue strengthens the body of the fly and gives this pattern a glassy sheen. Thanks to this little fly, I and others have had numerous double-digit days.

GREEN HALFBACK
Tied and contributed by Steve Harris

Hook: Size 8, Mustad 79580
Thread: Green 6/0 UNI-Thread
Tail: Pheasant tail
Body: Green chenille
Thorax: Green chenille

Wing Case: Pheasant tail
Hackle: Brown, palmered over thorax
Intended use: Wet fly for stillwater rainbow trout

Comments: The Green Halfback is a pattern that has been around for a long time. I don't know who first dressed this Green Halfback variation but I remember buying a couple of these flies 30 years ago from a resort store. This fly remains to be a very productive lake pattern. In large sizes it represents a dragonfly nymph or caddis pupa. In smaller sizes it could pass for a scud or snail. I once caught a seven-pound rainbow trout from Jim Smith Lake on this pattern. The trout touched the fly on two different occasions before finally taking the fly firmly enough to be hooked, played and landed. The Halfback works well on a fast-sinking line with a medium to fast retrieve.

Paul Jacobsen
received his first fishing rod from his father at the age of five. His father Irvin was an avid fisherman and often took him on weekend outings to the Little Campbell River in White Rock where Paul caught his first rainbow trout. From these father/son outings, Paul spawned a lifelong passion. One day, his father returned from work with a handful of flies from the Hamilton Harvey store that he was renovating. Paul, being a curious child, often
wondered how things were made, and upon seeing the flies he wondered how you could take some feathers, thread and a hook and make something that would catch a fish. He was seven years

old when he raided his mother's sewing chest for thread, opened a feather pillow to get materials, and tied his first fly with the aide of a pair of vise grips as a vise. His father took the fly on a trip to a Kamloops area lake and managed to convince a trout that the fly was food, and the rest is history. Paul is self taught in the art of fly-tying and he has been tying flies now for 38 years.

Paul's first fly-caught steelhead came from the Coquihalla River one magical morning. Using a Greased Liner and Bill Bakke's dragonfly he managed to hook and land five summer-run steelhead. He made several trips to the Dean River in the late 1980s where he managed his first fly-caught steelhead of twenty pounds. Paul worked for the Vancouver City Police, beginning in 1979, where he spent many hours talking fly-fishing with Bill Yonge, creator of the Yonge's Firefly. Paul now calls Nelson his home, where he continues with his career in law enforcement. He spends many days fishing the mighty Columbia River, tying flies and demonstrating tying at the Castlegar Fly Fishing Symposiums.

DARNER DRAGONFLY NYMPH
Adapted and contributed by Paul Jacobsen, Nelson, B.C.

Hook: Sizes 4 and 6, Mustad 79580
Thread: Monocord, 3/0, Light Olive
Tail: 10 to 12 strands of ring-necked cock pheasant tail, tied short
Body: Light olive seal fur in a copper wire dubbing brush clipped to shape
Thorax: Light olive dubbing to match the abdomen
Legs: 4 to 5 strands of natural colored ring-necked cock pheasant-tail centers on both sides of the fly, extending to the end of the abdomen
Wing case: Heavy clump of ring-necked cock pheasant-tail centers clipped into a V
Eyes: Black 3mm plastic bead chain
Intended use: Wet fly for stillwater rainbow trout using a full-sink line or sink-tip line; worked over shoal areas, sight fishing

Comments: I have adapted this fly from a pattern given to me many years ago by a friend named Jim. Jim related a story of fishing at Six Mile Lake in Kamloops. Having a rather fishless day he was approached by an older gentleman who was hooking fish regularly. The older gentleman handed my friend the fly with the proviso that he not show the fly to anyone. Jim returned from his trip and asked me if I had ever seen such a fly and asked if I could tie it. I pressed him on the identity of this "gentleman"; Jim did not know his name, however, went on to describe the man and his boat. He said the man wore an old white floppy-brimmed hat, sporting a rather large nose, and was a very knowledgeable fisherman. He described the boat as a small aluminum pram with a most unusual seat, a wooden frame with rope weaved across the part where one would sit. I knew then that this "gentleman" was most likely the famous Kamloops angler Jack Shaw.

I have adapted the fly to suit my tying style and needs. Jack used an underbody of clipped deer hair, over-wrapped with dubbed seal fur. He also used a piece of black felt, rolled like a cigar and figure-eight wrapped in, then cut close to the body, to form the large black eyes of the fly.

This is my go-to fly for many Interior lakes and has on only one occasion failed to produce fish. For best results to fish this pattern to actively feeding fish, I use a full-sink or sink-tip line in the shallows over marl beds to reach fish that nose down and create little clouds of mud as they root around in the marl looking for food. I cast out and allow the fly to sink fully to the bottom, leaving the fly on the bottom until a fish approaches. Once the fish is within 8 to 10 feet, I begin the retrieve with a short pull that causes a plume of marl to come up off the bottom. The fish key-in on this disturbance and rush the fly with such speed as to nearly cause me heart failure. If two fish are present they often attack the fly as two terriers would a rat....the take is heart-stopping. This is a very time-consuming fly to tie, but well worth the effort. A warning at this point is called for; do not fish this fly with anything lighter than 6-pound tippet, as the takes are often violent.

COLUMBIA CARPENTER ANT
Adapted and contributed by Paul Jacobsen, Nelson, B.C.

Hook: Sizes 6 and 8, Mustad 9671
Thread: Black 6/0
Body: Black coarse bucktail tied onto the hook shank and pulled back over itself to form the abdomen and thorax, then coated with a liberal application of head cement for durability
Legs: Approximately 4 to 6 hairs left over from the formation of the thorax left in place and tied to both sides splayed out as legs and cut to length, approximately half the distance of the abdomen
Wing: Ginger-colored Chinese cock hackle tips tied flat over the abdomen, delta wing style, and extending approximately 1/4 inch past the tip of the abdomen
Head: Two strands of full peacock herl and a rather large thread head
Intended use: Wet and dry fly for Kootenay-area trout

Comments: I fish this fly on a full floating line during the carpenter ant hatch, which typically begins during the first full week of hot weather in the month of June. This fly was adapted from a pattern tied by Don Freschi of Sport Fishing on the Fly, here in the West Kootenays. I have changed the pattern by not using an actual hackle to imitate the legs. I have made the legs more pronounced by using the left-over body material, thus saving the additional step of adding a hackle.

This pattern has met with great success over the years; both my fishing partner Jim Noiles and I have used this fly during June on the Columbia River. We have both enjoyed afternoons of fishing, using this pattern, that were so hot and heavy we stopped counting the number of fish we had taken.

One downfall of the fly is its rather fragile nature; unfortunately it is made of deer hair which tends to get chewed quickly. I have slowed the destruction of the fly by adding liberal amounts of head cement to the abdomen and thorax during the tie-in stage.

One should fish this fly as closely to the natural's actions on the water as possible. That is to say, don't worry about it floating high on the water. Ants tend to stay slightly submerged in the surface film. You should also let the river currents and seams pull the fly under on occasion. Some of our best fish have taken the fly when it is fully three feet under water, being swept under by a seam.

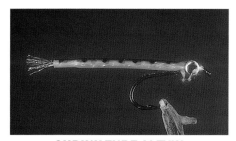

SHRINK TUBE ALEVIN
Adapted and contributed by Paul Jacobsen, Nelson, B.C.

Hook: Size 8, Mustad 7957 BX
Thread: Silver grey, 3/0, monocord
Tail: Ten strands of pearl Krystal Flash
Body: 3/32-inch translucent electrical heat shrink tubing (Note: Making the body is the most difficult part of this fly. Cut approx 1 1/4-inch piece of tubing. Insert a wire bobbin threader completely through the tube. Taper both ends of the tubing using the gentle application of heat from a Bic lighter; this will give the head and tail of the body a nice taper. Insert 5 strands of pearl Krystal Flash into the wire loop of the bobbin threader and double it back, creating 10 strands.

Pull the strands into the tubing until it clears the head end of the tube by approximately 1/4-inch. Cut the strands at the head end to free the bobbin threader, and tie the body onto the hook near the eye, cinching down both the tubing and Krystal Flash.)
Head: Silver grey thread with a thin coat of clear two-part 5 minute epoxy to build the head large enough to support the Mylar eyes
Eyes: 2 mm Mylar stick-on eyes
Egg sack: Red or orange ball of hot glue applied with a mini glue gun
Intended use: Wet fly for sea-run cutthroat trout

Comments: This fly can be fished on either a full-sink or sink-tip fly line, with the best results being in March when the fry have begun hatching. Fish a down-and-across method with a pause at the hang-down, then an erratic fry-imitating retrieve.

This fly can be a little tricky to master the first time on the vise, however, after tying half a dozen or so will you will easily master the technique. I will cover the tying in a little more detail here. Once the body material has been tied onto the hook shank and you have made a well-proportioned head, apply a thin coating of clear epoxy to the head. Rotate the fly to allow the epoxy to flow evenly until the head is symmetrical. This is going to be the base coat in which the eyes will sit. Position the eyes in place just prior to the epoxy setting up fully.

Remove the fly from the vise and clamp the bend of the hook in a set of hemostats.

Now, using a mini hot-glue gun with a red or orange glue stick, apply a small ball of hot glue under the throat of the fly, just to the rear of the head, at the place approximately where the gill plate would be. Rotate and manipulate the fly with the hemostats until a nicely formed egg sack is made, allowing the hot glue to cool. Apply a final thin coat of epoxy over the head and eyes; avoid coating the egg sack. You may color the dorsal surface of the fly body using any waterproof permanent marker, such as a Pantone. Olive green with brown par markings makes for a very good salmon alevin pattern, while dark brown to black makes an excellent whitefish alevin pattern.

My best cutthroat to date was taken on this fly. It was a 23-inch bar of chrome, fresh from the sea in a river that I shall keep secret. This fly has also proven itself deadly on coho in fresh water.

Grant Sapronoff
began his fly-fishing apprenticeship in 1969 under the watchful eyes of his father, Steve, and uncle Paul Gaverlick. They have spent many early mornings on the west arm of Kootenay Lake and late-summer evenings on the Columbia River. His neighbor John Goldsmith taught him to tie flies. After several years of

GRANT SAPRONOFF PHOTO

practice and experimenting with patterns, he began supplying local sporting goods shops. He was an early member of the West Kootenay Fly Fishing Club and served as President and Secretary from 1994 to1997. In the mid 1990s, his wife and he purchased their "Dream Home," a 1930s house on the west shore of the Columbia River in Genelle. With the opportunity to fish every day, Grant's fishing diary became considerably thicker. Presently he enjoys assisting new fly-fishers as well as fly-fishing with his 85-year-old father. He is helping his friend Joe Warren with the Canadian portion of a book that Joe is writing about the Columbia River.

MY CICADA 2003
Originated and contributed by Grant Saprunoff

Hook: Size 10 or 12, Daiichi 1270
Thread: Black 8/0
Tail: Turkey breast fibres
Body: Green medium Sparkle Chenille
Rib: Black hackle, palmered
Hackle: Black
Wing: Rolled mallard flank with a few strands of rainbow Mylar
Head: Peacock herl, Sparkle Dub with optional eyes
Intended use: Dry fly for Columbia River trout

Comments: This pattern represents the cicada hatch on the Columbia River and it usually goes through several modifications each season. We use this fly from April to June, and it fishes well either dry or wet. It is responsible for many large smiles on the faces of fly-fishers who get into my boat.

STEVE SPECIAL
Originated and contributed by Grant Saprunoff

Hook: Size 10 or 12, Mustad 94840
Thread: Black 8/0
Tail: Fox Squirrel
Body: Dubbed muskrat
Rib: Fine silver Mylar (optional)
Hackle: Black or dun, trim on bottom with a V cut
Wing: Grouse
Intended use: Dry fly for West Arm of Kootenay Lake trout

Comments: I developed this pattern for fishing on the West Arm of Kootenay Lake and named it after my father. It is very effective during small ant hatches, but continues to work throughout the summer.

SIMPLE SOFT HOPPER
Originated and contributed by Grant Saprunoff

Hook: Size 12, Daiichi 1270
Thread: Black 8/0
Body: Small yellow/tan vermeil
Wing: Deer hair with orange, red or
yellow mallard under wing
Intended use: Dry fly for Columbia River system

Comments: While fishing favourite waters when grasshoppers were around in August, September, and October, I noticed that the majority of the grasshoppers retrieved from fish were smaller and yellow-bodied, hence this soft hopper pattern.

GEORGETTI RED SHAD
Originated and contributed by Grant Saprunoff

Hook: Size 12, Mustad 94840
Thread: Black 8/0
Tail: Brown hackle fibres
Body: Red silk
Hackle: Brown, sparse
Wing: Brown/grey grouse
Intended use: Wet fly for local area waters

Comments: This pattern was tied for Chief Georgetti, who would have the Monseigneur bless the flies with holy water. He could be seen fishing off the big 80-foot wall in downtown Trail, during the hot summer months.

SUMMER CADDIS
Originated and contributed by Grant Saprunoff

Hook: Size 12, Daiichi 1270
Thread: Black 8/0
Tail: Orange deer hair
Body: Brown UV Sparkle Dub
Hackle: Brown
Wing: Deer hair, with orange deer hair and yellow Krystal Flash under wing
Intended use: Dry fly for Columbia River waters

Comments: With millions of caddis hatching each night on the Columbia I wanted a pattern that would stand out and attract the bigger trout. They do like the summer caddis, and in 2003 it accounted for 30 trout over 20 inches long.

BEAD ANT
Originated and contributed by Grant Saprunoff

Hook: Size 14, Daiichi 1273
Thread: Red 8/0
Body: Three black glass beads, epoxied
Thorax: Three beads: black, red, black, epoxied
Hackle: Black
Wing: Brown Indian hackle tips
Intended use: Wet fly for Columbia River trout

Comments: Inspired by Joe Warren, I put together this ant pattern, which is fished as an attractor when fish are not rising.

TERMINATOR
Originated and contributed by Grant Saprunoff

Hook: Size 16 or 18, Mustad 94840
Thread: Black 8/0
Body: Black Krystal Flash
Hackle: Black
Wing: Pearl Krystal Flash and Angel Hair
Intended use: Dry fly for trout in Columbia River back eddies

Comments: In early August there is a large hatch of black termites. I use this pattern in the dead water of the larger eddies.

BLUE ANT
Originated and contributed by Grant Saprunoff

Hook: Size 12, Tiemco 2312 or Tiemco 2487
Thread: Black 8/0
Body: Black window-seal foam, 1/8 inch in diameter
Hackle: Blue-dyed Hoffman
Wing: Brown Indian hackle tips with a few strands of blue Krystal Flash
Intended use: Dry fly for local area waters

Comments: This very durable carpenter ant pattern floats well in heavy currents. It is also best tied on a curved hook to help imitate a fresh-fallen struggling ant.

Cariboo

Region 5

Doug Porter

has been fly-fishing for nearly five decades and tying flies for nearly as long. He loves to fish but prefers to catch fish on flies of his own design. He was a charter member of the Kamloops Fly Fishers, where he wrote and edited their newsletter from 1974 to 1979, and he was the founder of the Grizzly Anglers in Clearwater. As a member of the executive in both organizations, he became

DOUG PORTER PHOTO

involved with the B.C. Federation of Flyfishers, through which he met more dedicated fly-fishers and conservationists from throughout the Pacific Northwest. Their collective influence, his own experiences, plus a strong desire to promote the sport of fly-fishing and conservation, led him on a path of writing, inevitably making it possible for him to contribute to *The Gilly* in 1985 and *Fly Fishing British Columbia* in 1999. For nearly 25 years he has been teaching fly-tying and casting and started teaching rod building in 1998. He is currently doing some contract teaching for Cariboo College in Williams Lake and is building a clientele as a fly-fishing guide in the Cariboo-Chilcotin.

DOUG'S DRIFTER
Originated and contributed by Doug Porter

Hook: Size 10, Mustad 9672
Thread: Light green monocord
Body: Dubbed green wool blend
Rib: Light green monocord
Hackle: Brown, palmered
Head: Peacock herl

Intended use: Wet-fly marl shrimp imitation for rainbow trout, also effective in imitating damselfly, or small dragonfly sedge pupae depending on retrieve

Comments: In the early 1970s, I, along with a few others from the Kamloops Fly Fishers, spent quite a bit of time on one of my favorite lakes in the Kamloops area. This particular lake had an extensive marl shoal that the trout frequented in low-light conditions to feed on the numerous Gammarus shrimp and other insects that lived in that rich environment. The clear shallow water allowed the angler to observe the trout's feeding patterns and reaction to various presentations. Trial and error led to the creation of many successful patterns that the trout took for various (or so I presumed, as fooling fish is a strong indicator of getting something right) insects and crustaceans.

All of the commercial shrimp patterns of that time used deer hair over the back of chenille with either a palmered or throat hackle, most having the hair coming down past the bend, leaving the shape of a curled-up shrimp. Observations I had made

indicated that swimming shrimp were stretched out straight, not curled up. I had read with interest an article about the invention of the Anderson Stonefly Nymph and its success in taking trout. The light underside and dark back over a palmered hackle seemed just the ticket for imitating a swimming shrimp. The only problem was, the colors were not right. The Anderson Stonefly pattern used brown wool for the back over a yellow body, and although yellow does turn green at a given depth in the water, I wanted colors that more closely matched the marl shrimp in the shallows. Thus began its evolution from a stonefly to a shrimp pattern.

With the use of the blender I began experimenting with different blends of greens and yellows to get the exact color I (or more importantly, the trout) wanted. Strangely enough, the most productive blend was made up of five different shades of greens and yellows in exact proportions. I had already found the exact shade of green wool for the back from a skein of medium olive that was left over from my wife's knitting.

Next came the hackle for legs. Irvin Ross and Doug Bleiler of the Kamloops Fly Fishers had fished with this pattern with great success, but Doug found that the brown hackle palmered was sometimes too much, so he palmered the front half of the fly and still found it produced well.

After two years of trial and error and some experimentation by me and others, the Drifter was perfected, and named by Irvin Ross as Doug's Drifter in 1975, following an unexpected take by a large fish as his rod was left sitting and the fly was not being retrieved. It was fished with most success using a floating line and long leader. It has taken fish on every lake I have fished it over light green marl bottoms in both the Kamloops and Cariboo regions. This is the first of my Drifter pattern family.

DRIFTER'S BROTHER
Originated and contributed by Doug Porter

Hook: Size 10, Mustad 9672
Thread: Light green monocord
Tail: Few strands of golden pheasant tippet (optional)
Body: Dubbed green wool blend

Hackle: Pheasant rump tied as collar extended 1/4 to 3/4 inch past bend
Intended use: Wet fly imitation of nocturnal sedge or large Gammarus shrimp for rainbow trout

Comments: Often, the particular lake I fished was in the evening when the trout moved in to feed. It had a medium-sized sedge that emerged then from the shallow marl shoal. While the drifter took fish consistently, I could see a number of fish refusing it when the sedges were emerging. This led to the 1976 development of the Drifter's Brother, so named because the body color was the same as the Doug's Drifter, but the shape was changed to more closely represent the sedge pupae. Instead of a palmered hackle, two turns of pheasant rump hackle were used over the dubbed body. It took fish more consistently, when sedges were emerging, than the Drifter.

DRIFTER'S LITTLE BROTHER
Originated in 1976 and contributed by Doug Porter

Hook: Size 12 to 16, Mustad 3666 or equivalent
Thread: Light green monocord
Body: Dubbed green blended wool
Hackle: Pheasant tail wrapped as
a collar extended 1/4 to 3/8 inch past bend
Intended use: Wet fly imitation of smaller *Gammarus* or *Hyallela* shrimp for rainbow trout

Comments: There were those times in the early spring and summer when the larger Drifter pattern would not produce as well. Stomach samples indicated that the fish were keyed on either small *Gammarus* or *Hyallela* shrimp. The colour of the natural was close to that of the Drifter, but the size was much smaller. I dubbed the body of a size-12 hook with the same blended material used for the Drifter, then used the same green wool for the back. I did not use hackle, but teased the fibers down to represent legs, and omitted the peacock herl head. This pattern was effective for representing the smaller shrimp swimming over the marl bottom. My best success was achieved fishing it with a full-sink or sink-tip line, keeping the fly right near the bottom, sometimes stirring up the marl as it was retrieved.

M&M
Originated and contributed by Doug Porter

Hook: Size 12 to 16, Mustad 3666 or equivalent
Thread: Black monocord
Body: Dubbed muskrat
Wing: Mallard breast feather
Intended use: Wet fly for Interior rainbow trout

Comments: During the '70s, there was always an international fish-out at Peterhope Lake, south of Kamloops. This involved many fly-fishing clubs from both B.C. and Washington State. It was always a great event to attend, with friendly competitions and club rivalries. The event was always held on the long weekend in May, with weather quite often on the miserable side, with snow, wind, and rain being the norm, between periods of sun and calm. Nonetheless, the weather did not deter all the dedicated fly-fishers who were set on winning the coveted trophy.

Peterhope did not relinquish its fish easily in the early season. Most events were held within three weeks of ice-out, and the water remained cold with no appreciable insect hatches other than small Chironomids (about which we knew little during that period, but were beginning to study as some dedicated fly-fishers were already aware of their importance in the trout's diet). The staples for the fish were shrimp and dragonflies. There were marl shoals on Peterhope, but the fish seemed to prefer

the drop-off areas where the dark green weeds predominated. I had been experimenting with various dubbing materials at that time, and found muskrat to be suitable. It had a light to medium gray hue, and good movement in the water. I had observed some gray sedge pupae, so thought it would be interesting to match the muskrat with a mallard wing in keeping with the green sedge pattern used so effectively in many lakes during that era.

While only an experiment, this fly proved to be successful in taking those early season trout in Peterhope Lake when fishing was at best, difficult and at worst, downright uncomfortable. It has since proven effective in many other lakes throughout the Kamloops and Cariboo.

PORTER'S PUPA (PP)
Originated in 1979 and contributed by Doug Porter

Hook: Size 8, Mustad 9672 or equivalent
Thread: Black monocord
Body: Olive-green chenille (varies from light green or brown to imitate emerger) tie in chenille 1/2 way up body and tie to bend to build up rear. If weighting fly, add lead to rear to keep fly positioned head up.
Rib: Light green thread, double wrapped to form wider segments
Shell Back: Pheasant-tail strands to
cover top half of fly
Hackle: Pheasant tail tied in at each side to represent paddles
Wing: Few strands of golden pheasant tippet for antennae
Head: Peacock herl
Intended use: Wet-fly emerging sedge imitation for rainbow trout

Note: Tie down back of fly using green thread, using two turns to provide ribbing effect.

Comments: This fly was a few seasons in creation, but has proven its worth time and again on many different lakes during the daylight hatches of the green or brown sedge. I always preferred using the pupa imitation over the dry fly, as experience had proven that, for the most part, the trout preferred to stay in the deeper water and not come to the surface where potential danger lurked. This being said, during the sedge hatch is one of the few times that large fish do seem to throw caution to the wind and rise to take sedges from the surface when ideal conditions present themselves.

I began with keeping the fly simple, as I prefer fishing flies than tying them. It kept evolving into a more and more complex pattern as I continued to experiment with body shape, legs, antennae, swimming paddles, back, and segmentation. Trial and error was the best teacher, with success being measured by fooling fish constantly on many lakes during varied conditions. This experimentation period lasted many years.

This fly pattern evolved in the 1970s, and reached a state of acceptance by both the fish and me sometime in the early 1980s. I have tried both dubbed bodies and chenille, but preferred chenille as I found it was easier to use and tie and was just as effective. The green sedges the PP imitates are found in most lakes, emerging from late June to early July, depending on the elevation. In clear lakes, I have found the light olive color to be most effective, while in the darker to stained water, the dark olive to brown shades take more fish. It is a durable fly (more to my liking, for, as I mentioned earlier, I prefer fishing to tying). I have fished it on both floating and sinking lines, but prefer the floating line as it is best fished in moderately shallow water with quick strips from the bottom to the surface. It is also effective fished drifted with the wind after casting 90 degrees to the wind direction. Weighting the tail of the fly with 6 to 12 turns of .0010 lead keeps the back end down during the retrieve and more closely represents the emergence pattern of the natural.

This has been a most productive fly during the past three decades in any stillwater which has a good sedge hatch. Colours and sizes must be varied to match the emerging species.

WATER BOATMAN
Originated in 1977 and contributed by Doug Porter

Hook: Size 14 and 16, Mustad 3666 or equivalent
Thread: Brown monocord
Body: Yellowish brown wool or Phentex
Shell Back: Dark brown mink tail
Intended use: Wet fly, water boatman imitation for rainbow trout

Note: Tie down mink hair butt first from head to tail on hook before tying in wool so that after the wool is wrapped, the hair can then be pulled up and over it and tied off at the head to form a shell back.

Comments: During the spring and fall I fished the shallows of my favorite lake in the Kamloops area with a small but effective pattern I tied out of yellow-brown wool for the body and dark brown cougar tail for the back. This fly worked on its first outing and did not require the same amount of tweaking as the Drifter and PP patterns, due in a large part to earlier experimentation with the boatmen patterns, when I was trying numerous different materials for paddles, none of which seemed to work.

I had observed water boatmen in the stomach samples of trout caught in the shallows, and a simple look at the bug showed it had a yellow-brown underside with a dark brown back. In those early days, I was not acquainted with weighting flies, so I fished it on a medium sinking line, even though the water I cast into seldom exceeded two meters in depth, most often less. The key to catching fish was to get the fly down to the bottom where the trout most often cruised and fed.

It has proven effective over the years for rainbow and brook trout, fished with both sinking and floating lines using either a hand-twist or quick-jerk retrieve.

BLOODWORM
Originated in 1996 and contributed by Doug Porter

Hook: Size 12, Tiemco 200R or equivalent
Thread: Maroon 12/0 Benecchi's or equivalent
Tail: Few strands of dark burgundy Angel Hair for flash

Body: Maroon wool
Rib: Red Larva Lace or stretch tubing pulled tight
Wing: Few strands of maroon marabou stripped and tied around the hook

Intended use: Wet fly, to imitate a bloodworm or small leech for rainbow trout

Note: Tie in stretch floss and wool at head and wrap over with thread to tail to keep body even.

Comments: I have often criticized the use of new synthetic materials in the construction of fly patterns, stubbornly refusing to use anything that was not traditional in fly-tying, namely fur, feathers, and other natural materials such as wool. I clung to this traditional fly-tying style until the '90s, when I began to realize that there were some new materials out there that produced patterns, especially Chironomid imitations, that looked absolutely realistic. The fish seemed to think so as well, as anglers around me took fish after fish while I watched. The urge to catch fish soon won out over my traditional views, and I began to study Chironomid pupae and larvae with a magnifying glass. This was an eye opener. I don't know how many different patterns I had previously tied using non-traditional materials, but they were in the hundreds. Some of them actually caught fish, but my desire to create the ultimate fly kept me going. At this point, I would like to add that I had lots of help along the way, from some very creative and innovative fishing partners, without whose inspiration I would still be using only wool and feathers, and missing out on a lot of fish.

The bloodworm/leech pattern I use now evolved over a few years of experimenting. As a working stiff, I could only get out to the lakes during holidays or weekends, consequently, as mentioned earlier, most of my patterns took a few years to perfect. Trial and error and variations on themes of patterns eventually led to successes, and this was one of them. The pattern works well in the spring and fall in the shallows of stillwater lakes where feeding fish cruise. It has taken numerous rainbows to five and brook trout to three pounds.

I find it best fished in water up to two meters deep on a floating line and long (six meter +) fluorocarbon leader. The long leader keeps the fly line from spooking the fish I am often stalking.

FIT FLY
Originated in 2000 and contributed by Doug Porter

Hook: Size 1/0 to 2, Mustad 36890 or equivalent
Thread: Black monocord
Tail &Back: Chartreuse rabbit fur tied at tail and head to form back and tail
Body: Orange Ice Chenille

Hackle: Fire orange, palmered
Intended use: Deeply sunk, wet fly that is highly visible for use in low-light conditions for steelhead. Also works well in cloudy water conditions during daylight hours.

Comments: While fishing the Kitimat River in April of 2000 with Peter Hepburn and Rob Gordon, for steelhead, I found I needed a fly that would be highly visible in low light conditions. After experimenting with various materials, I decided on the orange Ice Chenille and fire orange hackle for body colour and movement, topped with a chartreuse rabbit fur strip for better visibility and enhanced movement in faster water. While I only had one hit in the Kitimat, I have since caught both steelhead and bull trout in the Chilcotin River, and chum and pink salmon in the Bella Coola River.

Rob Brown

Living in Terrace for over thirty years, Rob Brown has been fishing the Skeena watershed waters for its trout and steelhead. He was an active member of the Northwest Branch of the Steelhead Society

for many years and acted as chair of the Society's Skeena Valley-based but world-wide-supported Wild Steelhead Campaign. Through his involvement in the Steelhead Society, the British Columbia Federation of Fly Fishers and as a journalist, representatives of industry and government bent on destroying fish habitat and over-exploiting salmon and steelhead runs have felt the sting of Brown's bite, both verbally and in print, on many issues, locally and province-wide.

Since the late 1980s, Rob has written under his Skeena Angler by-line weekly columns on a variety of environmental, conservation and fishing issues in the *Terrace Standard*. Besides his weekly column, Rob has written articles for *Field & Stream, Fly Rod & Reel, B.C. Outdoors, Steelhead Fly Fishing Journal, The Vancouver Sun* and *The Interior News* and he has written one book, *Steelhead River Journal: Skeena*. Furthermore, as the local fly-tying and fly-fishing teacher, he has been and continues to be instrumental in persuading many to become fly-fishers.

ZYMOSEDGE
Originated and contributed by Rob Brown

Hook: Size 8 or 10, TMC 2487 Scud Hook or Mustad C49S Caddis Curved
Thread: Black 6/0
Body: Olive-brown seal fur
Rib: Fine flat holographic gold tinsel
Legs: Brown partridge

Head: Black ostrich herl
Antennae: Two bronze mallard fibres
Intended use: Wet-fly steelhead nymph, but the pattern also appeals to rainbow and cutthroat trout in lakes and rivers, and has caught grayling as well

Comments: The progenitor of this pattern was a small olive sedge (#16) dressed to match the annual micro caddis hatch on the Lakelse River. The detailed paintings in Ernest Schweibert's *Nymphs* served as a template. On a whim, I built one of the pupae on a #8 scud hook, changing the rib from wire to flat tinsel. I stuck the bug in my fly wallet where it lay until one October afternoon

on the Zymoetz River where, on another whim, I knotted it to my tippet and consequently hooked fourteen steelhead. I've used the nymph confidently since then.

PARTRIDGE AND ORANGE
Originated by Finlay Ferguson and contributed by Rob Brown

Hook: Size 10, Tiemco 200
Thread: Hot orange 8/0
Body: Hot orange thread, over-wrapped with clear vinyl
Hackle: Gray partridge

Thorax: A small ball of hare's ear dubbing
Intended use: Wet fly (nymph) for summer-run steelhead and sea-run cutthroat

Comments: When he produced this modified version of the Partridge and Orange, Finlay Ferguson was clearly (and appropriately) inspired by the work of his Scottish countrymen, Stewart and Pritt. While the silk body of the Highland standby turns dark and buggy, when wet, Finlay's variant continues to glow brightly, a feature that has brought a lot of summer steelhead to his pattern over the years. The vinyl armor was installed to protect the fly from the serrated mouths of sea-run cutthroat. In his last years, Finlay dispensed with the thorax, with no appreciable decline in his catch rate.

MS. SCALES
Originated and contributed by Rob Brown.

Hook: Size 6 and 4, Daiichi 2161 or a similar Atlantic salmon fly hook
Thread: Brown 6/0
Tail: Golden pheasant tippet, dyed pink
Body: Black and claret seal fur or synthetic dubbing
Rib: Fine red wire doubled after the single-strand tag is completed

Hackle: Pink-dyed golden pheasant, palmered
Throat: Fuscia schlappen
Wing: Pheasant rump dyed hot orange
Intended use: Wet fly for summer and winter steelhead

Comments: Whether "dressed to kill" on a light wire hook and fished a few inches under the surface, or built on a heavier hook and fished near the stream bed, this is an effective fly for steelhead. It's built in the manner of the Dee flies, those elegant flies favoured by the Atlantic salmon fishermen who fished the Scottish river of the same name. I dedicated it to my wife, Karen Scales.

KIND OF BLUE
Originated and contributed by Rob Brown

Hook: Size 4, Daiichi 2161
Thread: Brown 8/0
Tip, Tag & Tail: Copper wire followed by blue tinsel, golden pheasant crest dyed orange
Body: Fine black wool aft; black seal fur fore
Rib: Copper wire
Hackle: Palmered blue grizzly, starting at the second turn of the rib
Throat: Hot orange
Wing: Black bear tied sparsely
Intended use: Wet fly for steelhead summer and winter

Comments: The model for this fly, with its Thunder and Lightning motif, was inspired by the design of some of Art Lingren's patterns that were published in the *Totem Topics*, the organ of the Totem Flyfishers, when Art was editing that newsletter. The fly owes its name to its blue accents and to the famous recording of Miles Davis' outing with John Coltrane, Cannonball Adderly and Gil Evans, which I was listening to at the time of its creation.

BOTTOM FEEDER
Originated and contributed by Rob Brown

Hook: Shank: size 2, Mustad 38960; Trailing Hook: Mustad 38971BR
Thread: Brown 6/0 or Danville's FlyMaster Plus in black
Tail: A tuft of owl, heron, or soft grizzled saddle hackle fibres
Body: Olive, light brown, and gray seal fur or substitute, in three sections
Head: Spun deer hair (olive and brown for adventurous tiers)
Hackle: Gray owl hackles, or large soft mottled grizzly wound fore, middle and aft
Gills: Red schlappen feather fibres
Wing: A pair of wide grizzly saddle hackles enclosing gray marabou and a few strips of pearl tinsel
Intended use: Wet-fly sculpin pattern for steelhead and bull trout

Comments: Insert the salmon hook in your vise then attach the trailing hook with the stiff, inelastic line called Fire Wire. After the fly is dressed, carefully snip the salmon hook at the bend with pliers. The red schlappen is tied in bunches on the sides of the lure to suggest gills. Tie a bunch of deer behind the head as a flared wing. This lure apes the mottled gray sculpin that is found in the Skeena and in the guts of that river's bull trout. It is a very good steelhead fly in the spring.

SKINNY SKUNK
Originated by Finlay Ferguson and contributed by Rob Brown

Hook: Size 6, salmon turned up eye
Thread: Black 6/0
Tail: Crimson hackle fibres
Body: Black floss
Rib: Fine silver wire
Hackle: Black saddle
Wing: Polar bear with one strand of pearl Flashabou
Intended use: Wet fly, to be fished "greased line" for anything with fins

Comments: Finlay Ferguson, retired hard-rock miner, log scaler and union activist, was the first angler to successfully fish flies on the main stem of the Skeena River. His arsenal of soft hackles and this anorexic version of Wes Drain's famous steelhead pattern belied his Scottish frugality. Offended by unnecessary expense, Finlay constructed his inexpensive flies then generously gave them away, along with angling secrets garnered over seven decades of fishing. Finlay fished a floating line and ten feet of ten-pound-test leader. His flies were designed to sink quickly. The Skinny Skunk caught chinook, steelhead, cutthroat, bull trout, Dolly Varden, and coho.

SUMMER MUDDLER
Originated and contributed by Rob Brown

Hook: Size 1 to 6, Tiemco 200
Thread: Brown 8/0
Tail: Mottled turkey
Body: Gold holographic tinsel, or gold braid
Wing: Mottled turkey, enclosing polar bear hair dyed hot orange
Gills: Red schlappen tied on the sides of the fly behind the head
Head: Spun deer with a short flared deer-hair wing
Wing: Bronze mallard on #1 and black squirrel on #2
Intended use: Wet fly for summer steelhead and cutthroat trout

Comments: This pattern is a hot-rodded version of Don Gapen's fly as tied in the manner popularized by Dan Bailey. The ring-eyed Tiemco hook is ideal for the minnow-like silhouette of the fly. Instead of using the full collar, flare the deer on top to enhance its action and ensure that air bubbles will stream off it in fast riffles. The colouration of the fly suggests the coho and cutthroat juveniles that frequent our rivers and streams, which in fact may explain the powerful allure the pattern has for cutthroat and steelhead.

MEENSKINISHT
Originated and contributed by Rob Brown

Hook: Size 4, Daiichi 2161 or any of those handsome Japanese salmon hooks
Thread: Chartreuse
Tail: A few fibres of chartreuse schlappen
Body: Chartreuse wool
Rib: Fine flat holographic gold tinsel
Hackle: Two turns of soft chartreuse hackle
Wing: Chartreuse marabou with some green sparkle tinsel mixed in
Intended use: Sockeye salmon, though it intercepts steelhead, coho, chinook, trout, and char as well.

Comments: Shortly after the Department of Fisheries and Oceans was persuaded to open Skeena River sockeye to sportfishing, local anglers scrambled to come up with a pattern that would actually prompt these notorious non-biters to bite. To this day, the majority of those fish are jigged.

Veteran steelhead fly-fisher Gord MacDonald told me that he had persuaded some sockeye to bite a bright green fly. Shortly after that conversation, I built a chartreuse pattern and actually had three sockeye bite it on its first time out. The fly is named for the part of the Skeena where that feat was accomplished.

FERRY ISLAND FANCY
Originated by Laurie Parr and Ed Chapplow, contributed by Rob Brown

Hook: Size 6 & 4, 2x long streamer
Thread: Red 6/0
Tail: Blue Krystal Flash
Body: Braided silver tinsel
Head: Coral pink chenille
Wing: Blue Krystal Flash
Intended use: Wet fly for Skeena River sockeye

Comments: Ed Chapplow caught enough sockeye with this pattern to create a considerable demand for it from the fly-fishing fraternity that gathers every year to fish the long bar at the head of Ferry Island between Terrace's Old and New bridges. The pattern, with its minnow-like appearance, would do well on cutthroat trout in estuaries, but its use is confined to the summer sockeye fishery.

BIG DADDY
Originated and contributed by Rob Brown

Hook: Size 8 to 4, Tiemco 7989 or any turned-up-eye light wire salmon
Thread: Black 6/0
Butt: Red seal fur
Body: Spun natural deer hair with a shellback
Back: Dense black foam
Throat: Teal or widgeon flank
Wing: Moose main split by the foam and turned into outriggers
Intended use: Surface fly for summer-run steelhead; caddisfly imitation in small sizes

Comments: The smart idea behind this waking monstrosity came from the brain of Pete Soverel, who showed up in Terrace with a skeletal version. Though Pete's spartan fly would have risen some steelhead, I reasoned that a larger silhouette might rise more. This led to the spun deer body coupled with the dense foam that serendipitously appeared in tackle stores at that time.

Because its stellar design made it nearly impossible to sink, the Big Daddy supplanted the Greased Liners and Bombers we'd been using to bring steelhead up and made the riffling hitch, with its anemic hooking properties, obsolete.

SOJI'S PILLOW
Adapted by Soji Inouye, contributed by Rob Brown

Hook: Up-eyed Mustad salmon in standard wire
Thread: Black 6/0
Tail: Gray squirrel tail over a tuft of red calf tail
Body: Badger hackle
Intended use: Dry fly for Babine River summer-run steelhead

Comments: This "bottle washer" was re-discovered by Soji Inouye, and his pal, Gary Wray, on the Bulkley River during the 1980s, when both of them lived in Smithers and fished the middle reaches of that river when very few people did. Gary and Soji fished the Pillow despite its bushy appearance and obvious floating properties, on one of those fast-sinking tips that were actually slow sinkers by today's standard. Since their leaders were of standard length, they were actually fishing just under the surface. They did well with this hybrid technique, and probably would still.
[**Note:** See Ray Mackowichuk's Sofa Pillow who originated the Bottlewasher type of flies for the Morice.]

CREPUSCULE
Originated and contributed by Rob Brown

Hook: Size 4, Daiichi 2161 or any of those Japanese salmon hooks
Thread: Brown 6/0
Tail: Dyed orange, tippet fibres

Tag & Rib: Fine copper wire
Hackle: Purple, palmered through seal fur alongside the rib
Throat: A turn or two of pink saddle

Wing: Dyed-pink golden pheasant rump feather
Intended use: Wet fly for steelhead late in the fall

Comments: It's a good idea to have pink and purple flies in your wallet when you're fishing dark-bottomed, tea-coloured coastal rivers. I fish a lot of these. I designed this fly with the idea of fishing it on the end of a long leader and a floating line. The pattern is tied in the manner of the reduced Atlantic salmon and summer steelhead patterns, but built upon a heavy hook to penetrate the fast flows in which one so often finds steelhead in the springtime. The colours reminded me of a twilight sky late in autumn, hence the name.

KITIMAT FIRE CHIEF
Originated and contributed by Rob Brown

Hook: Size 2, (clipped at the bend when the tying is complete) and a size 2 red Gamakatsu or Mustad bait hook attached to the shank by Tuff Line or Fire Line
Thread: Hot orange 6/0
Body: A butt of orange seal or substitute
Hackle: Marabou plumes with

one side stripped then wound on the shank in the following colour sequence: fluorescent yellow, then fluorescent red, finally fluorescent orange
Intended use: Sunk fly for winter steelhead on the Kitsumkalum River and late winter, so-called spring steelhead, on the Kitimat River

Comments: This pattern was shown me by Bill Dawson, the former fire chief of Kitimat. Bill's version was tied on a size two up-eyed salmon hook. I substituted the fluorescent coloured marabou for the regular colours Bill had used, omitted the silver tag, then built an articulated version. The result was an undulant, glowing fly reminiscent of the General Practitioner that I call the Kitimat Fire Chief or KFC.

Jim Butler

JIM BUTLER PHOTO

Born in North Vancouver in 1938, Jim Butler has been tying flies and fly-fishing since the age of 10. During a 1957 trip to Prince Rupert, Jim stopped to fish the Bulkley River, caught two steelhead and decided that that was the place for him. In 1968 he made the permanent move to Smithers and in 1971 he became a guide with his license stating "for the headwaters of the Skeena and Nass rivers." His home river was the Bulkley/Morice, but he also guided on the Babine and Kispiox and was one of the first to offer discounts to clients who practiced catch-

and-release. In his retirement years he is still involved with his first fly-fishing love and ties flies available for sale through his Nanika Fly Shop in Smithers.

FOAM-BACKED BOMBER
Originated and contributed by Jim Butler

Hook: Size 4 and 6, Tiemco 7989
Thread: Black Kevlar
Tail: White kip tail
Back: Grey closed-cell foam, trimmed to a triangular shape
Body: Spun Cariboo hair, clipped to shape and trimed top close to shank

Beard: Brown kip tail
Wing: White kip tail, divided and flared to sides about 1/2 inch past the hook eye (Note: Don't use too much tension when tying down the foam as the thread can cut it.)
Intended use: Waked fly for summer-run steelhead

Comments: This fly is the grey-and-white Bomber's cousin. It is one of the best-ever waking flies for steelhead. When I first started incorporating foam into a few dry flies, I offered to pay the guy at the garbage dump $5 if he would salvage a few rubber sandals for me. The flip-flop sandals were difficult to cut, but they came in a variety of colours and the soles of closed-cell foam floated well. When I returned to the dump a month later, I was presented with a box overflowing with mismatched sandals in the most riotous colours imaginable. I paid the young man his $5, thanked him and told him I wouldn't need any more. I think I kept four or five out of a total of 50. I made sure that the discarded ones were double-bagged and out of sight from anyone wanting to make another $5. The last time I used foam from a sandal was at Christmas Island. I cut out cylinders 1/2 inch in diameter by 3/4 inch long and with the aid of a needle, threaded my leader through the center and tied on a large bright fly and had a poor man's popper, on which I actually caught trevally. Some of the newer foams specific for fly-tying are denser and don't absorb water. However, if the fly starts to get a little soggy, simple squeeze the water out with thumb and forefinger and keep on fishin'!

1/2 N 1/2 (HALF 'N' HALF)
Originated and contributed by Jim Butler

Hook: Size 4 and 6, Tiemco 7989
Thread: Black Kevlar
Tail: Grey squirrel tail
Back: Grey closed-cell foam, trimmed to a triangular shape
Body: Orange wool

Hackle: Brown, palmered
Wing: Grey squirrel tail, divided and flared to sides about 1/2 inch past the hook eye then pull foam back over to eye, wrap thread in such a way that the squirrel tail extending

past the eye is stiffened and protruding upward at a 35- to 45-degree angle from the hook shank (Note: Don't use too much tension when tying foam as the thread can cut it.)
Intended use: Waked fly for summer-run steelhead

Comments: A good pattern for Skeena system summer-run steelhead. I always thought this fly to be1/2 stonefly and 1/2 caddis fly, hence the name. Steelhead love the way this low rider wakes through the surface.

HELGE
Dressed and contributed by Jim Butler

Hook: Size 4 and 6, Tiemco 7989
Thread: Black Kevlar
Tail: Dark moose hair
Butt: Fluorescent pink floss
Body: Cream floss
Beard: Dark moose hair
Wing: Dark moose hair with epoxy applied to stiffen the paddle that flares over the hook eye
Intended use: Waked fly for summer-run steelhead

Comments: In the fall of 1968 I recognized Helge Byman as the angler casting a fly on the Bulkley River's Strawberry Run. Bulkley and Morice river fly-fishers use a lift bolted to the stern of their boat which allows the boat operator to push down on the lift handle, raising the propeller high in the water column, thus permitting passage through shallower water. I wanted to get Helge's advice on building a lift for my aluminum car-top boat so I pulled into shore and watched him fish.

I couldn't help notice that Helge was fishing a floating line and the fly he was using was throwing a wake, the likes of which I had never witnessed before. Suddenly there was a boil behind the fly, Helge froze waiting, another boil, nothing, then the fish ate the fly on its third try and for the next few minutes tore the river apart. Soon a bright hen of about seven pounds was beached and released to fight another day. I asked Helge how he was able to get a little dry fly to throw such a large wake. He rewarded my curiosity by giving me one of his flies and the first thing I noticed was the clipped head that was much larger than anything I had ever tied. He had cemented and trimmed the head to what he referred to as a paddle. This fly turned out to be one of the most dependable dries for me through the next two decades. He didn't tell me its name and I never thought to ask so I just called it Helge.

LADY KRISTY
Originated and contributed by Jim Butler

Hook: Size 2 and 4, Mustad 80500
Thread: Black
Tag: Flat gold tinsel
Body: A rust-coloured mix (use a blender) of orange, red, brown wool, with short pieces or red and gold Krystal Flash
Rib: Fine gold wire
Hackle: Three turns of folded brown Spey hackle
Wing: Rolled mallard
Intended use: Floating-line wet fly for summer-run steelhead

Comments: This effective, early summer-run fly is a spin-off of the well-known low-water Lady Caroline Spey fly, introduced to Vancouver Island steelhead by Roderick Haig-Brown in the 1930s.

LADY CLARET
Originated and contributed by Jim Butler

Hook: Size 2, Mustad 80500
Thread: Black
Tag: Flat gold tinsel
Butt: Fluorescent fuchsia Depth Ray floss
Body: Blended dark claret wool
Rib: Fine gold wire
Hackle: Three turns of folded brown Spey hackle
Wing: Claret-dyed mallard flank
Intended use: Wet fly for summer-run steelhead

Comments: This fly works best fished deep on dark days or in lightly glacial-silted water and seems to have special appeal to Dolly Varden.

LADY BLACK
Originated and contributed by Jim Butler

Hook: Size 2, Mustad 80500
Thread: Black
Tag: Flat gold tinsel
Butt: Fluorescent pink, red or fuchsia Depth Ray floss
Body: Black floss
Throat: Three turns of black chenille
Rib: Fine gold tinsel
Hackle: As many turns as you can get from a folded black-burnt Spey hackle
Intended use: Wet fly for summer-run steelhead

Comments: This fly didn't fish very well until I added the chenille throat, which tends to hold the hackle away from the body, giving the fly a fuller appearance. I first dressed this fly as a follow-up to the Lady Kristy, but soon found out that it was an effective searching fly, fished either just under the surface or sunk using a sinking-tip line.

POOR MAN'S MUDDLER

Originated by Jim Wright and contributed by Jim Butler

Hook: Size 4 or 6, Tiemco 7989
Thread: Black
Tail: Two strands of medium flat pearl tinsel
Body: Orange or rust wool, sparse to give a thin body

Wing: Four small clumps of deer hair, spun, extending to the hook point only and trimmed to a small Muddler-type head
Intended use: Floating line wet fly for summer-run steelhead

Comments: This fly was given to me in 1969 by former Telkwa resident Jim Wright. Jim preferred to fish this fly under tension, just under the surface on a floating line.

HARD-EGG 'N' I

Originated and contributed by Jim Butler

Hook: Size 6 or 8, Mustad 36890
Thread: Black
Tail: Grey wool
Body: White rayon floss underbody to provide minnow body shape, followed by flat medium silver tinsel.
Back: Grey wool
Over body: Thin layer of white acetate floss

Egg sac: Small tuft of fluorescent red yarn
Finish: Submerge the fly in acetone for five or six seconds to make the acetate floss transparent (Note: the floss will harden when it dries)
Intended use: Wet-fly minnow imitation for rainbow trout

Comments: In May, 1985, I was fishing for trout in Rainbow Alley, the short river between Babine and Nilkitkwa lakes. Sockeye fry, some with a prevalent egg sac, were migrating through the alley to Nilkitkwa Lake. The most productive fly was the Egg 'n' I with a tied-down mallard flank feather for the back. The problem was that the rainbow's teeth would tear up the tied-down mallard feather, making it look ragged and less effective. This usually happened when it was too dark to tie on another fly. By replacing the mallard feather with grey wool, wrapping the body with acetate floss and dipping it into acetone, I had a fly that was virtually indestructible.

For cutthroat near tide water where the main migration is pink salmon fry, omit the silver tinsel and replace the grey wool with wool one shade lighter than kingfisher blue.

Fry imitations have been around for over a century and I'm amazed at how few anglers know how to fish a minnow fly properly. Migrating fry resting along the edges of a river and facing upstream are of no interest to feeding trout. Those swimming downstream in the main current are. They usually travel in bunches just under the surface and when a feeding fish breaks up the group it usually takes only a few seconds for the fry to regroup and continue their downstream journey. To mimic this migration, use a floating line and cast straight across the stream. Immediately mend downstream, let the belly in the line keep the fly pointing downstream and other than the occasional lift of the rod to raise a little line and slow down the fly's travel, keep the rod tip still. When I started fishing fry patterns in this manner my success improved tenfold.

CRAZY JIMMY-RED

Originated and contributed by Jim Butler

Hook: Size 4 or 6, Mustad 7970
Thread: Fluorescent red
Body: Fluorescent red chenille wound in a figure-eight around eyes
Eyes: Silver bead chain

Beard: White kip tail extending to hook point
Intended use: Wet fly for sockeye and Chinook salmon

CRAZY JIMMY-CHARTREUSE

Originated and contributed by Jim Butler

Hook: Size 4 or 6, Mustad 7970
Thread: Fluorescent chartreuse
Body: Fluorescent chartreuse chenille wound in a figure-eight around eyes

Eyes: Gold bead chain
Beard: White kip tail extending to hook point
Intended use: Wet fly for sockeye and Chinook salmon

Comments: This fly was discovered by accident. In August 1988, long before one could legally kill sockeye, I made the 2 1/2-hour drive from my Smithers home to the Babine River. When I arrived I attached a reel to a 9-foot, six-inch, 9-weight Sage. The line I threaded through the guides was an 8-foot 6-inch piece of 850 grain shooting head spliced to a floating running line. The leader was four feet long with a 15-pound tippet. When I looked for a fly to tie on I discovered that I forgot my fly box at home. All I had were three Crazy Charlie bonefish flies that I had used on Christmas Island the winter before and had casually thrown into a chamois reel case. They were tied on T.M.C. 811-S number six hooks and had gold bead-chain eyes, and three short strands of Krystal Flash for a tail. The gold tinsel body had an over-wrap of clear Larvae Lace. The beard was a sparse bit of orange kip tail with a few strands of Krystal Flash mixed in. My diary reveals that in five hours of fishing, many fish were lost due to the light wire hook straightening out or the fly being thrown by a leaping fish. Most of the fish took the fly with a solid strike or quick heavy pull. I beached 21 sockeye, 18 of which were hooked fairly in the mouth. One was snagged during the drift and two during the retrieve, when the fly tends to lie on its side. The day ended when I broke off the last of my three flies. I still use this fly when the overhead sun is beating on the water. The only change is I now use a Mustad 7970 hook.

Over the next few years I experimented with colour and size and finally settled on a size 4 Mustad 7970 hook with large silver bead-chain eyes on top of the shank, a body of fluorescent orange chenille with a white kip tail beard. A combination of gold eyes and chartreuse body works almost as well. I prefer red or fluorescent orange because the chinook are usually in the river at the same time as the sockeye and will respond to the fly with regularity.

My son was fishing one day with phenomenal success, hooking and releasing fish after fish. An angler hollered across the river, "What fly you using?" My son knew it was patterned after the Crazy Charlie bonefish fly and that I had tied it. Without hesitation, he shouted back, "Crazy Jimmy", and another spin-off from a great fly was born.

TRIPLE-H
Originated and contributed by Jim Butler

Hook: Size 1/0, Mustad 36890 trailer attached to a size 3/0 Mustad 3191 or 45 mm Waddington shank with 30-pound Spectra line (Note: In B.C. only a single hook is permitted; cut the main hook at the top of the bend after tying the fly)

Thread: Black Kevlar
Trailer and Main Hook Body: Black rabbit fur wound up shank
Eyes: Large bead chain
Head: Fluorescent red chenille wound in a figure-eight around eyes
Intended use: Deep sunk, wet fly for summer-run steelhead

Comments: A number of years ago, I watched two clients working their way down the Bulkley River's Airplane Run. As soon as there was room I waded in behind them and started casting a somewhat worn rabbit fur leech with a fluorescent red head and bead chain eyes. After a few casts, the fur came loose and unraveled, resulting in a two- or three-inch piece of rabbit strip training behind the hook bend. Too lazy to go back to the boat for another fly I started messing around, casting sidearm in order to see how big a belly I could cast in the fly line. The wrecked fly had just started to drift when all of a sudden it just stopped. Thinking that I had snagged a stick poking up from the bottom, I gave the line a hard jerk and found myself fast to a good fish of seven or eight pounds. I unhooked the fish, waded back in, cast and was promptly into another. This one was a large buck and as I led him to the beach, I applied a little too much pressure and broke him off. The last thing I saw was three inches of black rabbit strip undulating over a rose-coloured gill plate as the fish sped off downstream. After a great deal of thought I realized why, not only steelhead but, coho and chinook are attracted to long black flies.

Pacific lampreys inhabit almost every west coast stream from California to the Aleutian Islands. The young pass through a larval stage and I believe at that stage of life they become an important

food source for juvenile steelhead and salmon. Most lamprey larvae I found were between 2 1/2 to 5 inches long, black or very dark brown. To duplicate the larval form, I tried tying tube flies, but they didn't give me the action I wanted. String flies worked okay but they had the nasty habit of the tail hook fouling the leader when cast. I finally settled on an articulated fly four inches long and gave a few away to close friends. The fly worked so well for them, particularly in off-colour or water less than 44 degrees Fahrenheit, that they decided to confuse others by renaming the fly Triple-H from my original name of Hot Head Hinge. This fly outsells all others at my Smithers' Naninka Fly Shop.

Bob Clay

came to Kispiox Valley in the '70s from his Alberta home. He has a deep passion for the sport and was smitten on first sight with the Kispiox Valley, river and its fish and stayed, eventually building a beautiful house overlooking the river where he and Kathy have raised their fly-fishing family. A guide on the river for years, he knows the river intimately and now works for Wilfred Lee's Hook & Line Guiding. Bob is a man of many talents, one of them being his skill at turning Tonkin grass into bamboo rods. Clay builds double- and single-handed bamboo fly rods, custom orders only. Besides fishing the Skeena system, Bob can be found guiding or floating down the Dean River on a busman's holiday. Bob collected a number of patterns developed by himself and his friends for this book.

PINK & PURPLE MARABOU
Originated and contributed by Bob Clay

Hook: Size 1 to 4, Gamakatsu Octopus, Tiemco 105 or Mustad beak trailer hook
Thread: Red
Body: Purple marabou wound up hook shank

Collar: Hot pink marabou with a few strands of purple Flashabou
Head: 5/32 brass groovy eyes
Intended use: Wet fly for summer-run steelhead

Comments: Clay's marabou flies are dressed on a long-shanked hook with the trailer hook attached by 30-pound Fireline. This pattern is best fished sunk on a sink-tip. It's a standard for Bob on the Dean, Kispiox and other waters on the Skeena system.

DEAN RIVER LIGHT MARABOU
Originated and contributed by Bob Clay

Hook: Size 1 to 4, Gamakatsu Octopus, Tiemco 105 or Mustad beak trailer hook
Thread: Fluorescent red
Body: Orange marabou wound up hook shank

Collar: Light pink marabou with a few strands of pearl Flashabou and orange Krystal Flash
Head: 5/32 brass groovy eyes
Intended use: Wet fly for summer-run steelhead

Comments: This fly is best fished on a sink-tip line. Clay believes in the bright-day/bright-fly theory and for him this fly works well on the Dean River when the fish are fresh in from the sea.

BLACK & BLUE MARABOU
Originated and contributed by Bob Clay

Hook: Size 1 to 4, Gamakatsu Octopus, Tiemco 105 or Mustad beak trailer hook
Thread: Red
Body: Black marabou wound up hook shank

Collar: Black marabou with a few strands of blue Flashabou and blue Krystal Flash
Head: 5/32 brass groovy eyes
Intended use: Wet fly for Kispiox summer-run steelhead

Comments: Blue is a favoured colour on the Kispiox and this is Bob's staple blue-toned pattern for those big Kispiox monsters. It's best fished on a sink-tip.

GREEN THING
Originated & tied by Dirk Dirkson, contributed by Bob Clay

Hook: Size 4, Tiemco 105 trailer hook
Thread: Green, flat, waxed nylon
Tail: Black marabou with a few strands of green Flashabou and Krystal Flash

Body: Green cactus chenille
Hackle: Natural black Jersey giant schlappan
Head: Brass cone head
Intended use: Wet fly for Kispiox summer-run steelhead

Comments: This fly is another Kispiox favourite that needs to be fished deep.

STELLAR JAY
Originated and tied by Wally Bolger, contributed by Bob Clay

Hook: Size 4, Gamakatsu Octopus trailer hook
Thread: Black
Body: Blue marabou wound up hook shank

Collar: Black marabou with a few strands of blue Flashabou and blue Krystal Flash
Intended use: Wet fly for steelhead

Comments: This is another variation on the blue theme for the Kispiox River and is best fished deep on a sink-tip.

THE PERSUADER
Originated & tied by Todd Stockner, contributed by Bob Clay

Hook: Size 2, Gamakatsu Octopus trailer hook
Thread: Red
Body: Blue sparkle dub

Collar: Blue hackle followed by purple
Wing: Black rabbit strip with a few strands of holographic tinsel
Intended use: Wet fly for steelhead

Comments: Trailer hook attached to cut-off front hook with 25-pound braided stainless-steel wire. This fly is best fished on a sink-tip for Kispiox River steelhead.

KILOWATTS - BLACK AND BLUE
Designed & tied by Cliff Watts, contributed by Bob Clay

Hook: Size 1/0 Gamakatsu Jig 90 Degree Round Bend Heavy Wire
Eye: 3/16-inch nickol Dazl Eyes (7/32 inch as heaviest eye; large bead-chain as lightest)
Thread: Fluorescent pink Danville, size A, flat waxed thread
Tail: 20 to 25 strands of electric

blue Flashabou with a single black marabou feather
Body: Opal Black Estaz, palmered
Hackle: A single black schlappen
Wing: 70 to 80 strands of electric blue Flashabou tied on hook point side
Intended use: Floating or sinking line for anadromous fish

Comments: The jig design, when attached with a non-slip loop knot, has an added enticement that brings better results. It is very effective for Skeena Drainage steelhead.

The variable eye sizes make it a slow- to fast-sinking fly. The short-shank, Siwash jig hook has had a five-year landing percentage of over 75% on steelhead.

EGG SUCKING LEECH

Originated & tied by Jim Holcomb, contributed by Bob Clay

Hook: Size 2, Tiemco 7999
Thread: Three plumes of black marabou
Body: Dubbed black seal over wrapped lead
Head: Pink chenille
Intended use: Wet fly for summer-run steelhead

Comments: When I met Bob Clay on the Kispiox in 1983, I was struck by the giant white marabou leech he fished. I looked at my #4 Green Butt Skunk and vowed to try bulkier flies the next year. Some of us ran across a 1950's *Outdoor Life* with an Alaska theme and it showed a version of the Egg Stealing Leech, with chenille and marabou body with a chenille egg. In 1984 I showed up at the Kispiox with my weighted seal fur and marabou leech with the egg-head version as well as the weighted seal leech without the egg version. From that year on it has became a standard pattern and has put as many fish or more on the beach than most patterns up and down the Skeena. Versions dressed in purples and blues also work well.

STEALTH BOMBER

Originated & tied by Jim Holcomb, contributed by Bob Clay

Hook: Size 1/0, Daiichi 2441 or equal
Thread: Bright green
Wing: Black rabbit strip
Collar: Black rabbit with a few stands of blue Flashabou
Head: Foam bass bug
Intended use: Waked fly for summer-run steelhead

Comments: This fly was the result of my frustration with many of my steelhead pushing the dry fly away from it with the boil. I wanted the waking action of the riffled Bomber or Muddler but I wanted the fly to remain in the surface film. So I dressed the Black Leech on the back of a foam head, on a size 1/0 hook to keep it riding low and keep the fly from rolling as it is riffle-hitched and skated along the surface of the water. I prefer the small black foam head on a 1/0 hook, but I've had success with a number of color and size combinations. This has been the comeback fly on all the steelhead rivers I or my friends have fished. My experience is that every steelhead that's gone for it has grabbed it solidly. Not that it will always produce fish but I've never seen refusals, missed strikes, or the fly pushed away by the rise of a steelhead. This fly rocks.

MOOSE HAIR SKATER

Originated & tied by Dave Lambroughton, contributed by Bob Clay

Hook: Size 4 to 8, Tiemco 105
Thread: Red flat waxed nylon
Tail: Moose hair
Body: Purple crystal chenille
Back: Moose hair
Side wing: Moose hair stubs
Wing: Moose hair
Intended use: Waked fly for summer-run steelhead

Comments: Lambroughton's staple pattern for bringing up Dean River and Skeena system summer-run steelhead. It really kicks up a wake as it comes across.

DEER HAIR ON A HOOK

Originated by Jim Wright, tied and contributed by Bob Clay

Hook: Size 4 to 8, Tiemco 105
Thread: Black, flat, waxed nylon
Wing: Black deer hair
Head: Black deer-hair stubs
Intended use: Waked fly for summer-run steelhead

Comments: The forerunner of the Bulkley Mouse and, in small sizes, this is a great fly for glassy tailouts. Jim Wright believed in using the very basics in his flies. Back in the very early 1970s, Wright dressed two very basic patterns. His staple floating-line wet fly, called a Tar Baby, was dressed solely from the hair on a Tar Baby doll. His Mouse was just a clump of deer hair on a hook. If steelhead didn't like the Tar Baby then he would try the mouse and if they refused the Mouse he would leave them for another day. Bob Clay gives Wright credit for popularizing the waked-fly technique on the Bulkley.

Ray Makowichuk

A long-time resident of Houston, Ray has spent the better part of four decades pursuing steelhead with a fly on Skeena system tributaries but mostly on the Morice and Upper Bulkley. Mentored by the famous Houston guide Helge Byman, Ray began his guiding career in 1974. Each year he can be found on the Babine River during the May and June trout season, on the Morice and Upper Bulkley in July and August during the chinook season and then on those same rivers during the September to November steelhead season.

BLACK BI-VISIBLE
Originated and contributed by Ray Makowichuk

Hook: Size 4 or 6, Tiemco 7989
Thread: Black 6/0
Tail: A small clump of red hackle fibres

Body: Four eight-inch-long black Hoffman super saddle hackles
Intended use: Dry fly for summer-run steelhead

BROWN BI-VISIBLE
Originated and contributed by Ray Makowichuk

Hook: Size 4 or 6, Tiemco 7989
Thread: Black 6/0
Tail: A small clump of red hackle fibres
Body: Four eight-inch-long brown

Hoffman super saddle hackles
Intended use: Dry fly for Morice River summer-run steelhead

Comments: Bryan Williams in his 1935 book *Fish and Game in British Columbia*, when writing about steelhead flies, says that "the Bi-visibles are also very important" and recommends the dry-fly fisher have an assortment. The original dressings for this type of fly consisted of a hackled body followed by a couple of turns of white hackle. Because it was dressed as a two-toned light and dark fly, the dark showing up better in the day and the white in the evening, it was named Bi-visible.

The Bi-visibles have a long history on the Morice River. During his 1955 trip to that river, John Fennelly in *Steelhead Paradise* (1963), about a dry fly made of black hackles says:

On the same trip occurred the most unusual coincidence of my fishing career. I was casting into the river a short distance below the lake. On one of my back casts my fly was caught in the branch of a tree behind me. After considerable maneuvering I managed to yank it free and started to examine the fly for possible damage. To my amazement, I found that my fly had pulled out of the tree another dry fly with a small bit of leader. This fly was old and bedraggled and consisted of a bunch of long black hackles. The odds against this happening even on a highly fished stream would be enormous, but on a wilderness river like the Morice the odds must have been astronomical.

Somewhat facetiously I decided to treat this old fly as a good luck symbol, and to try fishing with it. After a few casts I had a rise and was fast into a good rainbow (about 2 1/2 pounds). On its first run this fish wrapped itself around a snag and broke off. Muttering a few curses

about good luck charms in general, I put on a fresh fly and started casting again. About 20 minutes later I had a second strike in almost the same spot as the first. This time I managed to land the fish. I could hardly believe my eyes when I bent over to extract my fly from the trout's jaw, and saw the old black fly hanging from the other side of its mouth. (p. 19)

Ray Makowichuk dresses his Black and Brown Bi-visibles with very long hackles which are wound so closely together that the fly sits high on the hackle tips when dead drifted to Morice steelhead. Once the dead drift part of the cast is complete, the bottlewasher Bi-visible dances on top of the water as it scurries across the surface, completing its drift as a waked fly.

SOFA PILLOW
Originated and contributed by Ray Makowichuk

Hook: Size 4 to 8, Tiemco 7989
Thread: Black 6/0
Tail: A few red hackle fibres
Body: Flame red Antron
Rib: None

Wing: Fox squirrel tail
Hackle: Brown
Intended use: Dry fly for Morice River summer-run steelhead

Comments: The Sofa Pillow has been a staple Morice River pattern ever since John Fennelly introduced it back in the 1950s. This version, first dressed by Makowichuk in 1968, with its fuller hackle, rides high on the dead drift and, like the Bi-visible, scurries across the surface as a waked fly.

ORANGE COMET
Contributed by Ray Makowichuk

Hook: Size 2/0 to 4, Eagle Claw 1197
Thread: Black 3/0
Tail: Orange bucktail
Body: An underbody of fine nylon floss to shape body, followed by flat silver tinsel

Hackle: Mixed orange and yellow hackles
Intended use: Sunk-line wet fly for Morice River chinook salmon

Comments: This California-originated steelhead pattern has been a popular chinook salmon pattern on the Morice River since 1969 when California fly-fisher Karl Mausser introduced it to Ray Makowichuk. About the fly's effectiveness Ray says that, "if I had four rods in my boat during that time of the year they would all have Comets on them."

MAUSSER MINNOW

Developed by Karl Mausser and contributed by Ray Makowichuk

Hook: Size 8, 6 or 4, Mustad 9672
Thread: Clear 6/0 to tie down tail and black 6/0 for head
Body: Underbody of white nylon floss with flat pearl tinsel over

Throat: Fluorescent red thread
Intended use: Floating-line wet fly for Babine River rainbow trout

Comments: Karl Mausser is famous in the steelhead world for his 33-pound, world-record Kispiox River steelhead caught in 1962. Massuer made his first trip to the Skeena system in 1957 and became a fixture on the Morice and Kispiox rivers. However, prior to the fall steelhead fishing, Mausser journeyed to the Babine to enjoy the trout fishing on that river at the lake's outflow. He developed his fry patterns years ago and this is Makowichuk's adaptation of the minnow, an effective fly to have when the trout are gorging on newly emerged salmon fry.

OWL NYMPH

Originated by Karl Mausser and contributed by Ray Makowichuk

Hook: Size 10 to 4, Mustad 9672
Thread: Black 6/0
Tail: Owl fibres from body
Body: Wrapped owl fibres

Wing case: Owl feather fibres
Intended use: Floating-line wet fly for Babine River rainbow trout

Comments: This is another of Karl Mausser's flies that he used for Babine River rainbows. Ray Makowichuk says that Karl and he "used it on a dry line when the water got choppy or in the evening just before dark." Ray believes the fly looked like a minnow to the fish and that it is a very effective fly when used in the right conditions.

Andrew Williams, Fred Seiler and Hugh Storey

This next group of flies was assembled by Andrew Williams and comes from Andrew's, Fred Seiler's and Hugh Storey's boxes. All are long-time Terrace and Kitimat area anglers. Andrew collected and put together the written documentation.

Andrew Williams'

fascination with fly-fishing started in 1972 when he pulled an Orvis cane rod and Hardy reel out of the Ausable River in upper New York State. When he caught his first trout on a fly the next spring, it was hard to tell who was hooked: the fish or him. Born in Southampton, England, home of the famous Test, Avon and Itchen rivers that gave birth to fly-fishing, Andrew did not have an opportunity to try the sport of the gentry until his family moved to Canada. The founding president of the Ottawa Fly Fishers and current president of the Skeena Fly Fishers, he is a frequent contributor to *B.C. Outdoors* and other fly-fishing magazines, and is currently working on a book on trout fishing.

Fred Seiler

was born and raised in Kitimat in northern British Columbia. He has been an outdoor enthusiast all his life, hiking all the nearby mountains while hunting, and fishing all the coastal streams from Kitimat to Rivers Inlet while working for Fisheries. He retired from logging several years ago to develop Silver Tip Ecotours, a fish guiding and bear-watching business. His extensive knowledge of the area, its rivers and its wildlife, especially grizzly bears, has contributed to making him an excellent wildlife photographer.

FRED SEILER PHOTO

Hugh Storey

was born in Deep Cove, and has lived in Kitimat off and on since 1952, working for Alcan. He began fly-fishing on the Nicomekl River near Vancouver in 1961, dabbled with it for 10 to 12 years and fished most of the lower mainland and Vancouver Island streams. He has fished exclusively with the fly for the last 20 years on the Skeena and Kitimat River systems. A self-taught fly tier, he has in recent years focused more and more on fly-fishing for steelhead with the dry fly, especially since his retirement in 2002.

HUGH STOREY PHOTO

CHICKABOU SALMON FRY
Adapted and contributed by Andrew Williams

Hook: Size 6 to 10, Tiemco 300
Thread: White 6/0
Tail: A few strands of pearlescent Krystal Flash and a chickabou feather: grizzly (sockeye), orange (coho), green (humpback)
Body: Gudebrod Electra Braid holographic rod wrap in pearlescent (sockeye), gold (coho), silver (humpback)

Back: Olive deer hair with few strands of matching Krystal Flash (sockeye), brown (coho), dark green (humpback)
Belly: White Neer Hair
Eyes: 1.5mm prismatic gold stick-on eyes
Intended use: Wet fly for trout in local Terrace-area rivers

Comments: In the early part of the season, many of the traditional fry patterns, such as the Rolled Muddler, Egg 'n' I, and Mallard and Silver, are effective, as is the wet fly technique of quartering downstream. As the season progresses, however, trout—especially the larger ones—in heavily fished streams become warier. That is the time to experiment with more realistic fly patterns and innovative casting techniques. Watching salmon fry drifting in the surface film, I realized I needed a fly pattern that more closely imitated their size, colouration and movement. That's how the Chickabou Fry pattern was developed. I varied the slim epoxy-coated body with its big eyes, slim silhouette and appropriate colours, to match the distinctive appearance of the different salmon fry. A tail of green, grizzly or orange chickabou gave the fly the wiggle of the hapless fry drifting downstream.

GRANTHAM'S SEDGE
Originated by Ron Grantham and contributed by Andrew Williams

Hook: Size 6 to 12, Mustad 9671
Thread: Black 6/0
Body: Weed wacker cord extended 1/4" past eye of hook, covered in dark brown dubbing

Wing: Deer hair wing tied on to extension, caddis-style
Head: Trimmed deer-hair butts
Intended use: Waked fly for summer-run steelhead

Comments: Waking patterns are popular on the Copper River in the early fall, but most require a double hitch to wake without sinking. Ron's pattern places the head of the fly before the eye and wakes well without a hitch. Rob Brown introduced me to this fly several years ago and I've found it works best in smaller sizes, especially when the water is clear and steelhead are put off larger flies.

ADAMS PARACHUTE
USA origin, contributed by Andrew Williams

Hook: Size 8 & 10, Tiemco or similar dry-fly hook
Thread: Black 6/0
Tail: Mixed grizzly and brown stiff hackle fibres
Body: Grey muskrat belly fur dubbing
Hackle: Mixed grizzly and brown

dry-fly hackle tied parachute style around post
Wing: White calf body hair tied as a post 1/3 back from head
Intended use: Dry fly (dead drift) for steelhead

Comments: During late August and early September, I have noticed steelhead actively taking large dark mayflies on the Copper River in the mid-afternoon. When this is happening, the fish ignore almost all other offerings. Surprisingly, the "trout-sized" Adams parachute when drifted over the steelhead will bring them up. Sometimes, I twitch the fly a little, like an emerging dun, and this does the trick.

ROLLED MUDDLER VARIANT
Originated by Tom Murray and contributed by Andrew Williams

Hook: Size 8 to 12, Mustad 9672 or similar hook
Thread: Red 6/0
Tail: Mallard flank fibres
Body: Medium flat silver Mylar
Rib: Medium silver oval tinsel
Hackle: Spun deer hair head with most fibres over the wing

Wing: Pearl Flashabou, followed by mallard flank, and then deer-hair fibres
Head: Silver bead, omit for flies to be fished just under surface
Intended use: Wet fly for cutthroat and rainbow trout, Dollies etcetera especially in springtime

Comments: This is a very popular pattern throughout the Skeena system and the Kitimat in the spring. Trout and char actively feed on the emerging salmon fry from February to May and the Rolled Muddler is an effective imitation of the various species. It is fished un-weighted to mimic the fry's struggling in the surface film, and weighted when trout, especially larger fish, are feeding near the stream bottom.

MARABOU SPEY
Contributed by Andrew Williams

Hook: Size 1 to 6, regular salmon
Thread: Black 6/0
Hackle: Pale blue marabou wound on as a hackle (or other colours)
Wing: Black marabou plumes tied in close to head, followed by black marabou or other colours wound on as a hackle with blue Krystal Flash and Flashabou added before the final hackle is wound on
Intended use: Wet fly for steelhead and salmon

Comments: This standard fly style is very popular on all of the Skeena River tributaries because it is both easy and cheap to tie and highly effective for all species of fish. The original Alaskabou series has been adapted and varied into dozens of colour combinations from reds and oranges, pinks and purples, to blacks and blues. These patterns are fished on sinking or floating lines and catch steelhead, salmon and trout throughout the year.

CRIPPLED HERRING
Originated and contributed by Andrew Williams

Hook: Size 1/0, Gamakatsu circle hook
Thread: Clear monofilament or 3/0 white
Tail: V-cut Mylar body tubing, epoxied
Body: Flat large pearl Mylar tubing
Head: Epoxied with large red stick-on eyes
Intended use: Saltwater wet fly for coho

Comments: I saw injured baitfish struggling on the surface when I was fly-fishing for coho off the Work Channel north of Prince Rupert. I designed a fly that flutters as it sinks and twists and turns when it is trolled or retrieved, to suggest the injured herring and needlefish that coho target.

CLOUSER MINNOW
USA origin, contributed by Andrew Williams

Hook: Size 1/0 to 8 Billy Pate Saltwater
Thread: White or black 3/0
Tail: White bucktail tied sparse
Head: Pearl Krystal Flash followed by dark bucktail, usually dark blue or chartreuse, tied on upside down
Head: Lead dumbbell with eyes painted on or with stick-on eyes
Intended use: Wet fly for saltwater coho fly-fishing

Comments: This pattern, originally developed for smallmouth bass fishing in lakes and rivers, has become a standard for saltwater fly-fishers targeting coho salmon and other species. The dumbbell head sinks the fly quickly and the upside-down

orientation of the hook virtually eliminates fouling on rocks or weeds. The fly should be tied sparse to provide the maximum movement of the bucktail. Many tiers use artificial hair for this pattern and tie it in a wide range of colours, a popular variation being hot pink.

NO-NAME TUBE FLY
Originated and contributed by Fred Seiler, written up by Andrew Williams

Hook: Size 2/0 or 1/0, Gamakatsu barbless salmon hook
Thread: Black 6/0
Tail: Chartreuse magnum rabbit strip about 3 inches long
Body: Hydroponic tubing wrapped
in cross-cut white rabbit strip, often weighted with lead wire
Hackle: Black schlappen
Head: Silver Diamond Braid
Intended use: Wet fly for in-river fishing for chinook salmon

Comments: Guide Fred Seiler designed this tube fly for his clients who fish in July for fresh-run chinook salmon in rivers down the Douglas Channel and in the Skeena system. He wanted a large, durable fly that he could fish with heavy shooting heads and Spey rods in the fast waters chinook prefer. The rabbit-strip tail provides an enticing action and the cross-cut rabbit body provides a bulky silhouette.

EGG-SUCKING LEECH VARIATION
Adapted and contributed by Fred Seiler, written up by Andrew Williams

Hook: Size 2/0 or 1/0, Gamakatsu barbless salmon hook
Thread: Black 6/0
Tail: Purple magnum rabbit strip about 3" long
Body: Hydroponic tubing wrapped
in large purple Ice Chenille, often weighted with lead wire
Hackle: Black schlappen
Head: Fluorescent red chenille
Intended use: Wet fly for in-river fishing for Chinook salmon

Comments: Seiler had adapted the standard Egg Sucking Leech, which is so popular in the Skeena region, to his tube fly style for salmon. The dark pattern provides a good silhouette in coloured water. The advantage of the tube-fly style is that the fly slides out of the way of the salmon's teeth, reducing wear and tear on the fly, and that the Gamakatsu salmon hook holds exceptionally well. A fly this size tied on conventional hooks would tend to lever a hole in the salmon's mouth and would be harder to penetrate a chinook's tough mouth.

GRIZZLY SEILER

Originated and contributed by Fred Seiler, written up by Andrew Williams

Hook: Size 4 & 6, Tiemco 7999
Thread: Black 6/0
Tail: Blonde or dark brown grizzly bear hair about the length of the shank
Body: Silver Diamond Braid
Wing: Pearl Krystal Flash, matching grizzly bear hair over, and black marabou over all
Intended use: A general wet-fly pattern that can be used for sea-run cutthroat, rainbows and steelhead in the spring when chinook salmon fry are emerging

Comments: Seiler tied this fly to match the large dark chinook fry he saw in the Kitimat River in the spring. When the pattern is wet, it provides a sleek realistic shape with a dark back and silver belly to imitate the natural. The long stiff bear hairs help to keep the marabou wing from wrapping around the hook shank. The pattern has proved effective for steelhead as well as trout. Seiler says the tail and underwing can be made of bucktail or other stiff hair, if grizzly bear is not available.

ALBINO ALEVIN

Originated and contributed by Hugh Storey, written up by Andrew Williams

Hook: Size 10 or 12, Tiemco caddis hook
Thread: Clear monofilament
Tail: Pearl Krystal Flash
Body: Tube fly lining (weight with 15 strands of fine lead wire) with extra Krystal Flash pulled back and tied down
Egg Sack: Light pink or orange chenille
Head: Wrapped in clear monofilament with red stick-on eyes covered in head cement
Intended use: Wet fly for trout and char during the spring salmon fry emergence

Comments: Storey noticed albino salmon fry swimming amongst the schools, during a visit to the local hatchery. He concluded that these lighter coloured individuals would be picked off easily by hungry trout feeding on the emerging fry in the rivers during the spring, and decided to tie an imitation. His pattern is extremely lifelike and works very well on his home river, the Kitimat, and nearby Skeena tributaries.

PUMPKINSEED SPEY

Originated and contributed by Hugh Storey, written up by Andrew Williams

Hook: Size 2 to 6, Tiemco 200R
Thread: Black 6/0
Tail: Small clump matching coloured deer hair, or none
Body: Small fluorescent green Antron butt followed by black emu plume strands wrapped around oval tinsel into a braid
Rib: A small grizzly saddle hackle
Hackle: Dyed ring-necked cock pheasant
Wing: None, or sometimes white calf tail, if tail is white calf tail
Intended use: Wet fly for steelhead

Comments: A style of fly, as much as a pattern, the Pumpkinseed was developed to provide lots of mobility with its long pheasant hackle and to be a durable fly that could be varied in colour and size. Storey uses an unusual body-making technique: he wraps 6 to 8 strands of coloured emu herl around a fine oval tinsel, making a braid that he wraps around the hook. This is followed by a short-fibred grizzly hackle. The end result is a bulky, but light, body which keeps the fly suspended just below the surface and provides an excellent dry-line pattern for steelhead.

Brian Smith

was mentored at the vise in the early 1970s by the late Jack Shaw of Kamloops. Most of his patterns continue to reflect the use of natural materials, as did Jack's. Brian is a past Northern Vice-Chair of the BCFFF, and a founding author and contributor to the B.C. Wildlife Federation's *Outdoor Edge* "Fly Angles" column from 1995 through 1999. Brian is a past vice president of both Westwater Flyfishers of Abbotsford and Polar Coachman Flyfishers of Prince George. He was raised at the Coast, lived in Kamloops country for ten years, and has lived in Prince George the past eleven years. He fishes for trout and "steelies" at any and all opportunities!

BLOOD BUGGER
Originated and contributed by Brian Smith, Prince George, B.C.

Hook: Sizes 10, 12, 14, Mustad 79580
Thread: Black Danville 8/0, or fine UTC
Tail: Black marabou
Body: Fine # 1 lead wire, 5 wraps behind the eye followed by Brushed

out Dazzle Dubbing "B.C. Blood"
Hackle: Black Saddle 1 1/2 times gap of hook, palmered
Intended use: Genera-purpose wet fly (leech pattern)—all seasons, smaller sizes through the summer & fall

Comments: This pattern is my variation of the very popular Woolly Bugger. It is my very favourite general searching pattern for all seasons and all lakes when there, is no visible hatch in progress, or no evidence of a previous days hatch. It is also a great choice after a good Chironomid hatch has ended.

After many adaptations of colours, materials, and hooks, I have used this fly for over fifteen years in any and all B.C. and Alberta stillwaters that I could find. If dad or mom is looking for a wet fly to let son or daughter troll around a lake, try this one on a sink-tip or # 2 sink line.

I use the float tube a lot for northern B.C. waters. I like to cast to the far shore with this pattern, utilizing a Cortland 444 Ghost Tip # 2 sink line, a 12-foot leader with 4- or 6-pound fluorocarbon tippet, and a slow hand-twist retrieve from deep to shallow water over a shoal. Late in the summer, a switch to a # 2 full-sink line is usually necessary.

My largest fish taken to date on this pattern is an 8 3/4-pound Blackwater-strain rainbow, caught and released at Dragon Lake in 1992. I expect a larger one on this pattern before I die. And Dragon is likely the lake the monster will come from. A buddy of mine took a 16-pound rainbow from Dragon in 1993 on a leech pattern. That fish more resembled a silver chrome steelhead than a 'bow! Leeches are big-fish flies.

TRANSLUCENT CHIRONOMID
Originated and contributed by Brian Smith, Prince George, B.C.

Hook: Sizes 12, 14, 16, Talon Pupa Hook or Curved Nymph Hooks in 14,16, and 18
Thread: UTC Fine to match body colour
Tail: None, but for near-surface fishing, add a few strands of clear or pearl Krystal Flash as a tail to imitate the protruding shuck
Body: Flat waxed Johnson's dental floss underbody, over-wrap dental floss with 5-7 wraps of fine nylon body material or floss (Note: Colours are black, olive, cinnamon

brown, grey, Maroon and red, and sometimes tags may be added)
Tag & Rib: Fine silver, gold, copper, or red wire
Thorax: Peacock herl
Wingcase: Primary wing feather strip, matched to body colour (dark or light)
Gills: White Glo-Yarn, 1/2 pencil-width
Exoskeleton 3 to 4 coats clear nail polish to the body and rib section
Intended use: Wet fly (Chironomid) for rainbow trout

Comments: The ultimate Chironomid pattern that is the result of a culmination of thirty-five years of experimentation. Deadly in early spring, I developed this variation in 1999, and have since been systematically replacing all of my Chironomid patterns for this one. Only a few members of the Polar Coachman Fly Fishers in Prince George have seen me tie it. The translucence is the fish trigger that took me years of thought and play, and only one lightbulb moment of glory to get right. Tied correctly, the dental floss underbody adds this elusive look of translucence to the entire body section.

The easiest way to tie the body materials together is to approach it a la slim-body/Steelhead style. Tie in the dental floss, body material, and rib all at the same time at the ¾ point of the hook. Wrap the dental floss over the body and rib material down past the hook bend, leave the body and rib in the material clip, and wrap the dental floss back up to the tie-in point. Then begin to bring the body and rib up the hook in even turns.

I fish this and all Chironomids without an indicator and with a dry line, or alternately, a Cortland 444 Ghost-Tip # 2 sink line. I like to use 12 to16 feet of leader, with a tippet of 4- or 6-pound fluorocarbon. I believe that the biggest fish of the day will be found at the midpoint of the slow hand-twist retrieve, in deeper water. I also believe I can cover more variations of depth without a strike indicator.

My largest fish released on this pattern is a beautiful 4 1/4-pound Tzenzaicut-strain rainbow at Hart Lake in 2000. The variation has been so positive that I cannot imagine a change that could improve this one, other than to perhaps add pro-legs when I am in the mood!

DEADLY DAMSEL NYMPH
Originated and contributed by Brian Smith, Prince George, B.C.

Hook: Sizes 10, 12, and14, Mustad 79580
Thread: UTC fine to match body colour
Tail: Grizzly hackle fibres, large bunch, splayed
Body: Seal fur dubbing, colours are Naples yellow, dark olive, pale olive, ruddy brown
Rib: Lemon yellow thread, 7 turns counter-clockwise to thorax
Thorax: Dubbing same as per body, but a little thicker

Wing case: Match body colour with an appropriate body feather or primary feather (mallard)
Hackle: To match body colour of ginger, Naples yellow, or grizzly olive, palmered
Eyes: Green, clear, or grey Larva Lace, wrapped on top and burn ends
Intended use: Wet fly all-around damsel pattern for June and early July when the damsels are migrating

Comments: An adaptation from the original pattern file of the late, great, master angler Jack Shaw of Kamloops. I never wet a line that I don't miss my fly-fishing mentor and friend Jack. The most noticeable variation that I have added to Jack's pattern is the protruding eyes, a very dominant characteristic of the damsel nymph.

This pattern is best fished on a # 2 full-sink early in the day, switching to a floating, intermediate, or 5-foot sink-tip line in mid-day when the damsels migrate to the surface to search for reeds to climb upon and evolve into adults. Fish them with a slow, steady retrieve, pausing frequently to let the fly drop deeper in the zone, then bring it back up through the feeding zone again.

I have used this pattern for about fifteen years. The damsel has always been one of my favourites to tie as they are so darn pretty, and very effective when conditions are right.

Most of my patterns take a little extra effort to tie. They are the result of much experimentation, and the extra time at the bench is usually rewarded with trophy trout. My largest fish on this pattern is a sleek 6 1/2-pound female Loon Lake Rainbow released at Dragon Lake in 1997. If one has ever caught a Loon Lake trout at Dragon, they are easily recognizable by the way they scream all over the surface of the lake!

CINNAMON MAYFLY NYMPH
Originated and contributed by Brian Smith, Prince George, B.C.

Hook: Sizes 14 and 16, curved nymph hook
Thread: Fine brown UTC
Tail: Three brown pheasant sword tail fibers
Body: Two brown pheasant-tail fibers
Rib: Fine gold wire

Thorax: Same as body, 1 1/2 times larger than body
Wing case: Three strands of peacock herl
Hackle: Brown partridge feather
Intended use: Wet fly (nymph) for trout

Comments: An essential early spring pattern for Northern B.C. lakes. However, watch the hatch. Some lakes have only pale grey nymphs, or muddy greys. The same tying methods and pattern can be applied to all colours, allowing for size compensation, down to size 16, and even 18 on shorter shank hooks. This fly is another original fly pattern from Jack Shaw that must be in your fly box if you want to fish lakes in B.C. The only adaptations I have made is to change hook style, and add the peacock herl wing-case instead of pheasant as in Jack's original. The reason

I added the dark herl is because the nymph, when mature and ready to migrate to the surface and hatch, becomes noticeably darker along the wing-case area.

A tying tip for the hackle, and all hackles tied under: my style is to select a correct size small body feather, strip the fuzz from the bottom, leaving only the best fibers. Stroke the fibers outward, and clip out the tip of the feather. You will now have a v-shape feather. Tie the whole feather directly under, binding it with two light-holding loops of thread. To adjust the length, pull the feather backward by the stem to achieve a perfect hackle position every time, then bind and secure the hackle.

This pattern is best fished up on the shoal with a floating line and long leader, during the hatch, and deeper off the shoal with a sink-tip or # 2 full-sink early in the day. Fish this pattern with a slow hand-twist retrieve, pausing often during the process.

My most memorable fish taken on this pattern is a nice five-pound Blackwater-strain rainbow taken at Marmot Lake in 1997.

CADDIS PUPA
Originated and contributed by Brian Smith, Prince George, B.C.

Hook: Sizes 10, 12, 14
Thread: Olive green UTC
Body: Light medium and dark olive "Dubbing Supreme"
Thorax: Medium brown dubbing
Rib: Lemon yellow rod-building thread

Hackle: Pheasant body feather
Wing case: Brown pheasant sword, over thorax
Head: Peacock herl
Intended use: Wet fly sedge pupa for rainbow trout

Comments: Effective shoal pattern during late June and early July. Fish deep on a dry or sink-tip line, occasionally raising the rod tip to imitate a rising pupa that cannot make up its mind what to do. The credit for this fine pattern belongs again to the late, great Jack Shaw of Kamloops, B.C. Jack used swimmerettes, which I have eliminated. My adaptation also uses herl in the head, and a dubbed thorax in a different colour than the body.

This pattern lends itself best to a sink-tip line. I have been a sink-tip-ine fan for many years, having found them to be the most versatile fly line of the bunch. I just do not feel right unless I know that I can reach the bottom of the lake with my patterns, plus be able to fish the top portion. Cortland's Ghost tip is as good as they come, and, matched with a fluorocarbon leader and tippet, is able to effectively probe 20 feet of water from top to bottom.

This pattern is capable of pulling in a limit of large fish when the caddis are on the prowl, or if they are hatching during the evenings. Keep an eye out for activity, and stick to 6 to 12 feet of shoal water for your presentation of the caddis pupa. I like to use a slow hand-twist retrieve, interspersed with pauses and complete stops to let the fly settle. The strike often comes when the retrieve begins again.

I had a banner day at Jimmy Lake near Westwold with this pattern in late June 2002. Ten fish, 4 over 23 inches, 8 over 20 inches, all over 16 inches. All on the same fly, with only cleaning up the tippet from the teeth marks was all that was required. Pretty durable. I still have the fly in my box, and am looking at it as I write this.

I pray that I may fish until my dying day!

Jim Fisher

A devotee of wild fish, Jim Fisher moved to the Okanagan area in the 1970s to make a living while at the same time honing his fly-fishing and fly-tying skills. They became his passions and have manifested themselves in many ways. Jim has been a long time fly-tying instructor, ardent fly-fisher, fly-fishing writer and a charter member of the Kalamalka Fly Fishers' Society in Vernon. He wrote a fly-tying column

for a number of years for the *Okanagan Sunday* and has had fly-tying articles appear in other publications. He also authored *Tying Flies for B.C. Game Fish*, an instructional fly-tying book for intermediate tiers taking the Kalamalka Fly Fishers' Society course at the local college. In his retirement and during the year when the trout are biting, Jim can be found fly-fishing his favourite lakes in the area, the Adams River for rainbow trout, as well as sometimes on Vancouver Island streams and estuaries in pursuit of pink and coho salmon.

ADAMS RIVER SPUDDLER
Tied and contributed by Jim Fisher

Hook: Size 6 or 4, Mustad 79580
Thread: White 1/0 nylon
Tail: Fox squirrel tail or reddish brown bucktail
Body: Wide flat gold Mylar, double wrapped
Rib: Five or six turns of medium gold wire, double wrapped
Wing: Under-wing of same material as tail, extending to end of tail with an over-wing of two matched pairs of wide and webby badger saddle hackles tied tent fashion over under-wing and barely extending past the end of the tail
Head: Large Muddler-style head and collar of spun and clipped deer hair, saturated with clear head cement and pinched flat on dorsal and ventral surfaces when cement has barely set
Intended use: River and estuary wet fly for Kamloops trout

Comments: I do not of course purport to have invented this fly, only to have named it and helped popularize its use on the estuary of the world-famous Adams River. I continue to use it almost exclusively each fall (and all the winter of 2002). This pattern is a variation of Don Gapen's famed Muddler Minnow via "Spuddler"as tied by Jack Dennis.

In 1992, I first wrote of the Adams River Spuddler in my "Fly of the Week" column in *Okanagan Sunday*, a supplement to the now-defunct *Vernon Daily News*. If memory serves me, when I wrote that column on this fly I had been tying and using this fly for about five years.

The Adams River Spuddler was also featured in the June 1999 issue of *B.C. Outdoors* and more recently in an article by Loucas Raptis which appeared in the September 2002 issue of the

BCFFF *Fly Lines*. The fly is also featured in my last Kalamalka Fly Fishers fly-tying manual, *Tying Flies for B.C. Game Fish*, published in 1996.

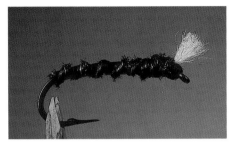

BRAD'S BLOOD WORM
Originated and contributed by Jim Fisher

Hook: Size 12 or 10, Mustad 9671
Thread: Black 6/0 nylon
Body: Red flat Mylar tinsel
Rib and thorax: Three or four peacock herls and a single strand of copper wire twisted together to make a thread
Gills: Sparse white Antron yarn protruding over hook eye
Intended use: A wet-fly pupal Chironomid imitator for Kamloops trout in Interior lakes

Comments: Tom Murray's excellent Tunkwanamid was the inspiration for this fly. I've probably taken more Kamloops trout on Murray's fly than any other pattern I have ever used. In a never-ending search, however, for the "ultimate" Chironomid imitator, I am continually trying to improve on the Murray design.

Three years ago I had tied a half dozen of these, then unused, Tunkwanamid variations, and placed them in my Chironomid box. On a subsequent and somewhat slow day on Campbell Lake near Barnhartvale, my son Brad found them, tied one on and began to take fish with alarming regularity. He was outfishing the old man by at least three trout to one before I relented and tied one to my much-shortened tippet. We finished the day tied at 24 released trout each!

I have continued to use this pattern on Campbell and, for me, it does outfish the Tunkwanamid. Whether it will do as well on other Interior lakes remains to be seen. However, the fly has produced on Eileen, Hidden, Scuitto and Woods lakes, but Chironomid larvae and/or pupae are nowhere near as important on these waters as they are on Tunkwa and Six-Mile, which are far more similar to Campbell Lake in littoral development, topography and water chemistry.

FISHER SEDGE
Developed and contributed by Jim Fisher

Hook: Size 12, 10, and 8, Mustad 94840 or 9671
Thread: 3/0 nylon to approximate body color
Body: Polypropylene dubbing in shades of green, grey, olive or brown (Note: a butt of insect green polly-dubbing may first be employed to suggest an egg sac)
Wing and head: Natural or brown-dyed deer hair in four layered segments
Intended use: Traveling sedge dry fly for Kamloops trout in lakes.

Comments: This fly is my representation of the scampering, adult phase of limnephilus. To the best of my knowledge, this fly appeared once in print in my "Fly of the Week" column during the spring of 1989.

This pattern is very similar to the Mikaluk Sedge but does not have a hackle. I don't know when the Mikaluk Sedge was first tied, but I have been tying and fishing my fly for maybe ten years before I heard of the Mikaluk. The Fisher Sedge is also quite similar to Clark Closkey's Simple Sedge. Both the Simple and Fisher sedge patterns have a higher propensity to land upright when cast than the Mikulak does. Properly tied and dressed, a deer-hair dry fly does not need a hackle to ensure it floats well. I have fished the Fisher Sedge to hatches on at least thirty Kamloops lakes and have enjoyed good success with it on most of those lakes.

HIDDEN LAKE PUPA # 1
Designed and contributed by Jim Fisher

Hook: Size 10, Mustad 9671 or 9672
Thread: Olive 6/0 nylon
Body: Dubbed light dun or tan seal fur
Rib: Four turns of medium transparent olive Swannudaze plastic lace
Hackle: Small ring-necked pheasant church window feather with one side stripped for sparseness
Intended use: A sedge pupa wet fly imitator for Kamloops trout in Interior lakes

Comments: About 25 years ago I designed this Carey Special variation to suggest the pupa stage of the brown-winged sedges that emerge each year in late May and early June on Hidden Lake, near Enderby, B.C. The fly continues to do well there during the pre-emergence hours but I have also used the fly a good deal on Woods and Jimmy lakes near Westwold, where I have found it equally successful. I normally fish this fly on a short sink-tip or intermediate line, with a slow hand-twist retrieve.

Hidden Lake Pupa #1 was featured in my "Fly of the Week" column on June 2, 1991. There is also a #1, #2 and a #3 version of this fly, though they have not proven to be as consistently effective as the Hidden Lake Pupa #1.

PINK BB
Originated and contributed by Jim Fisher

Hook: Size 6, Mustad 34011 stainless
Thread: Silver Mylar or clear nylon monofilament
Tail: Medium or hot pink marabou with four strands of pink Krystal Flash
Body: Medium flat silver Mylar
Rib: Five or six turns of small oval silver tinsel or silver wire
Head: BB-sized silver bead
Intended use: Wet fly for saltwater beach and estuary pink salmon fishing

Comments: The inspiration for the pink Beady-Bugger was Barry Thornton's Pink Eve, which was one of the first pink salmon flies that I enjoyed success with. I wanted a pattern that would have more action in the water than Thornton's fly, which employs stiff and lifeless FisHair for a tail. First tied in 1996, I found that marabou was the answer and the employment of a bead head caused the new pattern to jig enticingly on the retrieve.

I have used the Pink BB to best effect on Vancouver Island's Oyster River estuary, during the first ninety minutes of the ebb when I can fish the fly "greased line" in the main river channel. Takes are usually just a barely perceptibly stopping of the fly, and one has to really pay attention to hook fish.

The Pink BB has also produced well for me Nile Creek usually on a big flood tide. One evening two years ago, I was faring poorly at Nile Creek when a young fly-fisher appeared and took four quick fish. When I asked to see his fly I noticed it was almost identical to my Pink BB except it had two small bead-chain eyes instead of my single, larger bead head. I switched to the Pink BB and managed to beach three fish before dark.

Sam Saprunoff

began fly-fishing with his father Steve on the Lower Arrow Lakes in the late 1950s and grew up fishing the West Arm of the Kootenay Lake and Slocan Lake. In the 1970s he took time off fishing to work summers, get a university teaching degree and help his wife, Linda, raise a son and a daughter. In the early 1980s, when his children were old enough to go camping and fishing, he was reunited with his love of fly-fishing. His wife often jokes that he should have married a fish! His brother Grant, who lives on the banks of the Columbia River, was instrumental in helping Sam to learn how to tie flies. As well, many members of the Lonely Loon Flyfishers' Society of Kelowna helped him develop his fly-tying expertise. Over a 13-year period Sam served as an executive member and President of the Lonely Loons. He now shares his tying and fishing knowledge with the Penticton Fly Fishers. His favourite river is the Columbia, although he has made several trips to the Chilco as well as the Bulkley and Babine rivers. Recently he moved to Victoria and is thrilled to be able to fish for pinks at the Oyster River, coho at Nile Creek, sea-runs in the Sooke Basin and trout in Prospect Lake. He has been involved with the BCFFF for the past 15 years and often shares his tying abilities and patterns at their AGM symposiums.

SAM'S BEADED DAMSEL (SBD)
Originated and contributed by Sam Saprunoff

Hook: Size 12, Tiemco 100 or size 14 Daiichi1273
Thread: UNI-Thread 8/0 olive green
Tail: Olive marabou or light brown marabou
Body: Four or five Killer Caddis glass beads—small (11/0), olive (009), Caddis green (11/0, 051), root beer (11/0, 15/0, 135)

Rib: Olive ostrich herl strung between each bead
Thorax: Marabou casing over olive ostrich herl
Legs: Woodduck or mallard flank,

dyed woodduck lemon or light green
Eyes: Two red midge beads or green beads made with Bug Eye Sticks
Intended use: Wet fly for rainbow trout

Comments: This fly is best fished using a floating, slow-sink, or full sink line, depending on the depth of the water. While fishing I often saw damsel nymphs of various green to brown colours swimming at different depths in stillwater lakes. After experimenting with several Joe Warren bead patterns I wanted a fly that would sink quickly and could be fished with several types of fly line. By adding the ostrich herl and small bead eyes, the fly took on a very buggy look. It can be stripped to give it the damsel nymph motion or left dangling at the end of a short leader on a floating line. This fly has given good results on many of the lakes in the Okanagan/Merritt/Coquihalla Connector areas.

SAM'S DAMSEL IN DISTRESS (SDD)
Originated by Grant Saprunoff, modified and contributed by Sam Saprunoff

Hook: Size 10 or 12, Tiemco 5262
Thread: Olive green, then black 8/0 UNI-Thread
Tail: Dark brown marabou
Body: Dark brown marabou, can be weighted with .01 lead wire
Rib: Braided gold tinsel, twisted thin

Thorax: Light orange seal fur or lime green polar bear fluff
Wingcase: Hen pheasant tail; soft-side, folded over thorax, then 3- to 4 fibre for legs on each side
Intended use: Wet fly for rainbow trout

Comments: My brother Grant gave me a sample of a similar fly tied on a Tiemco 100 size 10 or 12 hook. He told me he had seen a leech attached to a damsel nymph but in his tie, he used brown marabou instead of black, normally used to dress leech imitations. I switched to the longer Tiemco 5262 (extra length allowed for lead wire to be used) and enlarged the thorax by using more dubbing of golden seal fur or bright lime green dyed polar bear fluff. This fly is my #1 fly for seeking out trout feeding areas in any lake in the Okanagan, Merritt, Cariboo, Chilcotin, Kootenays, and Babine areas. The gold rib acts as an attractor and the pheasant tail wings/legs, plus the marabou tail, give the fly great action. It has worked well on the Babine and Chilco rivers as well as Campbell, Pennask, Hatheume and Mellin lakes, to name a few. This fly works best with a sink-tip and short quick strips.

SAM'S BEAD BLOOD
Originated by and contributed by Sam Saprunoff

Hook: Size 12 and 14, Daiichi 1273 red nymph hook
Thread: 8/0 UNI-Thread; green for the thorax, black for the head

Tail: Optional of two short strands of red or natural pheasant tail
Body: On size 12 hook use 9 or 10 red beads and on size 14 hook use 8 red beads or 4 black beads alternated with 4 red beads. Killer Caddis Glass beads ID-Midge, 15/0, black (053), midge, 115/0

scarlet (138) (Note: The last bead at the curve of the hook must be secured with epoxy thus eliminating the use of thread to secure each bead)
Legs: Red or natural pheasant tail, length to match the hook body
Intended use: Wet fly blood worm imitation for rainbow trout

Comments: When Savas Koutsantonis of Trout Water Supplies introduced me to some new coloured Daiichi 1273 hooks, I knew right away that they were made for a bloodworm fly. I had experimented with some of Joe Warren's bead patterns but saw no combination of a red hook with red beads and I knew that this combination had to be a winner. Contrary to the actual bloodworm larva, I attached pheasant-tail legs which provided more life to the fly and produced more trout than a fly tied without legs. Besides fishing it as a Chironomid pattern in any stillwater lake, it has worked extremely well on Hatheume Lake when the fish are taking Chironomid emergers.

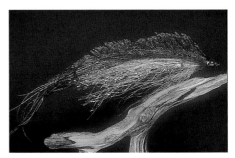

OKANAGAN BLUE BUCKTAIL
Originated by and contributed by Sam Saprunoff

Hook: For body a 2/0, Mustad 34011 or 1 Eagle Claw L1197N; for trailer hook, 2/0, Maruto 4310 or 2/0 or 3/0, Mustad 925544 secured with 50-pound mono or wire
Thread: Black Big Fly thread for attaching trailer hook line; 6/0 or 8/0 in green, black, or red mono-filament UNI-Thread for other fly parts
Tag: Several wraps over each other of red thread on hook end of main body
Body: Holograhic silver Mylar over

0.10 lead-wrap underbody
Underwing: White polar bear tied short, with layers of 3- to 4-inch long white polar bear, pearl Krystal Flash, blue bucktail, blue Krystal Flash or blue triple braid Flashabou
Throat: Red feather or wool
Wing: Two matching peacock swords (one will do)
Head: Braided blue Flashabou, #3 red holographic eyes coated with Devcon 2-ton epoxy
Intended use: Trolled wet fly for rainbow trout and lake char

Comments: Around 1985 I tried a very small silver-bodied, white-and-black bucktail to imitate kokanee fry that I found in the stomach of a 5 lb. rainbow. To my surprise this mini bucktail caught over a dozen rainbows that spring. After talking to my brother Grant about Kootenay Lake bucktails, I decided to design imitations of trout and kokanee up to 6 inches in length. I also wanted to dress a pattern that could be retailed to pay for my supplies. Using a silver Mylar body for the base I discovered that any combination of green, blue, or pink bucktail or dyed polar bear hair with a greenish-blue back would work. After seeing a fly with the peacock sword in the water slim down to imitate the back of a small kokanee I tied most of my patterns with a wing of one or two peacock swords. Once you have found a school of kokanee, the bucktail can be trolled, rowed or cast and stripped in the vicinity of the school. With this fly I and others have hooked fish from 3 to 25 pounds on Okanagan, Arrow, Adams, and Kootenay lakes.

OKANAGAN PINK BUCKTAIL

Originated by and contributed by Sam Saprunoff

Hook: For body use a 2/0, Mustad 34011 or 1, Eagle Claw L1197N; for trailer hook, 2/0, Maruto 4310 or 2/0 or 3/0, Mustad 925544 secured with 50-pound mono or wire
Thread: Black Big Fly thread for attaching trailer hook line; 6/0 or 8/0 in green, Blackor red monofilament UNI-Thread for other fly parts
Tag: Several wraps over each other of red thread on hook end of main body
Body: Silver Mylar over 0 .10 lead underbody

Underwing: White Polar bear tied short, with layers of 3- to 4-inch long white polar bear, pearl Krystal Hair, pink bucktail or polar bear, pink Krystal Flash followed by a smaller layer of olive green bucktail or polar bear and peacock Krystal Flash
Throat: Red feather or wool
Wing: Two matching peacock swords (one will do)
Head: Olive green Krystal Flash, #3 red holographic eyes coated with Devcon 2-ton epoxy
Intended use: Trolled wet fly for rainbow trout and lake char

Comments: Once I had a good imitation of a small kokanee then I set out in 1986 to develop a bucktail pattern to imitate a small rainbow trout. Using a silver Mylar body for the base, I discovered that a fly dressed with a combination of white polar bear for the main body, pink bucktail for the body stripe with a small amount of olive green bucktail, and peacock sword wing, imitated small trout up to 6 inches. Off a creek mouth or when a school of kokanee has been located, the bucktail can be trolled, rowed or cast and stripped in the vicinity of the fish. A one- to two-foot chop on the water can greatly enhance the action of the fly. It has consistently hooked large rainbows in the Okanagan Lake as well as rainbows and Dolly Varden in Arrow and Kootenay lakes.

OKANAGAN GREEN BUCKTAIL

Originated by Des (John) Goldsmith, re-designed and contributed by Sam Saprunoff

Hook: For body use a 2/0, Mustad 34011 or 1 Eagle Claw L1197N; for trailer hook, 2/0, Maruto 4310 or 2/0 or 3/0, Mustad 925544 secured with 50-pound mono or wire
Thread: BlackBig Fly thread for attaching trailer hook line; 6/0 or 8/0 monofilament UNI-Thread for other fly parts
Tag: Several wraps over each other of red thread on hook end of main body
Body: Silver Mylar over 0.10 lead underbody

Wing: Layers of 3- to 4-inch long white polar bear, pearl Krystal Hair, followed by two layers of green bucktail or polar bear, peacock Krystal Flash and a back of peacock Angel Hair
Throat: Red feather or wool
Head: Peacock Krystal Flash, #3 silver holographic eyes coated with Devcon 2-ton epoxy
Intended use: Trolled wet fly for rainbow trout and lake char

Comments: On May 30, 1993, I was out fishing near Peachland with fellow Lonely Loons member, Stan Juniper. After Stan caught and released a nice 3-pound rainbow on a green peacock sword bucktail, I switched my fly to a Kootenay Lake green/silver-bodied pattern given to me by Des (John) Goldsmith of Trail, B.C. This fly produced my most exciting and largest rainbow to date, a 13-pounder. I decided to redesign John's pattern adding more polar bear, pearl and peacock Krystal Flash and two layers of olive green bucktail. It has been a consistent producer of large rainbows in the Okanagan Lake and rainbows and Dolly Varden in Arrow and Kootenay lakes.

SUZIE BUCKTAIL

Originated and contributed by Sam Saprunoff

Hook: For body use a 2/0, Mustad 34011 or 1, Eagle Claw L1197N; for trailer hook, 2/0, Maruto 4310 or 2/0 or 3/0, Mustad 925544 secured with 50-pound mono or wire
Thread: Black Big Fly thread for attaching trailer hook line; 6/0 or 8/0 monofilament UNI-Thread for other fly parts
Tag: Several wraps over each other of red thread on hook end of main body
Body: Silver Mylar over 0.10 lead underbody

Wing: Layers of 3- to 4-inch long white polar bear followed by silver Krystal Hair or silver Krystal Flash with a back of black ear hair from black poodle, or black bucktail or polar bear substitute and topped with black Krystal Flash
Throat: Red feather or wool
Head: Silver Krystal Flash, #3 red or green holographic eyes coated with Devcon 2-ton epoxy
Intended use: Trolled wet fly for rainbow trout

Comments: In the 1990s, the kokanee in Okanagan were becoming smaller, so I wanted a real, silvery bucktail about three inches in length. As I groomed my poodle Suzie one day I realized that her lengthy black ear hair would make a perfect finishing back for a bucktail fly. The resulting Suzie Bucktail not only imitated small kokanee that fooled several trout in the four to five-pound range but in three separate locations on Okanagan Lake it produced three, three-pound kokanee! On a bright, sunny day, trolled at fast speed or stripped quickly during a black ant hatch this fly has consistently produced results on any lake that has trout feeding on kokanee.

Penticton Fly Fishers

For nearly a quarter of a century the Penticton Fly Fishers have actively promoted fly-fishing and supported and encouraged the preservation and development of lake and stream water for the practices of fishing with artificial flies. The club has been active in conservation work in their area, supporting projects which help them achieve their goals. Chris Cousins and Bob Davies represent their club's fly-tying talent.

Chris Cousins,

besides his passion for the sport, is the owner of Lakestream Flies and Supplies in Penticton. He has fly-fished since 1966, tied flies since 1968 and been a member of the Penticton Fly Fishers since the late 1980s. Flowing from that fervor for fly-tying, since 1973 he has taught fly-tying at Penticton Fly Fishers meetings and community events, as well as at the local college and schools. His first love is small stream and river fly-fishing, but he enjoys getting out and wetting

CHRIS COUSINS PHOTO

a line on the many stillwaters around his Penticton home and in other places in the province.

Bob Davies

started fly-fishing with a steel telescopic rod when he was about 12 years old. Shortly after that he started to tie flies and saved to buy a cane rod. His favorite spots were on the Columbia River, the Lower Arrow Lake and the West Arm of the Kootenay Lake. After graduating from university he moved from B.C. to Quebec and gradually got away from fishing. Thirty five years later he returned to B.C. and rediscovered fly-fishing. For the past seven years he has been active in the Penticton Flyfishers club. During that time he has fished extensively throughout the interior of B.C. but his favorite is still dry fly-fishing on the Columbia River. His dog Pal goes everywhere

BOB DAVIES PHOTO

with him and is quick to spot a rise and gets even more excited than Bob when a fish is on.

CHRIS' RELIANT STEELHEAD WORM--BLACK
Developed and contributed by Chris Cousins

Rear Hook: Size 2 or 4, Gamakatsu Red Octopus
Thread: Black 6/0 UNI-Thread
Tail: Black magnum, rabbit strip and six pieces of holographic Flashabou
Rear Body: Black chenille
Worm Body: Black magnum rabbit strip, through which is woven the connecting 20 pound black Dacron doubled backing
Head Hook: Size 4, Mustad 34011

Collar: Purple rabbit strip
Head: Devcon ½ hour two-ton epoxy
Intended use: Deeply sunk wet fly for steelhead, trout and char

[Note: For all flies dressed on two hooks you must cut off at top of bend after fly is complete. In B.C., the rule is one single-pointed hook only.]

CHRIS' RELIANT STEELHEAD WORM--PURPLE
Developed and contributed by Chris Cousins

Rear hook: Size 2 or 4, Gamakatsu Red Octopus
Thread: Purple 6/0 UNI-Thread
Tail: Red magnum rabbit strip and six pieces of holographic Flashabou
Rear body: Purple chenille
Worm body: Purple magnum rabbit strip, through which is woven the

connecting 20-pound purple Dacron doubled backing
Head hook: Size 4, Mustad 34011
Collar: Pink rabbit strip
Head: Devcon 1/2 hour two-ton epoxy
Intended use: Deeply sunk wet fly for steelhead and bass

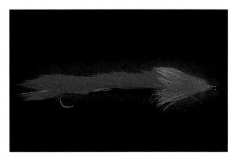

CHRIS' RELIANT STEELHEAD WORM – PINK
Developed and contributed by Chris Cousins

Rear hook: Size 2 or 4, Gamakatsu Red Octopus
Thread: Pink 6/0 UNI-Thread
Tail: Pink magnum rabbit strip and six pieces of holographic Flashabou
Rear body: Pink chenille
Worm body: Pink magnum rabbit strip, through which is woven the

connecting 20 pound pink Dacron doubled backing
Head hook: Size 4, Mustad 34011
Collar: Pink rabbit strip
Head: Devcon 1/2 hour two-ton epoxy
Intended use: Deeply sunk wet fly for steelhead, bass, trout and char

CHRIS' RELIANT STEELHEAD WORM--CHARTREUSE
Developed and contributed by Chris Cousins

Rear hook: Size 2 or 4, Gamakatsu Red Octopus
Thread: Chartreuse 6/0 UNI-Thread
Tail: Chartreuse magnum rabbit strip and six pieces of holographic Flashabou
Rear body: Green Ice Chenille
Worm body: Chartreuse, magnum rabbit strip, through which is woven

the connecting 20-pound chartreuse Dacron doubled backing
Head Hook: Size 4, Mustad 34011
Collar: Chartreuse followed by black rabbit fur
Head: Devcon ½ hour two-ton epoxy
Intended use: Deeply sunk wet fly for bass

Comments: This pattern came from my tying vise in 2002, with a great deal of input from Bill Bartlett of Terrace, B.C. Rabbit-fur string flies have been popular on Skeena system tributaries for a number of years. While I am reluctant to claim an original fly here, the method I use to assemble the fly is unique to me. This fly is effective for steelhead, bass, trout and char.

COLUMBIA RIVER CADDIS
Originated and contributed by Bob Davies

Hook: Size 14, Tiemco 100BL
Thread: Olive green
Body: Light mustard yellow dubbing
Thorax: Dull rusty-red dubbing
Wing and feelers: Stacked deer hair
Intended use: Dry fly for Columbia River trout

Comments: In mid-summer, the Columbia River has a fantastic hatch of caddisflies. They hatch in such numbers that they get under your glasses and up your pants. Don't open your mouth or they will get in there too. We started fishing with the typical flies—elk or deer hair caddis patterns—in sizes 14 and 16, but the fishing was slow. I had some luck with a Madam X fished as a hopper imitation, but we were still looking for something to represent the hatching caddis flies.

I take my fly-tying materials with me and like to tie on the river, so I set to work to dress a more representative imitation of the hatching fly. Deer hair matched the wing and feeler colour but the body was different. The underbody is a kind of mustard colour and the thorax a sort of rusty brown. There may be some variation in the natural insect's body colour, but these were the colours we observed. A size 14 hook was a reasonable match but size 12 was okay too.

I played around with several configurations, finally coming up with the dressing detailed here. We had some great success with this fly catching many 18- to 20-inch rainbow trout during the evening hatch. The fly even caught some fish during the mid-afternoon. It worked well fished either dry or wet. With the thousands of existing caddis patterns, it may be presumptuous on my part to claim a new one, but I can't recall seeing a pattern just like this one so I named it the Columbia River Caddis.

A lone Deer River angler casts a fly as the day comes to an end.

Other Patterns & Old Reliables

Harry Lemire

Washington State's Harry Lemire is one of the Pacific Northwest's premier steelhead fly-fishers. For nearly 50 years Harry has influenced steelhead fly-fishers with his innovative ideas on flies and fly presentation. He has spent parts of five decades fly-fishing British Columbia's running and stillwaters and has tested his flies on many of our waters. No book on British Columbia flies would be complete without some of his patterns.

GREASE LINER
Originated in 1962 and contributed by Harry Lemire

Hook: Size 4 to 8, Partridge Wilson salmon dry fly or 3 to 7, Alec Jackson
Thread: Black Nymo, size A or Kevlar
Tail: Fine chestnut deer body hair
Body: Black or any color to match egg-laying caddis in area fished
Hackle: Grizzly tied sparse and wet-fly style
Wing: Body hair from deer, elk or cariboo, leaving stubs at head to flare up
Intended use: Skating (waked) fly for summer-run steelhead

Comments: Dress line, leader and fly with floatant. This fly is used extensively in B.C., as well as Washington and Idaho.

Originated in 1962, the Grease Liner is the grandfather of fall steelhead waking flies. It was designed with its untrimmed stubble head to cause the fly to wobble and create commotion on the water's surface. It is allowed to swing across the current on a tight line, creating a wake and hopefully bringing out the killer instinct in the fish.

Waking or dragging a dry fly across the surface of the water was very unconventional back in the 1960s. But consider this: if you see a spider walking across a table, your response would be to watch it for a few seconds, then possibly get a napkin, pick it up, and throw it in the toilet. But what would you do if the spider was running across the table at you? You would react quicker and try kill it and this is the killer instinct I was talking about. This is the response that I was trying to get from steelhead as it came across the water's surface, and it worked.

The head of stubbles is the most important part of this fly and makes it different from all other surface flies. Any fly using this type of head is a sub-species to the Grease Liner. For example, some patterns that followed are the Elk Hair Caddis, X-Caddis and Bulkley Mouse. For a more complete account on the Grease Liner see *Steelhead Fly Fishing* (1991) by Trey Combs.

BLACK DIAMOND
Originated and contributed by Harry Lemire

Hook: Size 2 to 8, Partridge single salmon
Thread: Black
Tip: Fine silver tinsel
Body: Black dubbing
Rib: Flat, silver tinsel
Throat: Guinea hen tied as a beard
Wing: Guinea hen and gray squirrel mixed over four peacock sword fibres
Cheeks: Jungle cock
Intended use: Floating-line, wet fly for summer-run steelhead

Comments: Originated in 1963 and named after the town in which I lived for 30-plus years, the Black Diamond has filled the bill for those times when I felt I needed a little blackish bug. This fly is generally used as a change-up pattern but I sometimes use it all day. The Black Diamond has been a very reliable fly and I have caught many steelhead with it. It is used extensively in B.C., as well as Washington and Idaho.

GOLDEN EDGE YELLOW
Originated and contributed by Harry Lemire

Hook: Size 2 to 6, Partridge salmon
Thread: Yellow
Tip & tail: Fine flat silver tinsel and golden pheasant crest feather
Body: Yellow dubbing
Rib: Flat silver tinsel
Throat: Guinea hen beard
Wing: Mixed of bronze mallard and gray squirrel tail with a golden pheasant crest topping
Intended use: Steelhead wet fly

GOLDEN EDGE ORANGE
Originated and contributed by Harry Lemire

Hook: Size 2 to 6, Partridge salmon
Thread: Orange
Tip & tail: Fine flat silver tinsel and Golden pheasant crest feather
Body: Orange dubbing
Rib: Flat silver tinsel

Throat: Guinea hen beard
Wing: Mixed, bronze mallard and gray squirrel tail with a golden pheasant crest topping
Intended use: Steelhead wet fly

Comments: Both flies were developed in the very early 1970s. The Golden Edge Orange is identical to the Yellow except it is dressed with orange thread and has an orange head and body. I have always preferred the more natural or buggier looking patterns and there aren't very many bright flies in my boxes. However, I realize that bright flies are needed from time to time and I have settled on the Golden Edge Yellow and Orange. I also find them very aesthetically pleasing to the eye and I've used this pattern extensively in B.C., as well as Washington and Idaho.

FALL CADDIS
Originated and contributed by Harry Lemire

Hook: Size 4 to 8, Partridge Wilson salmon dry fly or 3 to 9, Alec Jackson
Thread: Black Nymo or Kevlar
Body: Burnt orange or light orange dubbing
Rib: Bronze Mylar or fine bronze wire
Hackle: Moose hair spun to form head and hackles

Wing: Under wing of gray squirrel and an over wing of tented game hen hackle
Intended use: A low-riding, waking fly (Caddis pattern) for summer-run steelhead

Comments: Developed in 1984 and used extensively in many B.C., Washington and Idaho rivers, this fly was my number two grease-lining fly for steelhead. It produced a lot of fish in the fall of the year when the fall caddis is on the river. However, it moved into number three spot after I developed the Thompson River Caddis and that fly sometimes pushes on the Grease Liner for my number one spot.

To successfully tie this fly's head and legs, spin moose body hair in a dubbing loop, trim 80% like chenille, leaving a dozen or so hairs at the neck to represent legs. Then wrap and trim head shovel-shaped, flat on top and bottom.

Fish with a floating line, and dress leader and fly with floatant. For more information see *Steelhead Fly Fishing* (1991) by Trey Combs.

THOMPSON RIVER CADDIS
Originated and contributed by Harry Lemire

Hook: Size 4 to 8, Partridge Wilson salmon dry fly or 3 to 7, Alec Jackson
Thread: Size A, black, Nymo or Kevlar

Body: Insect green, black, gray, golden yellow or orange dubbing
Rib: Black, tying thread

Rib: Black, tying thread
Hackle: Moose body hair spun to form head and hackle
Wing: Two green phase ring-necked pheasant back feathers, one shorter

than the other
Intended use: A low-riding, waking fly (caddis pattern) for summer-run steelhead

Comments: Follow the instructions to spin the moose hair head and legs and trim as per the fall caddis. Developed in 1986, this is one of my favourite skating patterns. Originally I dressed this fly with the insect green body but I have found that other colours work just as well. The fly has a great silhouette, suggesting a fleeting prey when skated across the surface. Fish with a floating line and dress leader and fly with floatant. Like my other steelhead patterns this fly has seen extensive use on B.C., Washington and Idaho rivers.

STEELHEAD SCULPIN
Originated and contributed by Harry Lemire

Hook: Size 2 and 4, Tiemco 7999
Thread: Black Nymo or Kevlar
Body: Gray wool or rabbit
Rib: Flat pearl Mylar with a copper wire over rib
Throat: Pine squirrel beard

Wing: Three ratty badger or grizzly hackle all flowing in same direction tied in Matuka style
Cheeks: Red wool
Intended use: Sunk-line wet fly for winter steelhead

Comments: Out of frustration with other sculpin patterns which in my opinion were too bulky and over-dressed, I first tied this fly in 1988. Over the years the Steelhead Sculpin has been a very good producer. I use it mostly in the winter months when I'm using sink-tips and fishing near the bottom but I have had good success with summer fish using it on a dry line and swimming it in the surface film. It has seen extensive service in B.C. as well as on Washington and Idaho rivers.

TRAVELING SEDGE GREASE LINER
Originated and contributed by Harry Lemire

Hook: Size 8 to 12, 2x long dry fly
Thread: Black Nymo or Kevlar
Tail: Gray-tone body hair from deer, elk or cariboo
Body: Watery green or gray

Hackle: Two turns of cree hackle tied wet
Wing: Same as Grease Liner but I prefer cariboo
Intended use: Dry fly for stillwater trout

Comments: This trout dry fly owes its origin to the Grease Liner steelhead fly. The Traveling Sedge Grease Liner has worked well for me and has become my favorite traveling sedge pattern for B.C. and Montana lakes, or for that matter, anywhere Travelers are found. It is an easy-to-tie and durable fly that floats well and has a good silhouette. For best results dress line, leader and fly with floatant.

Some Oldies and Reliable Standards

There are a number of old standards that have wide use in B.C. Some are B.C. developed, but many come from the USA and Great Britain. Georgi and Neil Abbott, Logan Lake Fly Shop, Kelly Davison of Babcock's Fly & Tackle gave me their deadly dozen flies. As well I jotted down my list of well-established oldies.

Georgi and Neil Abbott, owners of the Logan Lake Fly Shop, provide the following dozen of their bestselling flies:

Halfback	Zug Bug
Doc Spratley	Hare's Ear
Tom Thumb	Carey Special
Woolly Bugger	Butler Bug
Adams	Mikaluk Sedge
Pheasant Tail Nymph	Idaho Nymph

Kelly Davidson from Babcock's Fly & Tackle offers these as his deadly ten:

Cone Head Woolly Bugger	Egg 'n' I
Mickey Finn	Egg Sucking Leech
Glo Bug	Sea-Run Dry
Bead-head Rolled Muddler	(see Region 2, Kelly Davison)
Professor	KCK Red & Yellow
Tied-Down Minnow	(see Region 2, Kelly Davison)

Art Lingren's list:

Pheasant Tail Nymph	Egg 'n' I
Tom Thumb	Wintle's Western Wizard
Adams	Muddler
Rolled Muddler	Mallard & Silver
Doc Spratley (Lake version)	Elk Hair Caddis
Steelhead Doc Spratley	Green Wulff
Halfback	Mosquito
General Practitioner	

ELK HAIR CADDIS
USA origin, tied by Art Lingren

Hook: Size 8 to 18, Mustad 94840 or equal
Thread: Tan 8/0
Body: Dubbed hare's ear fur
Rib: Fine gold wire
Hackle: Palmered furnace
Wing: Tannish-cream elk
Head: Clipped elk hair butts
Intended use: Dry fly for river trout

Comments: Developed by Montana fly tier Al Troth, this pattern's use has spread throughout the Pacific Northwest. It is a reliable dry fly for trout in B.C. waters.

GREEN WULFF
USA origin, tied by Art Lingren

Hook: Size 8 to 12, Mustad 94840 or equal
Thread: Green
Tail: Deer hair
Body: Dubbed olive, seal fur
Hackle: Mixed brown and grizzly
Wing: Deer hair
Intended use: Dry fly for river trout

Comments: The famous USA angler, Lee Wulff, developed a series of dry flies which bear his name. Most B.C.'s rivers are not rich in nutrients and do not have prolific insect hatches. However, on the few rivers that are rich and have good hatches, some will have a hatch of large mayflies, called green drakes. The Green Wulff, although not an exact imitation, rides high and floats well on our rough western streams.

MIKALUK SEDGE
Originated by Art Mikaluk, tied by Art Lingren

Hook: Size 6 to 10 Tiemco 200R or similar long shanked hook
Thread: Olive or green 6/0
Tail: Elk hair
Body: Dubbed green or olive seal fur
Wing: Three clumps of elk hair stacked along hook
Hackle: Brown, clipped top and bottom
Intended use: Dry fly for Interior rainbow trout

[Image of Adams fly]

ADAMS
USA origin, tied by Art Lingren

Hook: Size 8 to 18, Mustad 94840 or equal
Thread: Black 8/0
Tail: Mixed grizzly and brown hackle barbules
Body: Dubbed grey muskrat
Hackle: One grizzly and one brown
Wing: Grizzly hackle tips
Intended use: Dry fly for trout

Comments: Developed by Michigan fly tier Leonard Halliday in 1922 and named after his good friend C. F. Adams, this fly has wide use wherever trout rise to dry flies. In B.C. this fly works well on lakes when mayflies are hatching, but is equally as good on rivers. This is a standard dry fly that will be found in many B.C. fly-fishers' fly boxes.

Comments: This fly, an imitation of the traveling sedge, came from the tying vise of Art Mikaluk from Calgary over thirty years ago. The traveler sedge hatch, common to many Interior lakes, is the highlight of many a stillwater trout fly-fisher's season. When the sedges are hatching, no insect common to the Interior lakes raises more interest from large trout than does the traveler.

TOM THUMB
Tied by Art Lingren

Hook: Size 8 to 16, Mustad 94840 or equal
Thread: Black
Tail: Deer hair
Body: Deer hair
Wing: Deer hair
Intended use: Dry fly for Interior rainbow trout

Comments: This is B.C.'s most popular and widespread dry fly. In use for half a century, it was first a stillwater dry fly used as a traveling sedge imitation. However, because it floats well, it has become a staple dry fly for river fly-fishers as well. I have had many memorable successes with a Tom Thumb on the end of my line and fresh in my mind is an experience that happened in the winter of 2002. I don't fish much through the cold of winter, but every week or so I like to get out for a few hours just to be in the outdoors. It was February 7, and I was wandering the Fraser sloughs in search of cutthroat. I didn't start fishing until noon and, as I started to cast, mayflies started floating on the surface and the trout were keying on them. I put on a size 14 Tom Thumb and between that pattern and Haig-Brown's Black Caterpillar I landed 10 of 15 cutts and rainbows in the next couple of hours.

BLACK TOM THUMB
Conceived by Vince Sweeney, tied by Kelly Davison

Hook: Size 8, Partridge K12 or equal
Thread: Black
Tail: Red deer hair
Body: Black deer hair
Wing: Black deer hair
Intended use: Waked fly for summer-run steelhead

Comments: Dr. Vince Sweeney makes annual trips to the Dean River in August. It is that month that offers the fly-fisher more stable water for fishing a waked fly in the surface film. Back in the mid-1980s, he asked Kelly Davison to dress him some red-tailed, black Tom Thumbs. This fly turned out to be a hit and has been Vince's most consistent Dean River waked dry fly. The Tom Thumb dressed with natural deer hair in sizes 6 and 8 is also a good steelhead waked dry fly.

MOSQUITO
Tied by Art Lingren

Hook: Size 8 to 16, Mustad 94840 or equal
Thread: Black
Tail: Grizzly hackle barbules
Body: One white and one black
moose mane hairs would concurrently
Hackle: Grizzly
Wing: Grizzly hackle points
Intended use: Dry fly for trout

Comments: This is a basic dry fly with fairly widespread use. However, it is doubtful that the trout take it as a mosquito imitation. That insect just doesn't frequent the waters where trout live in any significant numbers for fish to actively feed on it. Nonetheless, fish do like this little dry fly and probably take it for the Mosquito's cousin the adult Chironomid.

CAREY SPECIAL (OLIVE)
Originated by Colonel Carey, tied by Art Lingren

Hook: Size 6 to 12, Mustad 9671 or 9672
Thread: Black
Tail: Ring-necked pheasant rump feather fibres
Body: Dubbed olive seal fur
Hackle: Ring-necked pheasant rump feather
Intended use: Wet fly for Interior rainbow trout

Comments: Developed in the 1920s, this is a widely used stillwater wet fly. It works especially well when trolled or rowed on a sinking line. The tail and collar hackle are consistent in most of the variations, however, anglers have had good sport casting black, red, green, yellow and maroon-bodied Carey Specials, depending on their fancy.

DOC SPRATLEY
Originated by Dick Prankard, tied by Art Lingren

Hook: Size 2 to 14
Thread: Black
Tail: Guinea fowl fibres
Body: Black, wool, dubbed seal fur or chenille
Rib: Flat, silver tinsel
Hackle: Guinea fowl beard
Wing: Ring-necked pheasant tail
Head: Peacock herl
Intended use: Wet fly for Interior rainbow trout

Comments: This is another B.C. wet fly that has a large following. Primarily used as a lake fly for rainbows, its use has spread to rivers. In the larger sizes it could be taken by the fish as a dragonfly nymph and in the very small sizes as a Chironomid imitation. However, trout seem to like it in its many sizes. I had many successful days fishing this fly on lakes, however it is one of those flies that I pack with me when I am winter cutthroating in the Fraser sloughs and backwaters. Size 12 and 14 seem to work best there.

BUTLER'S BUG
Originated and tied by Glenn Butler

Hook: Size 6, Mustad 9672
Thread: Black
Tail: Deer hair
Body: Dubbed medium olive seal fur
Rib: Fine oval gold tinsel
Legs: Ring-necked pheasant-tail fibres
Head: Peacock herl
Eyes: Rolled fibres from a ring-necked pheasant tail
Intended use: Wet fly for Interior rainbow trout

Comments: Developed in 1980, this is one of B.C.'s more popular dragonfly imitations. Flies dressed with green olive, black and brown bodies are good producers. The fly-fishers should try match body colour to natural insect.

HALFBACK
Originated by John Dexheimer, tied by Art Lingren

Hook: Size 6 to 14, Mustad 9671
Thread: Black
Tail: Ring-necked pheasant-tail fibres
Body: Peacock herl
Rib: Fine gold wire
Wingcase: Ring-necked pheasant-tail fibres
Thorax: Peacock herl
Legs: Ring-necked pheasant-tail fibres
Intended use: Wet fly for Interior rainbow trout

Comments: This is a good all-around lake pattern, which was developed for Tunkwa trout back in the 1950s. In larger sizes it is representative of a dragonfly nymph, in medium sizes a mayfly nymph or shrimp and in smaller sizes a Chironomid or smaller mayfly nymph. Its use is widespread on B.C. lakes.

GOLD RIBBED HARE'S EAR
British origin, tied by Art Lingren

Hook: Size 8 to 14, Partridge G3A or Mustad 9671
Thread: Brown
Tail: Hare's ear guard hairs
Body: Dubbed hare's ear
Rib: Fine oval gold tinsel
Legs: Picked-out dubbing
Intended use: Wet fly for stillwater and river trout

Comments: The Gold Ribbed Hare's Ear fly owes its origins to the trout streams of Great Britain. The nymph form of this famous fly is one of the most popular nymphs used in North America. It is an excellent stillwater pattern, but works equally well in rivers. I have taken stillwater trout on this fly up to about seven pounds. Trout take this fly as a shrimp, mayfly, or perhaps even as a small damsel imitation. A popular variation has the addition of a gold bead head and a collar of brown partridge.

PHEASANT TAIL NYMPH
British origin, tied by Art Lingren

Hook: Size 10 to 16, Partridge G3A or Mustad 9671
Thread: Brown
Tail: Ring-necked pheasant-tail fibres
Body: Ring-necked pheasant-tail fibres
Rib: Fine copper wire
Thorax: Ring-necked pheasant-tail fibres
Wingcase: Ring-necked pheasant-tail fibres
Legs: Ring-necked pheasant tail fibres
Intended use: Wet fly (nymph) for stillwater and river trout

Comments: Frank Sawyer, river keeper on the Upper Avon, a famous British chalk stream, developed the Pheasant Tail Nymph in the 1950s. Wherever mayflies swim in rivers, fly-fishers have found Sawyer's nymph effective. It is a simple pattern to dress. This version is a little different than Sawyer's original, which he dressed using fine copper wire as the thread and he spun the pheasant tail on the wire. His thorax was built up using the spun pheasant tail on copper wire and he did not put legs on his nymph.

ZUG BUG
USA origin, tied by Art Lingren

Hook: Size 8 to 14, Partridge G3A or Mustad 9671
Thread: Black
Tail: Peacock sword barbules
Body: Peacock herl
Rib: Fine silver oval tinsel
Hackle: Furnace beard
Wingcase: Lemon woodduck fibres cut short to extend about 1/3 the length of body
Intended use: Wet fly for trout

Comments: Originated by Cliff Zug, this pattern is very effective fly and popular amongst river fly-fishers. It could be taken as a caddis larvae or mayfly and a shrimp in stillwaters.

IDAHO NYMPH
Tied by Art Lingren

Hook: Size 6 to 12, Tiemco 3761
Thread: Black 8/0
Tail: Black saddle fibres
Body: Black ostrich herl
Rib: Black floss
Thorax: Peacock herl
Hackle: Black saddle
Wingcase: Pearl Krystal Flash, 12 to 20 strands
Intended use: Wet fly for stillwater rainbow trout

Comments: The origins of the pattern are not clear, but it has been a popular B.C. lake fly for many years. Some people prefer to dress the fly with a plain white wingcase. This sample is the Krystal Flash Idaho Nymph.

MUDDLER MINNOW
Originated by Don Gapen, tied by Art Lingren

Hook: Size 2 to 12, Mustad 9671 or 9672
Thread: Black
Tail: Mottled turkey
Body: Flat gold tinsel
Wing: Mottled turkey enclosing grey squirrel, deer hair
Head: Spun and clipped deer hair
Intended use: Wet fly for trout

Comments: One of the most popular wet-fly patterns in North America and good fished deep on a sunk line. However, this fly can be used as a hopper imitation for trout and steelhead find it a delectable dish when fished just under the surface and also as a waked fly. You may have to add floatant to the wings to keep it on the surface when fished dry, or put a half hitch or riffling hitch as it is referred to and that ensures it leaves a wake.

ROLLED MUDDLER
Originated by Tom Murray, tied by Art Lingren

Hook: Size 2 to 12, Mustad 9671 or 9672
Thread: Red
Tail: Mallard flank
Body: Flat silver Mylar
Wing: Rolled mallard flank, deer hair
Head: Spun and clipped deer hair
Intended use: Wet fly for sea-run cutthroat trout

BEAD-HEAD ROLLED MUDDLER
Supplied by Babcock's Fly & Tackle

Hook: Size 8 or 10, Mustad 9671 or 9672
Thread: Red
Tail: Mallard flank
Body: Flat silver Mylar
Wing: Rolled mallard flank, Krystal Flash, deer hair sparse
Head: Spun and clipped deer hair
Intended use: Wet fly for sea-run cutthroat trout and coho

Comments: The Rolled Muddler, developed by Tom Murray back in the early 1970s as a stickleback imitation for beach sea-run cutthroat, is one of B.C.'s most popular silver-bodied flies for cutthroat. Originally dressed on a size 12 it is now dressed as large as a size two. Coho like this fly as well and it has been dressed with chartreuse, purple and black wings for that game fish.

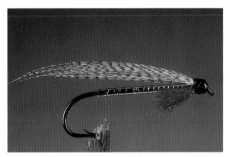

EGG 'N' I
Tommy Brayshaw, tied by Art Lingren

Hook: Size 6 to 10, Mustad 9672
Thread: Black
Body: Flat silver Mylar
Wing: Mallard flank
Throat: Fluorescent red Antron
Intended use: Wet fly for rainbow and cutthroat trout

EGG 'N' I (CHARTREUSE THROAT)
Supplied by Babcock's Fly & Tackle

Hook: Size 10, Mustad 9671
Thread: Black
Body: Silver Mylar
Wing: Mallard flank with a few strands of Krystal Flash
Throat: Chartreuse wool
Head: Stick-on minnow eyes
Intended use: Wet fly for cutthroat trout

Comments: A good all-around salmon-fry imitation, best fished on a floating line.

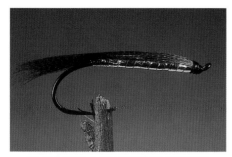

MALLARD AND SILVER (DARK)
Unknown originator, tied by Art Lingren

Hook: Size 2 to 8, low-water salmon or Tiemco 7989
Thread: Black
Body: Flat silver Mylar
Wing: Bronze mallard; apply head

cement or epoxy to wing over hook shank only
Intended use: Wet fly for rainbows, cutthroat and bull trout

Comments: The fly is derived from two of B.C.'s oldest silver-bodied salmon-fry imitations, the Mallard & Silver and Tinsel. The Mallard & Silver was a popular fly for Adams and Little rivers' trout back in the early days of that fishery and the Tinsel dates back to the early days on Vancouver Island. Salmon fry migrate downstream near the surface. This pattern has a low-lying wing kept in place by epoxy or head cement and provides a good silhouette to bottom-dwelling predatory trout and char always on the lookout for an easy meal. Best fished on a floating line.

TIED-DOWN MINNOW
Supplied by Babcock's Fly & Tackle

Hook: Size 8, Mustad 9671
Thread: Black
Body: Silver Mylar tubing
Wing: Bronze mallard tied down at

hook bend; apply coating of epoxy to wing over hook shank and body only
Intended use: Wet fly for rainbows, cutthroat and bull trout

MICKEY FINN
Canadian origin, supplied by Babcock's Fly & Tackle

Hook: Size 8, Mustad 9671
Thread: Red
Body: Silver Mylar
Wing: Yellow, red, yellow calf tail or bucktail

Intended use: Wet fly for cutthroat and coho

Comments: John Alden Knight popularized this fly with his Eastern USA writings back in the 1930s. In 1936 Knight made a trip to Canada where he fished with Gregory Clark on the Mad River Club water and Knight landed and released 75 brook trout with this red and yellow bucktail fly. On the way home they named this fly the Assassin but Greg Clark, war correspondent and feature columnist for the *Toronto Star* renamed it the Mickey Finn later that year. That name stuck and the fly's use has spread throughout North America.

WOOL-BODIED PROFESSOR OR WHAT ELSE
Scottish origin, supplied by Babcock's Fly & Tackle

Hook: Size 8, Mustad 9671
Thread: Black
Tail: A few fibres from a golden pheasant breast feather
Body: Dirty yellow wool or dubbing

Rib: Small oval gold tinsel
Wing: Mallard flank
Throat: Brown hackle
Intended use: Wet fly for cutthroat trout and coho

Comments: This fly is of Scottish birth, originated nearly 200 years ago by a university professor who wrote under the nom de plume of Christopher North. John Wilson was his real name. The Professor became a popular Eastern North American pattern and its popularity moved west as fly-fishers began exploring western waters. The Wool-bodied Professor also called a What Else for many years has been a popular sea-run and coho pattern on the Fraser River backwaters and Harrison River.

GLO-BUG
USA origin, supplied by Babcock's Fly & Tackle

Hook: Size 6, 1x short
Thread: White
Body: Light pink Glo Bug fuzz

Intended use: Wet fly for cutthroat trout and steelhead

Comments: This is a popular salmon-egg imitation that needs to be fished deep, close to the bottom.

WOOLLY BUGGER
USA origin, tied by Art Lingren

Hook: Size 2 to 12
Thread: Black
Tail: Black marabou
Body: Black chenille

Hackle: Black, palmered
Intended use: Wet fly for trout, steelhead, salmon

CONE-HEAD WOOLLY BUGGER
Supplied by Babcock's Fly & Tackle

Hook: Size 10, Mustad 9671
Thread: Black
Tail: Black marabou
Body: Black chenille
Rib: Red wire

Hackle: Black, palmered
Head: Silver cone
Intended use: Wet fly for trout, steelhead and salmon

Comments: The Woolly Bugger series of flies has been around for years and is dressed in many colours, with the more somber ones the more productive.

GENERAL PRACTITIONER (SIMPLIFIED)
British origin, tied by Art Lingren

Hook: Size 2/0 to 6, low-water salmon
Thread: Black
Tail: Orange polar bear hair
Body: Hot orange wool or dubbing

Rib: Medium oval tinsel
Hackle: Hot orange, palmered
Wing: Two hot orange hen neck feathers
Intended use: Wet fly for steelhead

Comments: A good all-round wet fly for steelhead.

DOC SPRATLEY (THOMPSON RIVER STEELHEAD)
Tied by Art Lingren

Hook: Size 2 to 8, Tiemco 7989 or Partridge low-water salmon
Thread: Black
Tip: Fine oval silver tinsel
Tag: Black floss
Tail: Guinea fowl fibres
Butt: Black ostrich herl
Body: Rear half of black floss, front half of black seal fur

Rib: Oval silver tinsel
Hackle: Black, one side stripped and palmered from second turn of tinsel
Wing: Ring-necked pheasant tail
Head: Peacock herl
Intended use: Floating-line wet fly for summer-run steelhead

Comments: This is a fancied-up version of the popular steelhead pattern used on the Thompson River for over thirty years. You can eliminate the tip, tag and butt and use fine chenille or floss for the body. As long as the fly is dressed thinly, steelhead will rise to the surface to take it.

BEAD-HEAD, WINTLE'S WESTERN WIZARD
Originated by Jerry Wintle, tied by Art Lingren

Hook: Size 2 to 10
Thread: Black
Tail: Deer hair
Body: Black chenille or seal fur

Hackle: Grizzly
Head: Copper or gold bead
Intended use: Floating-line wet fly for summer-run steelhead

Comments: With or without the bead head, this fly is one of the more productive floating-line flies for Morice and Upper Bulkley rivers' summer-run steelhead.

EGG SUCKING LEECH
USA origin, supplied by Babcock's Fly & Tackle

Hook: Size 8, Mustad 9671
Thread: Black
Tail: Black marabou with a few strands of black Krystal Flash
Body: Black Cactus Chenille

Hackle: Black, palmered
Head: Pink chenille
Intended use: Wet fly for trout and steelhead

Comments: Another variation of the ever-popular Egg Sucking Leech.

REGION 1, VANCOUVER ISLAND

Barry Alldred: *Squaretail Guide Service*. Phone 250 748-3929. Address: 4648 Howie Road North, Duncan, B.C., V9L 6N2

Shawn Bennett: *Moonlight Flies & Weigh West Marine Resort Fly-Fishing Guide.* Phone:1-800-665-8922. Address:P.O.Box 69,634 Campbell St., Tofino, B.C. V0R 2Z0. Website: www.weighwest.com

Mark McAnneely: *Fly Fishing Guide*. 4185 Discovery Drive, Campbell River, B.C., V9W 4X6

Art Limber: *Art's Flies*: hand-tied flies for Pacific salmon. Phone: 250 757-9882. Address: 6110 Island Highway West, Qualicum Beach, B.C., V9K 2E2

John O'Brien: *O'Brien's Fly Shop*. Phone 250 754-4655. Email: flyman@telus.net

REGION 2, LOWER MAINLAND

Scott Baker-McGarva: *Anglers West Fly & Tackle*, Licensed guide, fly-tying supplies and fly-fishing tackle. Phone: 604 874-FISH (3474). Address: 433 West Broadway, Vancouver, B.C., V5Y 1R4. Website: www.anglerswest.net

Kelly Davison: *Babcock's Fly & Tackle*: Licensed guide, fly-tying supplies and fly-fishing tackle. Phone: 604 931-5044. Address: #110-1140 Austin Ave., Coquitlam, B.C., V3K 3P5. Website: www.babcockflytackle.com

Dave O'Brien: *Michael & Young Fly Shop*, fly-tying supplies and fly-fishing tackle. Phone: 604 588-2833. Address: 10484 137th Street, Surrey, B.C., V3T 4H5. Website: www.myflyshop.com

Phil Rowley: *Fly Craft Angling Adventures*. Dedicated to fly-angler education "because you never stop learning!" Website: www.flycraftangling.com

Rick Stahl: *Michael & Young Fly Shop*, Licensed guide, fly-tying supplies and fly-fishing tackle. Phone: 604 588-2833. Address: 10484 137th Street, Surrey, B.C., V3T 4H5. Website: www.myflyshop.com

Dana Sturn: Private Spey Casting instruction and Spey casting forum. Website: www.speypages.com

REGION 3, THOMPSON-NICOLA

Georgi and Neil Abbott: *Logan Lake Fly Shop*: Offers a wide range of fly-fishing and fly-tying equipment and materials, as well as a great selection of stillwater patterns with unique local ties. Phone: 250-523-9711. Address: Box 629 Logan Lake, B.C., V0K 1W0. Shop is located in the lobby of the Logan Lake Lodge.

Hermann Fischer: *Translucent Flies by Hermann Fischer*. Phone: 250 554-3239. Address: 923 Invermere Court, Kamloops, B.C., V2B 7T3

Peter McVey: *Corbett Lake Country Inn*: Private fly-fishing, custom built bamboo rods. Phone: 250 378-4334. Address: PO Box 327, Merritt, B.C., V1K 1B8

REGION 4, KOOTENAYS

Steve Harris: *Wild Rivers Fly-Fishing Service*: Casting and flytying lessons and guided fishing trips. Phone: 250 489-3695. Address: 1608 3rd Ave. South, Cranbrook, B.C., V1C 2E1

Grant Sapronoff: *Flies*: custom-tied orders, 804 16th Avenue, PO Box 165, Genelle, B.C., V0G 1G0 Email saprunoff@netidea.com

REGION 5, CARIBOO

Doug Porter: *Chilcotin Wild Trout Adventures*: Guided Fly Fishing Trips, custom packages available. Phone: 250 394-4434 Address: P.O. Box 153, Alexis Creek, B.C., V0L 1A0

REGION 6, SKEENA

James Butler: *Nanika Fly Shop*: Specializing in fly-fishing gear for salmon and steelhead. Phone: 250 847-3064. Address: PO Box 3024, 3330 Simcoe Ave., Smithers, B.C., V0J 2N0

Bob Clay: *Riverwatch Fine Bamboo & Graphite Fly Rods*. Phone: 250 842-6447. Address: L-34, Kispiox Valley, Hazelton, B.C., V0J 1Y0

Ray Makowichuk: *Ray's Fly Fishing Services*: guided trout, salmon and steelhead. Phone: 250 845-2982. Address: Box 491, Houston, B.C., V0J 1Z0

Fred Seiler: *Silvertip Ecotours Ltd.* www.silvertipecotours.com Guiding on Skeena and Kalum rivers for wild steelhead, salmon and trout with 100% catch & release. Phone: 250 635-9326. Address: 3610 Cottonwood Crescent, Terrace, B.C.. V8G 5C7

REGION 8, OKANAGAN

Chris Cousins: *Lakestream Flies and Supplies*: Custom-tied flies, fly-fishing and fly-tying supplies. Phone 250 770-1696. Address: 107-1505 Main St., Penticton, B.C., V2A 5G7

Bibliography

Dirkson, Dirk (Ed.) *Fly Patterns of Alaska*. Portland: Frank Amato Publications, 1993.

Fennelly, John F. *Steelhead Paradise*. Vancouver: Mitchell Press, 1963.

Hafele, Rick and Dave Hughes. *The Complete Book of Western Hatches*. Portland: Frank Amato Publications, 1981

Helleckson, Terry. *Fish Flies*. Portland: Frank Amato Publications, 1995.

Lingren, Art. *Fly Patterns of British Columbia*. Portland: Frank Amato Publications, 1996.

__. *Famous British Columbia Fly-Fishing Waters*. Portland: Frank Amato Publications, 2002.

Rowley, Philip. *Fly Patterns for Stillwaters*. Portland: Frank Amato Publications, 2000.

Sawyer, Frank. *Nymphs and the Trout*. New York: Crown Publishers, 1973.

Stewart, Dick. *The Hook Book*. Intervale: Northland Press, 1986.

Surette, Dick. *Trout & Salmon Fly Index*. Harrisburg: Stackpole Books, 1976

Fly Index – By Fish

Appendix 3

NOTE: The flies are grouped into those for salmon, steelhead and trout but no distinction is made between those used in fresh and saltwater or those designated for a specific species such as pink, coho, Chinook or sockeye. Similarly for steelhead, the flies have not been segregated into wet or surface or for winter or summer-runs, as well the trout flies have not been segregated into those intended for river or lake or for cutthroat, rainbow, or bull trout. Many flies suit duo purposes for example, the many of the salmon patterns are good for sea-run cutthroat trout and many steelhead wet patterns work for other species. Check the contributor's information in the specific fly grouping and check what the contributor has put their Intended Use section and the write -up for more specific information.